Stanley Leathes

The religion of the Christ

Its historic and literary development considered as an evidence of its origin

Stanley Leathes

The religion of the Christ
Its historic and literary development considered as an evidence of its origin

ISBN/EAN: 9783337131326

Printed in Europe, USA, Canada, Australia, Japan

Cover: Foto ©Lupo / pixelio.de

More available books at **www.hansebooks.com**

THE

RELIGION OF THE CHRIST

*ITS HISTORIC AND LITERARY DEVELOPMENT
CONSIDERED AS AN EVIDENCE
OF ITS ORIGIN*

THE BAMPTON LECTURES FOR 1874

BY THE

REV. STANLEY LEATHES, M.A.

MINISTER OF ST. PHILIP'S, REGENT STREET;
PROFESSOR OF HEBREW, KING'S COLLEGE, LONDON

Second Edition

New York
POTT, YOUNG, AND COMPANY
COOPER UNION, FOURTH AVENUE
MDCCCLXXVI

CONTENTS.

LECTURE III.

The Christ of the Psalms.

"As it is also written in the second psalm, Thou art My Son, this day have I begotten Thee. . . . . Wherefore He saith also in another psalm, Thou shalt not suffer Thine Holy One to see corruption."—ACTS xiii. 33, 35.

LECTURE IV.

The Christ of Prophecy.

"And beginning at Moses and all the prophets, He expounded unto them in all the Scriptures the things concerning Himself."—LUKE xxiv. 27.

LECTURE V.

The Christ of the Gospels.

"The book of the generation of Jesus Christ, the son of David, the son of Abraham."—MATT. i. 1.

LECTURE VI.

The Christ of the Acts.

" For he mightily convinced the Jews, and that publicly, shewing by the Scriptures that Jesus was Christ."—ACTS xviii. 28.

LECTURE VII.

The Christ of the Pauline Epistles.

"Set your affection on things above, not on things on the earth. For ye are dead, and your life is hid with Christ in God."—COL. iii. 2, 3.

The certainty of the Pauline Epistles—What the Epistles prove—The identity of the Person of whom they speak—Jesus accepted as the Christ—It was thus with the Gentiles as well as with the Jews—The persuasion produced by the Scriptures—The Epistles corroborate the Acts and the Gospels—They show the general trustworthiness of the history of the Acts—The Epistles witness to the writer's faith—The events implied certain, especially when we take into account the means employed—These Epistles carry us back to an earlier time—Events cannot be imagined, but may be misunderstood—The import of the word "Christ"—The relation of the Epistles to the Gospels—Features common to the Gospels, Acts, and Epistles—The belief in Christ the product of two factors, but could not have been foreseen—The Epistles the product of belief in Jesus as the Christ—The agency of the Holy Spirit implied—The Pauline Epistles prove the life of Jesus, and the effects which followed His acceptance as the Christ—The contrast between the Epistles and the Gospels—They were not antagonistic—Facts which the Epistles presuppose—The conclusions which follow—The Christ-character of Jesus permanent—The seal of the Old Testament Scriptures

LECTURE VIII.

The Christ of the other Books.

"I Jesus have sent Mine angel to testify unto you these things in the churches. I am the root and the offspring of David, and the bright and Morning Star."—REV. xxii. 16.

The Christ-conception the net result of the New Testament—Original and unique—Pointing to a human life—Other aspects of the same idea—The Epistle of St. James—The Epistles of St. John—The First Epistle of St. Peter—The Second Epistle of St. Peter—The Epistle of St. Jude—The Revelation of St. John—The results that follow from all this—The expression, "The Holy Spirit"—Is the witness of a new fact—The points of contact in the Christian writings more important than those of contrast—The rapid development of the Christ-idea—The result of the human life of Jesus—The Christ-conception spiritual, producing results not to have been anticipated, which could have been produced by no one else—The evidence of origin afforded by it—Recapitulation—The consequent permanence of this religion—Conclusion

PREFACE.

We can do nothing against the Truth, but for the Truth.

St. Paul.

Die Weisheit ist nur in der Wahrheit.—*Goethe.*

PREFACE.

THE object of the following Lectures has been to unfold the significance, too often overlooked or forgotten, of the name Christianity, which is neither more nor less than the Religion of the Christ. As a matter of historic fact, the name by which this religion is known does not lead us back so much to Christ as its founder in the way that Muhammadanism leads us back to Muhammad for its founder, as it does to the Christ as the object and substance of the earliest ascertainable faith of the people called Christians. Whatever uncertainty, real or imaginary, may attach to the actual origin of this belief, there is and can be no question whatever as to its earliest expressions. These survive to us in literary monuments, which are imperishable and undoubted. The four great Epistles of St. Paul are themselves a treasury of evidence in this respect, and they must continue to be so until it can be shown on equal evidence, which as yet is not producible, that they represent only one phase, and that a partial and sectional phase, of early Christianity.

It is, however, commonly admitted now that we need not limit the genuine remains of the great Apostle to these four letters; and it is certain, whatever our opinion as to the formation of the canon of the New Testament, or the degree of authority attaching to it when formed, may be, that the Religion of the Christ, or the belief in Jesus as

the Christ, is not only common to every document comprised in it, but is alike the very backbone and essential
framework of all the documents.

We may take it therefore as a position which is unassailable, that the distinguishing mark of Christianity, from
the very first, trace it back as far as we can, was the belief
that Jesus was the Christ. So manifestly true is this
statement, that the mere expression of it has all the appearance of a truism. And yet it is not by any means
such; because, what is not involved in the fact, undenied
and undeniable, that a vast society was called into existence, and held together, by the confession and belief that
Jesus was the Christ, and that but for such a confession
and belief this society would and could have had no existence? There are involved at least these two principles—
1. That the conception of the Christ, whether right or
wrong, was a reality, and a reality fraught with the
mightiest consequences; and 2. That the features of the
human life of Jesus were adequate to setting in motion
the machinery which was latent in the Christ-conception.

And as to the strength and truth of this position, the
evidence of the New Testament, whatever the date and
authorship of its various parts may be, is conclusive and
unimpeachable. Taking the very widest possible margin,
we may say that within the first century and a half of our
era this simple formula, *Jesus is the Christ,* had called into
existence the whole of that literature, whatever its value,
which is comprised in the New Testament. Within that
period of time, from which we must of course deduct the
thirty years of our Lord's own life, there had, as a matter
of fact, come into existence the four Gospels, the Acts of
the Apostles, the Apostolical Epistles, and the Revelation;
that is to say, we have certain literary monuments which
must have come into existence between A.D. 30 and A.D.
150, and their actual existence is the problem to be solved.

Practically, this period may be considerably lessened. No one wishes to prove the existence of any Christian document prior to A.D. 50, and it is making unnecessary concessions to suppose that even the latest book of the New Testament is so late as A.D. 150. Within a period, then, probably at the most of seventy or eighty years, our existing documents were produced. To what was their production owing? Solely to the belief that Jesus was the Christ. It is alike impossible to eliminate this fundamental tenet from any one of the books in question, and to account for their existence without pre-supposing its belief.

The religion or belief, then, of which the books may be taken as the actual, and in some sense the natural expression, may be called the Religion of the Christ. The immediate result of that religion or belief was the creation of a unique literature, for which no parallel can be found in the literary history of the world. The literature was the product, and is the witness to the existence, of a particular society known to us also from extraneous sources as the Christian society, whose very name brings us back again to the idea which was latent in every one of the books, that the Christ had come, and that Jesus was the Christ. It matters not now whether the society authenticates the books, or the books authenticate the society. To a certain extent the books, it must be allowed, have a testimony of their own; they are a fair index of the society which created them, and their relative position with respect to other books which were produced by the society is a proof of the estimate in which they were held by it; while in the case both of the society and the books it was not possible for either to have existed without the previous acceptance of the underlying principle that Jesus was the Christ. This was at once the germ of the society's existence, the means of its cohesion and support when formed, and the root-principle to which the books bore witness, and to which alone they owed their being.

Not, however, that the maintenance of this principle was the direct object of all the books. It was so with the four Gospels only. We may say of them that the purpose for which they were written was to proclaim Jesus as the Christ. St. John said of his own record of events, *These are written that ye might believe that Jesus is the Christ.*[1] And the same might have been affirmed by the other Evangelists. But with the rest of the books this is not so much the purpose as the cause of their being written. In every one the position is accepted as a foregone conclusion which can only be referred to incidentally, but which is none the less present to the writer's mind and to the minds of all for whom he writes. Eliminate from him and them the belief in Jesus as the Christ, and you destroy the peculiar and essential features of their existence.

And this, it must be observed, is altogether independent of the abstract truth of the principle they accepted. Here we have this obvious literary fact, the creation and existence of a new and original literature solely in consequence of the belief in Jesus as the Christ. The rise of the Christ-religion proclaimed itself by the rise of a new literature which gathered round the central thought of Jesus as the Christ. This is an undoubted fact, independent alike of the genuineness and authenticity of the several books and of the actual truth of their central thought.

Nor can it for a moment be maintained that the movement thus expressing itself was trivial or unimportant. We cannot pass it by as an insignificant or an uninteresting phenomenon. As a matter of fact the movement which so early produced these literary monuments, and resulted in what we call Christianity, has lasted to the present day; it has played a most prominent part in modern history;

[1] St. John xx. 31.

by some means or other it supplanted the dominion of the Cæsars, and established itself on the imperial throne; it has penetrated all the framework of our social, political, and educational existence, and intertwined itself with our civilisation, morals, and government. Moreover, it is even now from time to time forcing itself into inconvenient prominence, and superinducing complications with which it is by no means easy to deal, and suggesting problems it is hard to solve, and yet not easy to put by.

The fact, therefore, of the rise of this Christ-religion and Christ-literature derives unquestionably an additional significance from the nature of its subsequent history. It cannot be treated as a merely transient or passing incident. Whether or not it was calculated tb be followed by consequences so tremendous, these are the consequences by which it was followed. It is possible that the haze of distance may have concealed from view many of the circumstances connected with the rise of this religion which it must be hopeless for us ever to discover; but the results produced are independent of this obscurity, and are what they are, neither more nor less, even though somewhere in the first origin of the movement there may have been something faulty, or which, at all events, science now regards as unsatisfactory.

In the long run, however, it is a sound maxim that the work proves the workman, and it is an inference not altogether hasty or unreasonable that a movement such as that of the Christ-religion, which has wrought so marvellously, cannot have been inherently defective from the first. No human agency or combination of human agents could have sufficed to produce the effects which have notoriously been produced, and therefore the effects may be estimated, not as the designed production of one or of many individuals, but as those great problems of history which are fraught with their own significance, and demand their own solution.

We may hold our judgment in suspense as to whether this particular work is of Nature or of God, but at all events it unquestionably is not of man.

And the alternative is named advisedly, of *Nature* or of *God*, because this with regard to Christianity is really the issue at stake. If the actual phenomena of the rise of the Christ-religion can be accounted for naturally, then there is an end to its claim to be in any sense the special exponent of the Divine will. Nature may be indeed another name for God, but God and Nature are not convertible terms, and to attempt to make them so is to destroy the special characteristics of both. God may have spoken, and doubtless has spoken, by all the religions of the world, but He has done so in a negative way, by showing us where they failed to apprehend the fulness of the truth, or to supply the actual craving of man's heart. If He has spoken by the Religion of the Christ, He has done so in a special and a positive way, which differs alike in the answer given to the wants of humanity and in the manner of His giving it. If the Religion of the Christ can be resolved into a mere expression of natural religion—a mere variation of other expressions—then it forthwith comes to an end, because there is no room for the Christ-function, and no meaning in the Christ-idea; then, in that case, God and Nature are absolutely identical, and what is done by Nature is done by God, and what is done by God is only done by and in and through Nature; and then Christ is an anomaly in Nature, interfering not only with the free action of her laws, but antagonistic in the very principle and idea of His existence, as proposing to discharge a function for which Nature has no need.

It must be observed, however, that, supposing God to have spoken by all the religions of the world, and to have spoken in the same sense by Christianity too, then the message of Christianity must be in virtual harmony with the message of other religions; it may surpass or excel, but it cannot contradict them. Now, the question whether or not it does contradict them is unhappily not a matter of opinion, but a matter of fact, and capable of conclusive demonstration. The history of Christianity from the first has been a history of conflict—of conflict, however, not sought, but encountered; and the severity of this conflict was originally felt in the contact of Christianity with the elder religion from which it sprang, or at least with those who were the professed and devoted adherents of that religion. Nor has Christianity proved to be more acceptable to the other religions with which it has been brought in contact—whether with the paganism of Greece and Rome, or with Islam, in the middle ages, or with Brahmanism or Buddhism in the East. It has never been received as an ally, but always been rejected as a foe. We may assume, therefore, that the message of Christianity is not in accordance with, but opposed to, the message of other religions. There is a point where it comes into collision with and contradicts them on their own showing; and this is the point which is expressed in the foundation and central idea of it as the Religion of the Christ. As long as Christianity is content to be placed on a par merely with other religions, there is no offence; it is when she asserts her inherent superiority because of her Divine election, it is when she takes her stand upon Jesus as the Christ or chosen of God, that the cause of offence arises. Then it is that the Master's words begin to verify themselves, as they so often have, *I am not come to send peace, but a sword.*[2]

And Christianity may historically be regarded as the Religion of the Christ. The earliest monuments of it show that its most essential feature was the recognition of the Christ character of Jesus. But when we come to examine

[2] St. Matt. x. 34, 35; St. Luke xii. 49, 51.

this Christ character we find it was by no means peculiar to Christianity, but was in fact the legitimate and special offspring of Judaism, so that Christianity grew like a young and tender plant out of the soil of Judaism. This also is a fact which cannot be denied. If the Christ idea had not existed in Judaism, the actual foundation of Christianity would have been wanting, and its rise would have been impossible. The Religion of the Christ, therefore, may be regarded as reaching both before and after the time of Jesus of Nazareth; for it is certain that the very earliest records of the Jewish nation either exhibit traces of the Christ idea or manifest features which supplied the actual foundation of the idea. The Religion of the Christ, then, is not merely that which we commonly understand by Christianity, but much more the complete phenomenon of the idea regarded as a whole, and embracing the earliest traces of it, as well as its full development in the writings of the New Testament. And this phenomenon is a literary fact established by literary monuments extending on the lowest possible computation over a period of a thousand years, from the earliest document in the Old Testament to the latest in the New. It is alike impossible to account for the literary existence of the New Testament without assuming the reality of a Christ element in the Old, and to account for its existence on the assumption that it is a mere exaggeration and the natural development of that Christ element.

It is obvious, moreover, that these two positions are mutually destructive. If the books of the New Testament can be accounted for on the supposition of the intensity and fanatical ardour of the Messianic anticipations of the Disciples, then those anticipations presuppose a sufficient foundation for them in the books of the Old Testament, inasmuch as they can be referred to nothing else; we must acknowledge the existence of a Christ idea, which can only have been derived from them. If, on the other hand, we may assume the non-existence of any such element, then it is clear that the New Testament cannot have been caused by the exaggerated development of this element. Or if, once more, it is affirmed that the Disciples had indeed these anticipations in an extravagant degree, but that there was no valid foundation for them in the Scriptures, which can be critically explained otherwise, then we must admit that historical phenomena which are most remarkable, and literary phenomena which are unique, were alike the direct and natural consequences of a misapprehension so complete, of a blunder so palpable and gross.

It appears, therefore, that the actual historic rise of faith in Jesus as the Christ, and the historic and literary results of that belief, may legitimately be allowed to have a retrospective value as evidence of the true meaning of the Scriptures. It is hardly possible to account reasonably for the character and prevalence of the Messianic anticipations, of which we have literary proof in the first century of our era, on the assumption that these anticipations were not warranted by the language of Scripture— were even a deviation from it. At all events, the Scriptures alone must be held responsible for their existence. It is surely, therefore, a daring course to adopt, to say that the historic result was one which ought never to have been produced. May we not rather say, that if the voice of God is ever to be heard in history, it may be heard in this historic result? And is it not a further confirmation of its actual truth, that these ancient Scriptures, even when read now-a-days after so long an interval, are still found to be replete with an inexhaustible treasury of meaning which they could not have had for their original possessors, but which is derived solely from their relation to and association with Jesus as the Christ? If He has thus shown Himself the light of prophecy, may we not infer that His was the light for which prophecy waited, and to which it was designed to point?

But if so, nothing can be more obvious than that such a combination of results is not to be reckoned as the product of nature; because the only interpretation of it can be, that this is the expression of personal will manifesting itself through the results of history and the facts of literature. Given the phenomena of prophecy as they are, and the human life of a person in whom, supposing his Christ-character to be a true one, their meaning is not only realised, but inteusified and heightened to an iufinite and before inconceivable degree, is it possible to regard the juxta-position of the two as an insignificant and casual incident? If it is fraught with any meaning at all, the meaning is one which can only be other than natural and above nature. It is an expression of God's will such as is not elsewhere found, in the order and harmony of the natural world, in the ordinary course of history, and the like; it is expressive of moral and spiritual truths which are not to be derived from other sources, and it teaches lessons which nature is incompetent to teach.

Now this is the position which we claim for the Religion of the Christ. It finds its place naturally among the religions of the world, for it was the direct descendant of one of the oldest of them, and it has been brought into contact with all of them. But it stands on a different footing from all. For no religion can point to the same historic and literary development which the Religion of the Christ can show. In no other case has the supposed fulfilment of the promises of an earlier religion produced anything like the phenomena which were produced by the first preaching of Jesus as the Christ; in no other case has the similar proclamation of such a fact, or supposed fact, produced within fifty years after it was first proclaimed anything like the literary phenomena which we know for a certainty were produced in various writings of the New Testament. These two features, the one historic and the other literary, are unique in the case of the Religion of the Christ. May we not then fairly claim this historic and literary development of the religion as a patent evidence of its origin? It is useless to point to any other literary monuments—such as the Vedas, the Kuran, or the like— because, independently of the inherent and intrinsic differ- ence of their substantive message, they differ fundamentally in the known circumstances of their origin. The Kuran, no less than the Christian books, may be regarded as the literary offspring of the Old Testament; but who has ever found in Muhammad the analogue or antitype of the Jewish Messiah, and who would for a moment compare the literary origin of the New Testament with that of the Kuran? One was the spontaneous growth of circumstances, and the product of many minds; the other was the deliberate production of a single mind for a definite and deliberate purpose. To confound in any degree the two productions would be to lack altogether the faculty of discrimination —the critical faculty. But if their literary and historic difference is so great, it is impossible that the two religions they represent can stand on the same basis. To imagine that they do is to reject the evidence of facts.

And it is to this broad evidence that we point in attestation of the claims that were undoubtedly advanced by those who first proclaimed the Religion of the Christ. We have a marvellous historic and literary result distinctly traceable to no other cause than the supposed fulfilment in a particular person of the obvious and known require- ments of prophecy. Of the nature of this fulfilment we are to some extent competent judges ourselves. According to one view, the degree of the fulfilment is only to be regarded as infinite; it is continually revealing itself to every independent student and disciple. According to another view, the fulfilment is simply *nil*, and purely imaginary. But this we may safely affirm, that the known results of the supposed fulfilment of prophecy in Jesus of Nazareth cannot be accounted for on the supposition that there was no more apparent correspondence between the person of Jesus and the character of the Messiah than those who hold this latter view would have us believe, or on the assumption that the correspondence was unreal. The Gospels, as we have them, which point to this correspondence, may more properly be regarded as the outcome of the belief in Jesus than as the cause of it. The belief itself is still to be accounted for, even if we reject the Gospel view of the character of Jesus, and so likewise are the consequences which followed the belief.

It is important, therefore, to remember that it is not merely with literary monuments that we have to deal, but with the known historic fact of great results produced, of which the literature itself, however regarded, is the surest proof. Can the supposition of falsehood in the character and claims of Jesus adequately account for these results? or, rather, can they adequately be accounted for on this supposition? Certainly not.

There must have been other causes at work which we are at a loss to conjecture for these known results to have been produced, on the supposition that there was a lie in the alleged character of Christ; while, on the supposition that His character was what it is represented to have been, all the phenomena to be accounted for are fully explained.

The question of the genuineness of particular books is altogether a separate matter, to be decided on other grounds; but it would appear that these considerations are still of weight, however, in particular cases, this question of genuineness may be determined.

And the wholly anonymous character of the first three Gospels would seem to corroborate this position. That the first Gospel is known by the name of St. Matthew does not pledge us to establish his traditional right to be the author of it before the narrative can be received as one substantially trustworthy, any more than it can be justly regarded as a claim advanced by him to have written it. And unless it can be shown that the original results produced by the preaching of Jesus were owing solely to the publication of this and the other existing Gospels, which is absurd, it cannot be maintained that we are bound to substantiate their genuineness as veritable productions of the men whose names they bear, before we can insist upon or appeal to their authority; because, as a matter of fact, the acknowledgment of these Gospels from a very early period as authentic narratives by the Christian society can be proved,[3] and because the known existence and phenomena of that society cannot be accounted for but on the supposition of substantial identity between the narrative of the present Gospels and the very earliest Gospel narrative that was proclaimed. The existence and peculiar features of the earliest Christian society as we know them can only be explained on the supposition that a particular story was everywhere accepted, the central facts of which it is easy to discover. This story was unquestionably proclaimed by the first disciples of Christ; and whether the record that we have of it emanated immediately from them or not, it is absolutely impossible that it should be substantially different.[4]

---

[3] See Dr. Westcott on *The Canon of the New Testament.*

[4] Compare, for example: "If the Gospel of St. Matthew, such as we now possess it, is undoubtedly the work of the publican who followed our Lord from the receipt of custom, and remained with Him to be a witness of His ascension; if St. John's Gospel was written by the beloved disciple who lay on Jesus' breast at supper; if the other two were indeed the companions of St. Peter and St Paul; if in these four Gospels we have inde-

For example, it is impossible that the story of the resurrection should not have been a substantive part of the primitive and original Gospel. Wherever St. Matthew preached, we know as a fact that this is what he must have preached. Whether, then, or not he wrote the Gospel that bears his name is a matter of secondary importance, compared with the absolute certainty there is that his testimony on such points as the resurrection and Messiahship of Jesus cannot have been intrinsically divergent from that of our existing record. This consideration, which is perfectly valid, is quite sufficient to show that a doubt thrown on the genuineness of one or more of our existing Gospels is inadequate to disprove the essential truth of the Gospel, because certain known effects could not have been brought about but by an agency in all material and important

pendent accounts of our Lord's life and passion, mutually confirming each other; and if it can be proved that they existed and were received as authentic in the first century of the Christian Church, a stronger man than M. Renan will fail to shake the hold of Christianity in England."— Froude, *Short Studies*, i. 242.

Of St. John's Gospel he himself observes afterwards: "It is enough to say that the defects of external evidence which undoubtedly exist seem overborne by the overwhelming proofs of authenticity contained in the Gospel itself."—*Ibid*, p. 252.

This latter is a very considerable admission. If it is granted that there are "overwhelming proofs" for the Gospel of St. John being written by the beloved disciple who lay on Jesus' breast at supper, then we have in the admitted genuineness of the Gospel a strong ground for its authenticity, the strongest that can be desired. It may be a matter of question how far the credibility of the ordinary events recorded in the other Gospels is dependent on the fact of their being by the several authors whose names they bear. It is certain that no one of them professes so much of itself. But at all events we must not forget that there are certain features of our Lord's life and character for which we are not dependent upon the fact that St. Matthew's Gospel was written by St. Matthew, or St. Mark's by St. Mark, but much more upon the known phenomena of an early Christian society, whose very existence would have been impossible without the underlying framework of the life of Christ, and whose phenomena determine within certain limits what that life and character must have been.

points identical with that which they represent and express. When, however, it is borne in mind that any such doubts are virtually baseless and unwarrantable, it is satisfactory to know, not only that the main issue is independent of them, as it really is, but also that, if it were not, they are not deserving of the serious attention we are willing to bestow upon them.

In like manner, when it is asserted, as one has heard it asserted, on ostensibly high authority, that we have no materials for a critical life of Christ because the evidence is not adequate to showing that our present Gospels existed as they are[5] much before A.D. 170, one is naturally disposed to enquire, How is the position of the ordinary Christian of the present day affected by any such statement, supposing it to be valid, as he has neither the time nor the power to determine? And here likewise the consideration of Christianity as the Religion of the Christ will materially assist us. Given the assumption that we cannot rely upon the detailed facts of our Lord's life as stated in the Gospels, because the accounts vary, because some particulars are of later accretion, and because the generally miraculous character of the narrative is alone fatal to its credibility—how far are we dependent on any such assumption? It is certain that the earliest form of Christianity was directly and immediately connected with the belief in and acceptance of Jesus as the Christ. This position is absolutely impregnable. The evidence of it is documentary; it is abundant, it is unvarying, and it is conclusive. What, then, do we know of the Jesus who was thus accepted as the Christ? We know that He was

---

[5] Cf. *e.g.* only, not as the case alluded to in the text. "The four Gospels, in the form and under the names which they at present bear, become visible only with distinctness towards the end of the second century of the Christian era."—Froude, *Short Studies*, i. 248. Small edition.

crucified, we know when and where and under what circumstances He was crucified. We know that this death by crucifixion, which was a central and universally common feature of the belief concerning Jesus, was also a feature the most unpromising for the proclamation of His being the Christ to be built upon. And yet the two are found uniformly combined, both among the Gentiles and the Jews. Now, if we knew nothing more of Jesus than this fact, we might, considering what we know of the faith itself, draw certain inferences which would not only be legitimate but inevitable. For instance, we should be safe in concluding that the Jesus who was thus accepted as the Christ was a person who had really lived. His death also on the cross must have been a fact. The reality also of those expectations, whatever they were, which are implied in the epithet Christ, is established beyond a doubt; and that these expectations had been the net historic result of the Scriptures of the Old Testament is a remarkable fact which has no parallel. We can point to no other literature which has produced so striking and manifest an historic result. It is unique in the history of literature. But, further, we must infer also that if the death of Jesus was an unfavourable basis for the establishment of His claims to be the Messiah, then the features of His personal character must have been such as to counteract all these unfavourable conditions. He can have been no ordinary man. There must have been very remarkable characteristics attending His person and His career which alone would have made it possible that He should be recognised as the Messiah. Under the circumstances, the mere fact of His dying the death of crucifixion would simply have been fatal to it. There is evidence, however, to show that, as a matter of fact, instead of its being fatal to it, this was the very cause of His being so recognised. We are compelled, therefore, to the inference that there must have been something very remarkable in His life or in His death, or after His death, to account for a circumstance so anomalous as that His death on the cross should be the principal cause of belief in His Messiahship, or at least an element inseparable from that cause, whatever it might be. Consequently, we are safe in the conclusion that the personal character of Jesus was unquestionable, that He must have been pre-eminently virtuous. There is, however, abundant evidence to show that the character of the Messiah was not one that the disciples of Jesus had invented for Him, but also one to which He Himself laid claim. We know nothing of His history if we do not know that He claimed to be the Messiah. For example, we cannot account for His death but upon this supposition. Consequently, we have these three elements: first, His known death; secondly, the claim which we must assume was advanced by Him; thirdly, the integrity of personal character essential to any wide recognition of the claim. But the last two must stand or fall together. It is impossible that Jesus should have claimed to be the Messiah, and have been content to die for the claim, and yet have been personally upright, if He was not justified in advancing the claim. In that case the integrity of His character comes to an end, and the only estimate we can form of it is one which will throw Him open to the charge of gross and deliberate imposition. We must determine, therefore, whether, in the face of the evidence, we are prepared to form this estimate of the personal character of Jesus. With regard, however, to the elements without which a belief in His Messiahship could not have been established, we may say that while His death on the cross would naturally have been fatal to that belief, it would also materially have corroborated the supposed integrity of His character if His character had previously had the appearance of blamelessness; and, coupled with the fact that He had openly claimed to be the Messiah, it would tend to establish its integrity. But the death of Jesus, together with His claim to be the Messiah, which, combined with the integrity of His personal character, it seemed to establish, could not alone have given the impulse to that belief in His Messiahship which we know to have been so widely diffused. We must throw in the announcement of His resurrection, which was universally made and within the Christian body uniformly believed. Indeed, when all things are considered, it is impossible to account for the general spread of the belief in Jesus as the Christ, without supposing that it was mainly occasioned by the announcement that He had risen from the dead. The question, then, we have to decide is simply this: Is it more easy to account for the phenomena of the early Christian society on the supposition that the resurrection of Jesus was a reality, or on the opposite supposition that it was not? And in reply, it cannot be denied that, on the supposition of its being a reality, all these known phenomena would be at once and amply accounted for; whereas, on the supposition that it was not, a known effect is left without any adequate cause, and it may be reasonably doubted whether it is theoretically possible to account for it.

For in that case we should be reduced to the admission of these causes as really and efficiently operative: The death of Jesus; His claim to be the Messiah; the integrity of His personal character; the belief among His immediate followers that He had risen from the dead; and the announcement persistently made by them and others to that effect. .Of these causes the death of Jesus was most unlikely to produce belief in His Messiahship, as we have seen; His personal claim to be the Messiah was not likely to be more operative; the integrity of His personal character alone would have been insufficient; and therefore we are compelled to assume that the known phenomena of the first Christian society were produced merely by an intense belief in that which was not true. That is to say, the faith of the disciples produced results which, but for it, they were themselves unable to have produced.

To what, then, is this faith of the disciples traceable? To suppose that they were intentional deceivers is impossible; we can only imagine they were the victims of delusion. How did they themselves become possessed of the conviction that Jesus was the Christ? Two causes are at once apparent—the actual teaching of Jesus, and His personal character. They could not have been for any considerable time in His society, and have arrived at the conclusion that He was the Christ, unless His personal character had been in accordance with His claims. Nor would they have been very likely to adopt the notion of His being the Messiah unless it had been encouraged by Him. When, however, they had seen their Master expire on the cross, there must have been an end to all their anticipations about Him, for it was precisely this death of His which was the least likely to convince them of His Messiahship. We are constrained, therefore, to postulate the occurrence of something after His death which had the effect not only of reviving their hopes, but of establishing on a secure basis their conviction that He was the Christ, in which they never afterwards wavered. If this was not His resurrection, it was at all events the belief common to all of them, that He had actually risen. His resurrection, however, does not appear to have been an event for which they were prepared; on the contrary, it took them one and all by surprise; they were not, it seems, without difficulty brought to·believe in it. To what, then, was this belief owing? The fact of the resurrection would at once account for it? Can it be otherwise accounted for? In their case also, therefore, we have certain known results produced which point us to a particular cause, but are not easily to be explained by the supposition of any other cause. And when to these results we add the others, equally patent— of the peculiar life the disciples forthwith adopted of going about preaching the story of the resurrection, and of the remarkable consequences which followed their preaching— it becomes by no means easy to accept the answer that the belief of the disciples is a sufficient explanation of all the phenomena, on the hypothesis that the resurrection was not a fact, when it is absolutely certain that had it been a fact there would remain nothing which required to be accounted for. We are able, then, to determine how far a critical life of Christ is an indispensable preliminary to our belief in Him. Even on the assumption that we had no materials for such a life, it would not follow that belief in Him was an impossibility; for it is certain that the results which actually followed the first proclamation of Jesus as the Christ are such as to lead us up to a few broad and definite facts as their necessary cause, and to make us virtually independent of all others. Whether one blind man was healed at Jericho, or two, may be more or less uncertain; but the uncertainty attaching to that event is no measure at all of the degree of positive knowledge we possess as to the death of Jesus and the prevalence of belief in His resurrection.

In like manner we are enabled, by a due consideration of the historic and literary phenomena of the Religion of the Christ, to arrive at a more correct idea of the position attaching to miracles in the scheme of revelation. It is not true to say that "the Revelation rests upon miracles, which have nothing to rest upon but the Revelation."[6] The

---

[6] "Miracles, of the reality of which there is no evidence worthy of the name, are not only contradictory to complete induction, but even on the avowal of those who affirm them, they only cease to be incredible upon certain assumptions with regard to the Supreme Being which are equally

revelation is recorded in a literature which presents features altogether unique that no concatenation of purely natural causes is sufficient to account for. Here then we have a solid basis for the miraculous to rest on, for we are confronted with phenomena which were not merely exceptional but above nature. It is not this or that detail, this or that text or expression, which cannot be explained, but the vast and complex whole is so remarkable as to challenge to itself the special tokens of a Divinely ordered work. We have the appearance of an historic person, whose position in history, as a matter of fact, whether rightly or wrongly, has been determined by His relation to the ancient literature of His country. That literature did not create His character, but it did create the part He played in history. Stupendous consequences have ensued from His relation to the Scriptures. These consequences themselves are out of the ordinary course of nature. They may well be termed miraculous.[7] Had there been nothing miraculous in the Old Testament, the character of Jesus and the Religion of the Christ would have been alike impossible. Had there been nothing miraculous in the person and character of

opposed to Reason. These assumptions, it is not denied, are solely derived from the Revelation which miracles are intended to attest, and the whole argument, therefore, ends in the palpable absurdity of making the Revelation rest upon miracles which have nothing to rest upon themselves but the Revelation. The antecedent assumption of the Divine design of Revelation and of the necessity for it stands upon no firmer foundation, and it is emphatically excluded by the whole constitution of the order of nature, whose imperative principle is progressive development."— *Supernatural Religion*, ii. 480. First Edition. Longmans. 1874.

[7] "When the man of science can find a natural cause, he refuses to entertain the possibility of the intervention of a cause beyond nature."— *Froude*, i. 234.

By all means; but surely the converse must hold good likewise; and when no natural cause can be discovered, and when it plainly does not exist, then let us admit, not only the possibility, but the fact of the intervention of a cause beyond nature. It is that which we find in the Religion of the Christ.

Jesus, the New Testament, as a mere literary phenomenon, would have been impossible, and so would the existence of the Christian church. These things singly are evidences of the miraculous only short of demonstration; taken together they furnish the completest possible moral proof of what can only be regarded as a miracle. But having arrived so far, it is not hard to see that what is miraculous as a whole may also be miraculous in its parts. What is in itself miraculous may be fraught with miracles. Any one of such miracles may be beyond the reach of scientific proof, and must be.[8] The resurrection of Lazarus at this distance of time cannot be investigated, and therefore cannot be proved; but who shall say that the resurrection of Lazarus was

[8] "Every thinking person who has been brought up a Christian, and desires to remain a Christian, yet who knows anything of what is passing in the world, is looking to be told on what evidence the New Testament claims to be received. The state of opinion proves of itself that the arguments hitherto offered produce no conviction. Every other miraculous history is discredited as legend, however exalted the authority on which it seems to be rested. We crave to have good reason shown us for maintaining still the one great exception."—*Froude,* i. 264.

If there is any value in the considerations now offered, it is plain that the whole surroundings of Christianity, in its known historic and literary development, are so remarkable as to constitute, at all events, a sufficient claim to our most earnest attention. When we have determined the amount of deference that is due to its moral and spiritual teaching, then, and not before, it will be time to decide about its miracles. If we can determine that the authority on which this teaching rests is merely human, that it is not rooted in the Divine, then we may reject the miracles by which it is accompanied as human likewise, that is to say fictitious. If we are constrained to admit that the teaching is Divine, that the circumstances under which it was communicated and the method of its communication were highly exceptional, and in fact unparalleled, then we may be willing to allow, not only that the revelation affords a presumption in favour of the miracles, but also that the miracles themselves, if true, would even tend to confirm the revelation. The essential history of the revelation, in all its bearings, itself involves a miracle, the greatest miracle of all. If this miracle is rejected, it is impossible that any other can be received; if it is acknowledged, it may even carry others in its train.

Bearing on this matter are the thoughtful words of Mr. Henry Rogers, in

beyond the power of one who should Himself rise from the dead? If His resurrection from the dead was the ostensible and the declared spring of a movement which in all its features cannot be accounted for on the supposition that it was unreal, is amply accounted for on the supposition that it was real, we have then, surely, laid in history a substantial basis upon which |the resurrection of Lazarus may rest, upon which it becomes intelligible, and not only intelligible but consistent. The resurrection of Christ carries with it the resurrection of Lazarus; and though the resurrection of Lazarus does not prove the resurrection of Christ, it may fairly be regarded as a link in the chain of preparation for it, and to those who have already believed in a risen Christ it comes with the force of an additional confirmation of that which has otherwise been found to be true. Miracles were regarded by our

his recent work, *The Superhuman Origin of the Bible*, which I had not the pleasure of reading till after these Lectures were in print, but in which I am thankful to find so many of the sentiments expressed in them confirmed. "As to those more extensive excisions which demand the surrender of all that is supernatural in the Bible (however interfused with all its elements, and as incapable of being rent from it without destroying it, as the system of bones or arteries from the human body without destroying *that*), the advocate of the Bible will justly require, before even listening to such a demand, that science shall not affirm, but *demonstrate*, the impossibility or incredibility of miracles. When she has done that, I for one acknowledge that it will be time to shut the book as a hopeless riddle of fable or falsehood, or both, which it will be hardly worth while to open again. Meantime he who admits in any degree the reasoning in these lectures; namely, that the Bible is not to be accounted for by merely human forces, ought not to feel much difficulty in this last matter; for if he concedes a revelation at all, in which are discovered truths and facts undiscoverable by human faculties, and conveyed in modes and forms for which human nature will not account, he has already admitted a *miracle*—a fact as much in the face of that 'invariable order' of nature, and 'those immutable series of antecedents and consequents' on which the objector to miracles insists, as any that can be conceived. The only difference is, that the miracle here has been wrought in the sphere of mind, and not in that of matter—a difference which, to a man who knows what the objection to all miracles logically involves, will not affect the question."—pp. 422, 423.

blessed Lord as a subordinate proof of that mission which He was content to rest on the truth of His spoken word: *And if I say the truth, why do ye not believe me?*[9] But though subordinate, He appealed to them as a valid proof: *The works that I do in my Father's name, they bear witness of me."*[1] The person of Christ, the character of Christ, the teaching of Christ, must ever be the highest evidence of Him. If that evidence is not accepted as in the truest sense miraculous, in the truest sense Divine, no miracles can suffice to prove His mission; but it may be that the truth of His spoken words implies also the truth of His accomplished works; and if so, we cannot truly accept Him without accepting also the message of His works.

It remains only to observe that, in proportion to the value of the evidence which the historic and literary development of the Religion of the Christ supplies as to its true origin, will be the prospect of its permanence in the world. If this religion is indeed Divine, as no other is Divine, then it cannot die. As Hooker says, "Truth, of what kind soever, is by no kind of truth gainsaid." We are therefore in no degree careful as to the issue of the various questions which science may from time to time propose. It is possible that these questions can receive no conclusive answer. The answer, however, so far as it is true, must be consistent with the Truth. Or they may remain, at the best, nothing more than theories which are but partly attested by facts. How, then, can the reality of that religion be affected thereby which is based not upon theories but upon facts? If the coming of Christ was the explanation of a marvellous literature which must ever remain otherwise a hopeless enigma, and if the rise of Christian literature, and the development of history for eighteen centuries since, have tended to prove and confirm the truth of that explanation as nothing else can prove it,

[9] St. John viii. 46.   [1] St. John x. 25.

here is a manifest and gigantic fact in the world's history, which cannot be set aside, however it may be interpreted. There is, and can be, no consistent interpretation of this fact but one. It is impossible to contemplate it fairly and deny its significance. The very existence of the Religion of the Christ is itself a message from God. No discoveries as to the ultimate origin of man, the unity of the human race, the antiquity of the earth, or what not, can avail to set aside that message. On these and other points it is possible we may be mistaken. As to the meaning of the message, if indeed it is from God, we cannot. At least in the message we have a truth which may suffice to be the guide of life, a truth that we can live and die by. Those who have not this conviction may hold their judgment in suspense, and live if they can without a religion they can trust, undecided about everything, and chiefly about the nature of God and the claims of Christ; but to others the belief that in the person of Christ we have the assured fulfilment of the promises of God will be evermore the pledge that they *"shall not walk in darkness, but shall have the light of life.*[2]

Such, then, as it seems, is the inexhaustible significance of that name which in the wisdom of God was joined inseparably to the human appellation of His dear Son; and as long as Christianity retains the name which it thus derives from Him, it will bear upon its surface the mark of its Divine origin, the evidence of its difference from and superiority to all other religions, in being the Religion of the Christ, the Religion of Him whose way was Divinely prepared before Him, and *whose goings forth have been from of old, from everlasting.*[3]

[2] St. John viii. 12.   [3] Micah v. 2.

89, St. George's Square, S.W.,
September 29, 1874.

PREFACE TO THE SECOND EDITION

A SECOND edition of the following lectures having been called for, it is needful to make a few observations in order to remove some misapprehensions with regard to the intention of the argument. It must be obvious to everyone that that argument makes no pretensions to being new; on the contrary, it is as old as Christianity itself; but the form in which it has been presented is perhaps more or less original. I have endeavoured to look at the Christ-character of our blessed Lord in the light of the various recent theories that have been advanced with respect to Him and to the origin of Christianity. At the same time, I have endeavoured to suggest rather than define the exact bearing of the argument upon any of those theories. I have developed it in relation to the *tone* adopted by those who have been influenced by them, and manifested that influence in the current literature of the day. If the argument is sound, it is impossible that those theories can stand. In proportion as the weight of it is admitted, it will serve to correct them and to counteract their tendency. The general tendency of the thought of the present day is to accept Christianity so far as it is naturally good, but at the same time to divest it of and to disengage it from all that is supernatural and not to be distinctly referred to causes that we can satisfactorily trace and accurately define.

Now the importance of keeping steadily in view what is virtually meant by the Religion of the Christ, and what is implied in the very word Christianity, is seen in the fact that the entire framework of the supernatural is involved in the due recognition of it. The very idea of a Christ is impossihle without such a framework. It is impossible to affirm that the notion of a Christ is to be found outside the pale of revelation. It is impossible to say that it is not to be found in the Old Testament; for if not found in the Old Testament, it could not exist in the New. In fact, the mere existence of the New Testament is a proof of the existence of the Christ-idea in the Old. But the existence of this Christ-idea is itself an evidence of the fact of prophecy; for that which the Christ-idea implies is a promise conveyed to man by a series of operations that cannot be accounted for by the mere working of nature. We may be at a loss to account for the Messianic expectation among the Jews; we cannot deny its existence, and we cannot explain it naturally. In proportion, therefore, as we acknowledge its reality, we shall be compelled to assume its supernatural origin. No nation could have had the sort of expectation which the Jewish nation had, unless it had been imparted from without; and in confirmation of this is the fact that no other nation had any such hope. The mythology and theology of various other nations show us how far they could advance naturally towards the formation of the hope, and show us likewise the point to which they could not advance. The history and literature of the Jewish nation show us that they had advanced very much further than this, and in fact had advanced so far that without a supernatural and Divine revelation, however imparted, it would have been impossible for them to have done so. The index of this degree of advancement was the fact of the Christ-idea. The Jewish doctrine of the Messiah became the register of it for all time; and it is a register that we cannot obliterate, and may not, without injury to ourselves, refuse to read.

And in order to estimate this degree, we have only to imagine what our condition would be if we were able to blot out of existence the entire history of the Christian church, and the entire literature of the New Testament. The contrast between the Old Testament and the other literature of the world would still be as great as it is now, but the book would be a singularly strange and incomplete one. It would be the record of a nation's mental condition for the period of a thousand years, who had believed themselves exceptionally near to God, and throughout that period ever on the verge of some great event which should place them at the summit of power and glory. Their law, their history, their poetry, their prophecy, would alike bear witness to this impression; and what is more, we should be able to mark the exact period at which the nation ceased to produce those documents which gave expression to the hope. We should also be able to affirm, that for more than a thousand years after the latest book of the Old Testament was written, the people did not cease to be animated with the same hope which had been the stay of their forefathers. But we should also be able to say that the whole thing had been proved a delusion, for that the stream of history had gone on and had left their hope an unrealised dream, till they had grown utterly ashamed and weary of it, and had begun to regard their national history as a romance, and their national literature as a mistake.

But we cannot thus blot out of existence the literature of the New Testament, or the history of the Christian Church; and consequently the existence of this literature and history has completely altered the relation in which the world must ever stand to the literature of the Old Testament. The book which before was singularly strange and incomplete has now become invested with an improbable and unexpected significance. And yet it was not possible for any man, or any combination of men, designedly to bring about this significance; it was wholly and entirely the work of history, and the gradual result of the progress of events. The kind of supplement the New Testament has supplied to the Old is unique in the literature of the world.

What then is the interpretation of this fact? The rise of Christianity has given a meaning to the Old Testament which it never had before, and which nothing else could give it. History has shown that there was something in the national life of Israel which there would not otherwise have been. It is, however, beyond the power of any nation to anticipate its own future as Israel did, no less than it was beyond the power of Israel to fulfil its own anticipations. The fact that the anticipations were both cherished and fulfilled can only be accounted for on the assumption that the development of history is not a blind succession of events, but a connected chain of circumstances, arranged according to a plan, and arranged for a particular purpose, and on this assumption there is only one way open to us of explaining the phenomena in question. The plan which is so clearly marked was designed by God, and the purpose He had in view was the indication of the one Man who should receive the homage and adoration of the world. To this end the hope of a Messiah was given to Israel, and the course of history demonstrated the fact that the hope was not fallacious, but was confirmed by the development of events in a way which it was greatly beyond the power of man or nature to bring about or to anticipate. And if it is asked what right we have to make such an assumption, it is sufficient to reply that the assumption is forced upon us when we contemplate the known facts of secular and sacred history. In no branch of the history of the world is there any instance of the kind of correspondence between the facts of Christianity and the history of the Jewish nation, and the kind of relation there is between the literature of Israel and the literature of the New Testament that we meet with in the history and literature of the Bible. The broad features of both are markedly distinct. Supposing, therefore, that we had a theory that was adequate to solve the problem of the entire history of the world, such a theory would be totally inadequate to the solution of the problem before us, arising from the facts of Bible history. Consequently this would be the crucial test which would serve to falsify our theory. This particular problem would still demand an entirely different solution. Nor would the difficulty be lessened by any attempts to place the phenomena of sacred history on the same footing with those of secular history, because the facts to which we now allude are precisely those which obstinately resist all such attempts. The argument adopted is of the broadest possible character, and is absolutely independent of all narrow interpretations and partial issues. If, therefore, we would find a theory that is capable of application to the facts of sacred no less than those of secular history we must adopt the assumption in point. In fact we must make two assumptions, neither of which is capable of absolute proof, but both of which are in the highest degree reasonable. First, we must assume that there is a God; and secondly, we must assume that He has spoken and revealed Himself in history, so that we may be enabled to arrive at some knowledge of His purposes through the clear message of history. Granting these two assumptions, the argument of the following lectures may be regarded as virtually conclusive. If God has spoken in history, He has spoken in the broad facts before us in a way that He has spoken nowhere else; and the result is that the testimony thus given to Christ is such as has not been given in any second instance, and it is a testimony that is unmistakable. The evidence is of a highly elaborate and complex character ; it is cumulative and convergent to a degree that is entirely without parallel. It is of the nature of a perfect arch which rests on the independent foundations of a twofold history and a twofold literature.

It must be understood, therefore, that the stress which is laid upon the Messianic character of Jesus is so laid for its ulterior rather than its primary importance. It has been said that we have nothing now to do with the Messianic character of Jesus which had reference to a past condition of thought. That may or may not be true. Into this question we have not intended to enter. The Messianic character of Jesus was that to which Christianity historically owed its existence. But the Messianic character of Jesus is impossible without the agency of the supernatural before and above and beneath and around it. In accepting that character, as we are bound to accept it, as the historic and originating impulse of Christianity, we are committed to a recognition of the supernatural. We cannot escape from it. We are placed in its immediate presence. It may be very true that the Messianic character of Jesus is not His only character, nor that character which has most direct reference to ourselves, nor that which is ultimately destined to have the greatest influence upon the world, but it is one which is inalienably and unalterably His, and therefore it is one which compels us to acknowledge the supernatural in Him, and serves to assure us that whatever aspect we regard Christ in must be a faulty and a perverted aspect, if in it the operation of the supernatural is lost sight of or obscured.

To acknowledge that Jesus is the Christ, is tantamount to acknowledging Him as the chosen of God ; but He cannot be the chosen of God unless God has not only selected Him from among men, but also made the fact of His choice known to man ; and He cannot have made His choice known to man but by special and direct revelation, which involves the agency of special and supernatural means of communicating His will. It is impossible, therefore, that we should accept Christ, or accept Jesus as the Christ, without accepting also the agency of the supernatural. But if we once accept the supernatural in the Christ idea, and acknowledge Christ as a supernatural person, we can have but little hesitation in acknowledging the presence of the supernatural in the words and actions of Christ; and hence the acknowledgment of the Christ functions as a *part* only of the character of Jesus becomes a sufficient guarantee for our due submission and allegiance to all that comes to us on the approved authority of Christ, and with the full sanction of His name; for the actual presence of the supernatural in Jesus is the proof that what He so has He has for ever. He cannot have been a supernatural person once, and have ceased to be so now. His authority must be permanent until it is superseded by authority equally supernatural. A wider acquaintance with the sphere of the natural cannot avail to set aside the supernatural, or intrinsically to modify our relation to Christ; *for He must reign, till He hath put all enemies under His feet. The last enemy that shall be destroyed is death.* And not till *all things shall be subdued unto Him, shall the Son also Himself be subject unto Him that put all things under Him, that God may be all in all.*[1]

It is obvious that if Jesus was indeed the Christ whom God had promised to send, then the historic manifestation of Jesus becomes the type and pattern of His continual method of action, and of His permanent relation to us. He is not only the starting-point of our renewed existence, the source of our regenerated life, but He is also the goal to which we must ever return, the anchor of our souls both sure and steadfast, in faithful and firm attachment to whom

[1] 1 Cor. xv. 25-27.

our bark may at all times ride securely amid all the changes and chances and the storm and sunshine of life. He is not only the express image of the Father, manifested once for all in the person of a man, but, in as far as He is the true manifestation of God, He is a manifestation which can never be altered, which must be independent alike of essential modification and of continual development. He must be the abiding centre and source, the enduring token and pledge, of all the promises of God. He must, in one word, be *Jesus Christ the same yesterday, and to-day, and for ever.*[2]

It can hardly be needful to remind the reader that I have purposely endeavoured in these lectures to divest myself of all Christian predilections, and have tried to frame the argument from an entirely independent point of view, in order to give the greater weight to those conclusions which appear to me to be unavoidable. I can truly say of my *method* of writing as St. John said of his *design: These things are written, that ye might believe that Jesus is the Christ, the Son of God; and that believing ye might have life through His name.*[3]

[2] Heb. xiii. 8.   [3] St. John xx. 31.

89, St. George's Square, S.W.,
     June 1, 1875.

LECTURE I.

*ANTICIPATION OF THE CHRIST IN HEATHEN
NATIONS.*

THE registering of doubts hath two excellent uses: the one, that it saveth philosophy from errors and falsehoods; when that which is not fully appearing is not collected into assertion, whereby error might draw error, but reserved in doubt: the other, that the entry of doubts are as so many suckers or sponges to draw use of knowledge; in so much as that which, if doubts had not preceded, a man should never have advised, but passed it over without note, by the suggestion and solicitation of doubts, is made to be attended and applied. But both these commodities do scarcely countervail an inconvenience which will intrude itself, if it be not debarred; which is, that when a doubt is once received, men labour rather how to keep it a doubt still, than how to solve it; and accordingly bend their wits. Of this we see the familiar example in lawyers and scholars, both which, if they have once admitted a doubt, it goeth ever after authorised for a doubt. But that use of wit and knowledge is to be allowed, which laboureth to make doubtful things certain, and not those which labour to make certain things doubtful. Therefore these kalendars of doubts I commend as excellent things; so that there be this caution used, that when they be thoroughly sifted and brought to resolution, they be from thenceforth omitted, discarded, and not continued to cherish and encourage men in doubting.—BACON, *Advancement of Learning.*

LECTURE I.

*As the hart panteth after the water brooks, so panteth my soul after
thee, O God.*—Ps. xlii. 1.

THE origin of Christianity has often been found an
interesting and a fruitful subject of inquiry in our
time. Many treatises have been written, and many theories
advanced, about it. Any one who could invent an entirely
new theory, whether plausible or not, would probably meet
with many persons who would be willing to listen to him.
For, whatever may have been its actual origin, there can
be no question that Christianity in itself is the most
remarkable phenomenon that history presents to our contemplation. It has already far outlived in its duration the
utmost limits of time that can be assigned to the dominion
of ancient Rome. Though its position in the world has
ever been one of antagonism, and therefore of peril, it has
survived the most desperate assaults whether from without
or from within; and now, in the nineteenth century of its
existence, shows no signs of a slackening interest for the
imagination, or of a declining influence on the human
mind.

Nor is it hard to see the reason of this. For Christianity
appeals alike to the deepest instincts and the highest
aspirations of mankind. It lays its hand upon the moral
nature, the social constitution, and the undefined and
mysterious spiritual sensibilities of man. It concerns
itself not only with life here, but professes also to have the
promise of life hereafter; and, notwithstanding the almost

endless variety of answers that might be given to the
anterior question, What is Christianity?—no two independent minds probably understanding thereby or deriving
therefrom ideas in all respects identical—that which the
term implies is sufficiently definite to be easily intelligible
to all, however widely their theoretical conceptions or their
individual sympathies may differ.

Indeed, it is no slight indication of the fascinating
power exercised by Christianity, that men abandon with
extreme reluctance their personal connection with the
name of Christian. Those who have broken loose from all
commonly received and traditional forms of belief, and
those also who live in habitual disregard of the one
ordinance which was designed from the first to be the mark
of Christian fellowship, are yet jealously sensitive as to
the appropriation of this name. "All who profess and call
themselves Christians," to adopt the large-hearted language
of our collect, would embrace a considerable number that
could not conveniently be assigned to any recognised
denomination. Some of those who are uncompromising in
their treatment of many things that large bodies, or even
the great mass of Christians, hold most dear, are yet second
to none in their zeal to retain the name.

We have no wish to narrow or to limit the claim of any
man to be so who desires to regard himself as a disciple
of the Son of man. It is He to whom all judgment has
been committed, and with whom, therefore, we would
gladly leave it; but we may safely observe that a Christianity which repudiates Christ is a contradiction in terms,
and that consequently, first or last, the doctrine and person
of a Christ must be a prominent feature of Christianity,
however interpreted. Whatever may have been the origin
of Christianity, it was intimately associated with the person
of Christ, for Christianity is the religion of the Christ.
Whatever differences may have existed between the teach-

ing of Christ and the subsequent developments of that teaching among His disciples, it will probably not be denied that the impulse known as Christianity is rightly and directly traceable to His teaching and influence. At all events, we cannot dissociate Christ from the subsequent and existing phenomena of the religion which bears His name. He is Himself the most prominent and conspicuous feature in connection with it.

The name of Christ, however, suggests an office rather than a person. It implies the supposed fulfilment of various preconceived ideas. The correspondence of Jesus with the ideal person and character of the Christ was the position assumed by the earliest preachers of Christianity. And as this is a fact which admits of no rational doubt, it is clear that there must have been certain predisposing causes to render the spread of Christianity possible. A belief of which one of the main features was the realisation in Jesus of a character at once clearly defined and readily intelligible could not have achieved any progress in the world, if there had not been adequate preparation made for it in the dissemination of such previous ideas.

Because it was not the personal character of Jesus that won its way among mankind, but the fact that in His character was fulfilled the conception of the Christ. In the case of the Jewish nation this is sufficiently manifest, since in that nation there had existed for many centuries the conviction that a person known as the Messiah was eventually to arise. The whole conflict of Christianity with Judaism consisted, not in the maintenance of the doctrine of a Christ, but in the establishment of the claims of Jesus to be regarded as the Christ.

Nor can it have been very different even with the Gentiles, who were led to believe in Jesus. We cannot affirm of them that there were certain definite notions of a coming deliverer existing in their minds, and that they believed in Jesus because He fulfilled those notions; but we may truly say that in 'every case their belief in Him involved the conviction that He was the Messiah to whom the Jews looked forward. Of this there is abundant evidence. It does appear, however, that there were sundry latent ideas prevalent in the ancient world, which may have had the effect in no small degree of disposing the popular mind to accept more readily the announcement of One who especially claimed to realise the anticipations of His own people. When we look back over the mass of current traditions afloat in the ancient world, the attitude of expectation indicated in many ways, the impression conveyed by poetry, mythology, philosophy, and literature, that a want was felt in our nature, and a hope that it might be supplied was cherished, we can see that there was much even in the heathen world that answered to the Jewish anticipation of a Messiah, and that this condition of mind was one specially favourable to the preaching of a Christ, who was proclaimed as the good news of God to mankind.

And indeed to the Christian, who is fully persuaded that Jesus Christ was all that He professed to be, and that in Him there is the present possession of as much happiness as our condition admits of, and the future promise of all that we can desire, it is not possible to survey the monuments of religious thought in any nation or language, and not discern indications of a mental state that bears collateral witness to the reality of the want which Jesus came to supply; if, indeed, it does not manifest what may fairly be regarded as the unconscious hope of His coming. There is independent and corroborative evidence borne to Him by many writers that were ignorant of His name and by many religious systems that are antagonistic to Him. What St. Paul says to the Romans is doubtless more or less true of every nation, and of all religions, that *that which may be known of God is manifest in them; for God hath shewed it unto them.*[1] It is not given to all to bear equal testimony, but there are continually traces of a testimony borne, and in its general results it is neither discordant nor incomplete.

And we may briefly characterise it as twofold. First, there is the universal consciousness of a deep and radical defect in our constitution, which, if not openly confessed, is at any rate sufficiently betrayed. And secondly, there is frequently revealed a kind of spontaneous impression or conviction that help, if it comes at all, must come from without; that it is not competent to human nature to regenerate or emancipate itself. It is not, of course, affirmed that either of these propositions is distinctly and broadly stated in so many words, but that, turn where we will, we are continually being confronted with that which tends to establish them. And, in fact, this testimony is the more remarkable, from the manifestly undesigned and unintentional manner in which it is borne. Human nature, in spite of itself, bears witness to the depth of its own wound. There can, one would think, be no question about this. Every form of ancient civilisation bears evident token of sin, and also of the consciousness of sin. Rites and ceremonies, laws, manners, and customs, which, after all possible allowance has been made for diversity of feeling and opinion, can only be regarded as indications of moral corruption, are common enough in the records of every ancient nation. Whether we look to Egypt or Assyria, to Persia or to Greece, to India or to the north of Europe, the witness is unfaltering, not only as to the depravity of man, but also as to a certain misgiving within the heart that all was not right. The hideous forms of sacrifice which confront us in many quarters are doubtless to be interpreted thus, and cannot fairly be interpreted otherwise.[2] If sacrifice implies a desire to

[1] Rom. i. 19.

[2] See, for example, G. W. Cox, *Mythology of the Aryan Nations,* ii. 144,

surrender what is most precious, and so far expresses a good intention and a noble effort, it implies likewise a conviction that to do so is absolutely necessary. But why necessary, unless because no other apparent means are open whereby to redress the balance of right which conscience declares to need and to demand rectification ? All analysis of the theory of sacrifice must ultimately result in this, that it is a witness to disorder within, for which it appears to promise the only available remedy. And when sacrifice takes the more awful and revolting form that it assumed among the Phœnicians and the Aztecs, it only shows the more plainly how deep and terrible the disorder is. But there can be no question that, long before the commencement of the Christian era, human nature had borne the most conclusive testimony to the existence of such disorder, and by many a blood-stained rite had confessed to the consciousness of it. Wherever, therefore, the Gospel of Christ came, it encountered a condition of mind which, being keenly alive to a sense of want within, was so far prepared to receive it. To make use of the vivid expression of an anonymous writer, every one who embraced the Gospel found that it "supplied a positive to the negative in himself."[3]

When, however, we pass to the consideration of the other kind of testimony which was borne rather to the hope than to the need of a Redeemer, it is perhaps possible to speak with less confidence. A vast field at once opens out to our contemplation, which we can only glance at in the most cursory manner. There have been three principal

---

and the note; also the elaborate essay of Dr. Kalisch on Sacrifice, prefixed to his *Commentary on Leviticus ;* and the *Dictionary of Science, Literature, and Art*, art. "Sacrifice." See also Hardwick's *Christ and other Masters*, part ii. p. 157 *seq.*

[3] A reviewer in the *Edinburgh Courant*, quoted by S. Baring-Gould, *Origin and Development of Religious Belief*, part ii. p. 8.

methods of interpreting the mythological legends of Greece. They have been interpreted on rationalistic principles, as Lord Bacon[4] and others have explained them ; or they have been regarded as distorted versions of historical occurrences, or in some cases as perverted accounts of historical events. Latterly, however, the tendency has been to look at them in their relation to the mythological tales of other countries, as portions merely of a vast whole. And so it has been supposed that one principle pervades them all. This method of interpretation is known as the solar theory.[5] The daily natural phenomena of dawn and daybreak, sunrise, noontide, and sunset, and of the varying seasons in their perpetual recurrence, having been originally expressed in sensuous language, which the mind afterwards outgrew, became ultimately invested with those very passions and accidents which the language literally suggested. And thus the foundation was laid of a copious mythology, in which the repetition of the same ideas in various forms is perpetually discernible. This theory may or may not eventually be regarded as a satisfactory explanation of the rise of the various myths; it is not even imagined that it expresses the way in which they were actually understood either by the poets who gave them their existing form, or by the people who took delight in the repetition of them. However true it may be as a conjecture of their origin, it cannot for a moment be accepted as the actual message which they bore to the world at large. It would be quite as reasonable to assign to them a directly Christian meaning, as to pretend that their recondite etymological significance was that commonly understood. The poetical interpretations of comparative mythology are the natural fruit of comparative philology, and could not have been originated

---

[4] In *The Wisdom of the Ancients*, and elsewhere.

[5] Cox, i. 53, *seq.;* ii. 108, 109, *et passim ;* Gubernatis, *Zoological Mythology,* &c.

till it had given them birth. We are therefore at liberty to regard the ancient mythological legends in their literal form, as we may be sure they were popularly regarded, and consider to what extent they may have served to prepare men's minds to receive the doctrine and religion of the Christ.

And here it cannot be questioned that all mythologies represented the gods as holding intercourse with men. They had their offspring among men, their friends and companions among men, their enemies among men. The teaching of mythology clearly was, that the notion of communion with the gods was neither absurd nor inconceivable. And so far as this mythology expressed on the one hand the popular sentiment, and on the other served to create and foster it, we may believe that to a certain extent it acted favourably rather than unfavourably in predisposing men to receive the message of the Incarnation. In like manner, the notion of assistance bestowed in an unexpected and supernatural way was by no means unfamiliar to mythology, and would therefore be subservient to the doctrine of a Divine Redeemer, who came to succour the weak, and to raise the fallen.[6] And, finally, the natural inference derived from mythology, when regarded in its widest survey, is suggestive of the truth that there are sources of wealth and strength for man in heaven which are not to be found on earth; and that, if he is to be delivered at all, it must be by a power exerted from without him, and not merely by strength developed from within.

It appears then, that we may fairly say that, notwithstanding much that was in the highest degree revolting in mythology, and much that had undoubtedly begun to pall upon the taste of the healthier and the loftier minds, there

---

[6] Cf. Hardwick, *Christ and other Masters*, part ii. p. 160 *seq*. The passage is too long to quote, but it is well worthy of reference.

was also that in it which would serve as a sufficiently prepared basis whereon to rear the superstructure of faith in a Divine Son of God and Redeemer of men, who should save His people with a mighty salvation, when His advent was proclaimed upon sufficient testimony.

While, however, the effect of the ancient mythology, both as regards the disgust and loathing it must have excited, and the relations of beings of a higher nature to man with which it may have made men's minds familiar, may have been on the whole favourable as a preparation for the preaching of the Gospel, it does not appear that at any time it had sufficed to arouse the distinct anticipations of a Redeemer to come, which obviously did exist among the Jews. We do indeed discover tokens of such anticipations from time to time;[7] but these were probably derived rather than original, and are perhaps to be referred mainly to the influence of the Jewish Scriptures when they had become widely extended by means of the Alexandrine version. The effect of mythological teaching, therefore, would not be so much of a positive as a negative character, regarded as a preparation for Christ. It would have prepared the mind for the reception of the idea, but could not have communicated the idea itself. Still, we must carefully bear in mind what it could not do, in order that we may

---

[7] The *vetus et constans opinio* of Suetonius (*Vesp.* iv.; cf. Tac. *Hist.* v. 13) must refer among others to Daniel's prophecy of the seventy weeks, then more than 500 years old. Cf. Josephus, *B. J.* vi. 5, 4, etc.; also the third Sibylline Oracle.

$$\text{καὶ τότ' ἔθνος μεγάλοιο Θεοῦ πάλι καρτερὸν ἔσται,}$$
$$\text{οἳ πάντεσσι βροτοῖσι βίου καθοδηγοὶ ἔσονται.} \qquad \text{194–5}$$

$$\text{καὶ τότε δὴ Θεὸς οὐρανόθεν πέμψει βασιλῆα.} \qquad \text{286}$$

$$\text{ἔστι δέ τις φυλὴ βασιλῆϊος, ἧς γένος ἔσται}$$
$$\text{ἄπταιστον· καὶ τοῦτο χρόνοις περιτελλομένοισιν}$$
$$\text{ἄρξει, καὶ καινὸν σηκὸν Θεοῦ ἄρξετ' ἐγείρειν.} \qquad \text{288–290}$$

$$\text{καὶ τότ' ἀπ' ἠελίοιο Θεὸς πέμψει βασιλῆα}$$
$$\text{ὃς πᾶσαν γαῖαν παύσει πολέμοιο κακοῖο.} \qquad \text{652–3}$$

the better understand what was actually done. In proportion to the poverty of the soil will be our astonishment at the beauty and luxuriance of the plant which afterwards took root in it.

We need not in any degree be anxious to dispute the position that fragments of truth are to be found in all religions. The reverse is rather the case; for it is the very presence of these elements of truth that constituted the natural basis on which alone it was possible for the Gospel to be reared. The points, however, on which it is desirable to arrive at clear and definite notions, if we can, are these : The way in which we are to regard the rise and development of these elements of truth as we find them existing, and the way in which they may be compared and contrasted with other elements that we recognise in the Old and New Testaments.

It may surely then be accepted as an axiom, that whatever of truth there is in any man, or in any nation, is derived from the fountain of truth, and is not an independent possession of the mind itself. The eye perceives the light; there is no light in the eye but that which it perceives, or, having perceived, retains. So in the human mind, there is no truth but that which it derives and appropriates from the fountain of truth. The mind is naturally constituted to apprehend the truth ; and when the channel is unimpeded truth flows in and is apprehended. The truth reveals itself. The mind rejoices in the consciousness of having discovered the truth; but with equal or with greater propriety we may say that the truth has revealed itself to the mind. And if truth is the exclusive possession of the Divine Being, every such manifestation of truth may be regarded as a true revelation from Him. Whatever indications, therefore, we find of a sense of sin, and of the undefined terrors incidental to it, notwithstanding the hideous forms it may have at times assumed, we may justly regard as revelations of a truth, even as St. Paul says, *The wrath of God is* revealed *from heaven against all ungodliness and unrighteousness of men who hold the truth in unrighteousness.*[8]   We need not, therefore, in any jealous or niggardly manner refuse to acknowledge the operation of the Divine Spirit of Truth in all nations and in all mythologies.   Everywhere and always, from the first dawn of intelligence on the earth, we may believe that the Spirit of Truth has been struggling to gain admittance into the minds of men; and as far as the *fact* is concerned, it matters not whether we speak of His success as the natural achievement of human effort or as the result of Divine revelation.   But unquestionably the latter is the more correct, because otherwise we should be at a loss to account for the various degrees of results, where there is every reason to believe that the human effort has been the same.   He has favoured some more highly than others, and the effects are manifest.

What was historically the actual primeval condition of mankind it will never be possible for us to determine. The Mosaic narrative may or may not commend itself to us as the most probable; it is absolutely certain that if we reject it we can discover none that shall be on the whole more satisfactory or more probable.   We may ask, How did the idea of God or a god first suggest itself to the human mind?   We may decide that the ever-present vision of the heavens, or the sky, or the light, or the sun,[9]

---

[8] Rom. i. 18.

[9] "One of the earliest objects that would strike and stir the mind of man and for which a sign or a name would soon be wanted is surely the sun. . . Think of man only as man . . . with his mind yet lying fallow, though full of germs—germs of which I hold as strongly as ever no trace has ever, no trace will ever be discovered anywhere but in man; think of the sun awakening the eyes of man from sleep, and his mind from slumber!   Was not the sunrise to him the first wonder, the first beginning of all reflection, all thought, all philosophy?   was it not to him the first

supplied a natural expression, borrowed from a natural object for the idea when it arose. But how did the idea arise? Was it spontaneous? Was it original? or Was it altogether secondary or suggested? This question we have really no means of deciding one way or the other. To draw an inference from the phenomena of language which decides it, obliges us to adopt the inconceivable hypothesis that the earliest individuals of our race were incapable of any other ideas than those of natural objects; that the first man was a merely sensuous being, who had no language but for the objects of sense, and no need for any other language. If this really were so, then it is inconceivable that the idea of God could ever have arisen. If, on the other hand, the idea of God was a primary and original idea, it must have found an original expression in language, whether or not the traces of such an expression are discernible in any of the existing forms of language. The analogy of the Aryan languages may indeed point us to the former inference; but it is one which may be modified, if not corrected, by the analogy of the Semitic languages. There the name for God is not derived from any visible object, but is itself expressive of an attribute that may naturally have been adopted as an original symbol for an idea which was original. To have called God the strong or mighty one, would seem to have been at least as simple and primitive as to have borrowed the idea of God from the sun, or the sky, or the light, or to have used the names of those objects for the expression of that idea. It may be impossible, on scientific principles, to decide whether or not the idea of God is original to man, without a very much larger induction than we at present possess; but these two considerations appear at least to be worth our

revelation, the first beginning of all trust, of all religion?"—Max Müller, *Science of Religion*, p. 368. Cf. also Hardwick, *Christ and other Masters*, part ii. p. 12, n. 2.

notice; namely, that it is difficult to conceive how the thought of God could ever have been framed if it was not from the first innate in man; if there had not been that in man's nature which responded to the external fact of God's existence.[1] We cannot imagine how it could have dawned upon the human conception which had before been devoid of it; and if it had lain dormant, then we may doubt whether mere earthly phenomena would have sufficed to arouse it. If, on the other hand, we accept the Mosaic record as authentic, and as furnishing as true an idea of the constitution and condition of the first man as we can obtain elsewhere, if not a truer one, then this question is practically solved for us, for that narrative represents the first man as possessed of free and uninterrupted communion with God.[2] He can have lacked, therefore, neither the full

---

[1] The analogy of human growth from childhood to maturity may suggest the supposition that the idea of God may have existed from the first in man, but potentially rather than actually. There was a capacity for the conception of God, though that conception existed only in germ, and was undeveloped, just as there was a capacity for all kinds of knowledge, though the knowledge was undiscovered. And thus it may be supposed that natural phenomena, operating on this capacity, developed the idea of God, which was not otherwise original or innate. But it appears that the thought of God is as vivid in childhood as it ever is afterwards, and the tendency of mental development is to expel rather than encourage that thought. The earliest races of man are the most religious, and the effect of intellectual development and mental culture is, at least in many cases, rather unfavourable to religious conceptions than otherwise. It would seem, therefore, that analogy points rather to the opposite conclusion, that the existence of the idea of God in the human mind can only be accounted for on the supposition that it was original and not derived, that it was innate in the first man, and not developed in him by the teachings of external nature. We cannot claim for human nature the power of inventing God, when the history of experience shows us that man's natural tendency, even under the most favourable circumstances, is to forget Him, or even to deny His existence.

[2] Gen. ii. 16, 17; iii. 8, 9, 10. Comparing these passages, we are led to infer that the effect of sin was to impair the freedom of man's intercourse with God.

conception of the idea, nor the language in which to clothe it.[3]

If, however, it is hard to believe that the idea of God was originally suggested to mankind by the teachings of external nature; if the spectacle of the brilliant and boundless heaven either developed in man the conception of a god, or at least furnished him with the earliest mode of expressing the hitherto unexpressed idea; can we suppose that the thought of *sin* owed its origin in the same way

---

[3] The opposite theory has found an eloquent exponent in Professor Max Müller. "The first materials of language supply expressions for such impressions only as are received through the senses. If, therefore, there was a root meaning to burn, to be bright, to warm, such a root might supply a recognised name for the sun and for the sky. But let us now imagine, as well as we can, the process which went on in the human mind before the name of sky could be torn away from its material object and be used as the name of something totally different from the sky. There was in the heart of man, from the very first, a feeling of incompleteness, of weakness, of dependence, whatever we like to call it in our abstract language. We can explain it as little as we can explain why the new-born child feels the cravings of hunger and thirst. But it was so from the first, and is so even now. Man knows not whence he comes and whither he goes. He looks for a guide, for a friend; he wearies for some one on whom he can rest; he wants something like a father in heaven. In addition to all the impressions which he received from the outer world, there was in the heart of man a stronger impulse from within—a sigh, a yearning, a call for something that should not come and go like everything else, that should be before, and after, and for ever, that should hold and support everything, that should make man feel at home in this strange world. Before this strange yearning could assume any definite shape it wanted a name: it could not be fully grasped or clearly conceived except by naming it. But where to look for a name? No doubt the storehouse of language was there, but from every name that was tried the mind of man shrank back because it did not fit, because it seemed to fetter rather than to wing the thought that fluttered within and called for light and freedom. But when at last a name, or even many names were tried and chosen, let us see what took place, as far as the mind of man was concerned. A certain satisfaction, no doubt, was gained by having a name or several names, however imperfect; but these names, like all other names, were but signs—poor, imperfect signs; they were predicates, and very partial predicates, of various small portions only of that vague and vast something

to the suggestions of natural phenomena? What, are the natural phenomena calculated to develop the notion of sin? It is impossible to determine. But it is likewise impossible to deny the manifold evidence of a knowledge of sin which meets us in the world. The sense of sin, therefore, if it was not prompted by the phenomena of nature, must either have been spontaneously developed, or it must have been caused by the presentation from without of some rule or standard which declared it. But if it was spontaneously

which slumbered in the mind. When the name of the brilliant sky had been chosen, as it has been chosen at one time or other by nearly every nation upon earth, was sky the full expression of that within the mind which wanted expression? Was the mind satisfied? Had the sky been recognised as its god? Far from it. People knew perfectly well what they meant by the visible sky; the first man who, after looking everywhere for what he wanted, and who at last in sheer exhaustion grasped at the name of sky as better than nothing, knew but too well that his success was after all a miserable failure. The brilliant sky was, no doubt, the most exalted, it was the only unchanging and infinite being that had received a name, and that could lend its name to that as yet unborn idea of the Infinite which disquieted the human mind. But let us only see this clearly, that the man who chose that name did not mean, could not have meant, that the visible sky was all he wanted, that the blue canopy above was his god."—*Science of Religion*, pp. 269-272. And again: "It was by a slow process that the human mind elaborated the idea of one absolute and supreme Godhead; and by a still slower process that the human language matured a word to express that idea. A period of growth was inevitable, and those who, from a mere guess of their own, do not hesitate to speak authoritatively of a primeval revelation which imparted to the Pagan world the idea of the Godhead in all its purity, forget that, however pure and sublime and spiritual that revelation might have been, there was no language capable as yet of expressing the high and immaterial conceptions of that heaven-sent message."—*Chips from a German Workshop*, i. 240.

More simple, and, on the whole, not less probable, appears to be the notion of a first man as yet unsinning, who could receive and therefore express the commands of the Almighty, and give names to all His creatures.

The idea of God is no less simple than it is stupendous or profound, and it was surely capable of being apprehended in its simplicity ages before thought or speech could frame or utter the "idea of one absolute and supreme Godhead."

developed, there is nothing to show that it may not from the first have been a delusion. There is nothing to show that it may not be a delusion now. There is nothing to show that we as sinners are individually guilty before God, unless there has been authoritatively declared to us an outward law that we have violated. The law may indeed be *written in the heart*,[4] but it must still be the counterpart of a reality which exists in God. Our consciences may accuse us; but why do they accuse us, unless because they reflect a law external to and independent of themselves, which says—Thou shalt not, or Thou shalt? What the historical rise of this consciousness was we know not, and science cannot discover it to us; but our own nature tells us that there the standard was long before there was any human consciousness to recognise its existence. It is impossible that the natural development of the moral faculties can both have invented the standard, and also have arrived at the knowledge of it. If they arrived at the knowledge of it, there it must have been to be known; they may have perceived it, or rather it must have revealed itself unto them; but if they invented it, then, being the invention of the moral faculties, we have no guarantee that the standard is not an incorrect one, our very perception of it may be an entire mistake: but then, of course, the inference follows, that if it is an entire mistake we have no right to insist upon our faculty of determining what is just or true.

Or we may state the matter thus. If God has given us a revelation, then He must also have given us adequate indications of its truth, and He must further have given us the power of recognising them as adequate when given. For if He has not given us this power, then any indications of a revelation, even if given, would be useless. We should be incapable of receiving it. If, on the other hand,

<hr>

[4] Rom. ii. 15.

He has not given us adequate indications of the truth, then the exercise of our faculty of discrimination is impossible. There is no higher sphere for its exercise. But we know that we do, as a matter of fact, possess this faculty of discrimination in some things, and to a certain extent, and we do habitually exercise it, even though at times it may mislead or fail us. Consequently, the possession of this faculty and the power of exercising it in all things but the highest, is reason for believing that we have it also in the highest if the opportunity of exercising it should occur. If, therefore, we possess a faculty of discriminating between truth and falsehood, then, on the supposition that God has given us a revelation appealing to that faculty, we are manifestly competent to recognise it when given; but the widest possible induction of facts leads us to confess that we do recognise a shalt and a shalt not, an ought and an ought not. This shalt and shalt not, this ought and ought not, cannot be true, we cannot know it to be true, it must be uncertain and unreal, if it is merely the result of our own invention and fancy, and not God's revelation. If, therefore, the shalt and the shalt not, the ought and the ought not, are true; if the difference between them is a reality; then that which assures us of this reality is the revelation of God. That is to say, it is by the revelation of God that we recognise the difference between right and wrong, truth and falsehood. God hath showed it unto us.

We are surely warranted then, in saying not only that the power of recognising this difference is given by God, but that it is one which could not be given through nature or the teachings of natural phenomena. It was not by the suggestions of these phenomena that man rose to a conception of morals or to the perception of the Infinite and the idea of God. It does not appear that the contemplation of any natural objects could reveal the moral difference between right and wrong, the beauty of truth or the hatefulness of falsehood. Nor can we believe that the first revelation of God was derived from gazing on the splendour and infinitude of the sky, or on the vastness of the ocean. It did not come from nature or through nature, but from beyond nature, from God Himself.

On the other hand, it is obvious that it is only by language derived from natural objects that we can express those ideas which are beyond the sphere of nature. It is only by metaphor and analogy that we can speak of the unseen. The eye of the mind has no language, but that which is required and has already been used to denote the impressions derived through the eye of the body, or through the other senses. And language thus employed has unquestionably a tendency to react on thought, and to debase thought; it has a tendency also to fetter and confine it. And it is probable that to this influence of language upon thought we may more or less directly ascribe many of the dreams of mythology in all nations; but then we must remember that if the true origin of mythology is to be found in language—if, as has been so finally said, mythology is the "dark shadow which language throws on thought"[5]—we have to face the question, Why is it that conceptions originally so pure and noble, so true and beautiful, suggested by the glorious phenomena of nature, should not have been preserved in their integrity, or at least from time to time have been renewed by the same inspiring influences? But, on the contrary, accepting this as their true origin, it cannot even be pretended that every trace of it did not soon vanish, like the dewdrops of the dawn before the rising sun, never to reappear but in

[5] " Mythology is inevitable, it is natural, it is an inherent necessity of language, if we recognise in language the outward form and manifestation of thought: it is in fact the dark shadow which language throws on thought, and which can never disappear till language becomes altogether commensurate with thought, which it never will."—Max Müller, *Science of Religion*, p. 353.

debasing and unworthy legends. In short, we can discover no tendency in mythology to regenerate itself. It follows therefore, from the evidence afforded by this method of mythological interpretation, that the natural tendency of man is to deteriorate. His first conceptions of the Infinite were truer and worthier than his latest; for, whether or not he originally identified the visible heavens with God, he subsequently learnt to confound God with the sensuous images language had associated with the visible heavens. And here was a moral fall.[6]

May we not say, then, that the witness of mythology is clear not only to this moral fall in itself, but also to the reality of that fallen condition of which it was at once the proof and the result? Why is there a tendency in human nature to deteriorate, an inability to rescue and restore itself, as the development of mythology and as practical experience alike testify, unless because of an

[6] " There are two distinct tendencies to be observed in the growth of ancient religion. There is, on the one side, the struggle of the mind against the material character of language, a constant attempt to strip words of their coarse covering, and fit them, by main force, for the purposes of abstract thought. But there is, on the other side, a constant relapse from the spiritual into the material, and, strange to say, a predilection for the material sense instead of the spiritual. This action and reaction has been going on in the language of religion from the earliest times, and is at work even now."—Max Müller, *Science of Religion*, p. 268.

And again, " The first step downwards would be to look upon the sky as the abode of that Being which was called by the same name; the next step would be to forget altogether what was behind the name, and to implore the sky, the visible canopy above our heads, to send rain, to protect the fields, the cattle, and the corn, to give to man his daily bread. Nay, very soon those who warned the world that it was not the visible sky that was meant, but that what was meant was something high above, deep below, far away from the blue firmament, would be looked upon either as dreamers whom no one could understand, or as unbelievers who despised the sky, the great benefactor of the world. Lastly, many things that were true of the visible sky would be told of its divine namesake, and legends would spring up, destroying every trace of the deity that once was hidden beneath that ambiguous name."—*Ibid*, p. 273.

original twist or wrench in our nature from the effects of which we cannot recover ourselves? All things bear witness to this fact, wherever we turn. All societies, religions, institutions, experience the effects and bear witness to the truth of it. Is it not as useless to deny as it is impossible to explain it? We may find it difficult to say what we mean by the Fall, and may not care too narrowly to define; but the evidence of facts for the reality and truth of a Fall is irresistible. And if the natural growth of mythology is itself a witness to this tendency to decline, how much more is the mythology full grown! Can anything afford more conclusive evidence of the depravity of the human heart than the ultimate form assumed by many of the legends of Greece, to say nothing of those of India? Is it possible to excuse or to condone the practices which were the immediate outcome of the cultus associated with those legends, and the deities to whom they referred? We may try to believe that their origin was more innocent than their result, but there can be no mistake about their result. The Pauline account of the heathen world in the Epistle to the Romans is too vivid not to be true, and is too true to be disputed. And that was the actual outcome of mythology, for of religion properly speaking there was none.

And can we believe that this was the method adopted by God for developing the growth of Christianity? Was Christianity the natural flower and fruit of such a seed and such a plant as this? Is Christianity what this developed into? Because, if we are to eliminate all but purely natural causes, we shall be constrained to confess that the Gospel as it appeared at first was the direct outcome, the spontaneous production, of germs and forces such as these. The hideous and the impure originated the 'lovely and the pure. The unholy generated the holy. If mythology was but the progressive development of religious ideas spontaneously conceived in man, it must have been a direct link in that chain of which the pure Gospel of Christ was the ultimate result.   And when we bear in mind the yet grosser and more openly revolting interpretation, which by some has been unhesitatingly assigned to universal mythology, construing its ever-varying development in the east and the west and the north and the south as but the unvarying repetition of the same ever-recurrent foul idea,[7] one shudders to think of the awful blasphemy that is involved in any position which implies or seems to imply that the very life-blood of Christianity has been deduced through channels such as these, and owes its natural origin to the same ultimate causes.   We may indeed say this may be science so called, but it cannot be truth.   Or rather, we may boldly say, this manifestly is not true; and therefore it cannot be science, for science is the handmaid of truth and leads to truth.

No!   What God has taught us through the patent and only too obvious facts of the heathen world and the ultimate phases of mythology, is sufficiently clear.   He has shown us written thereon in unmistakable characters the actual condition of the human heart, its naked deformity, its real depravity, its natural tendency, when left to itself. He has shown us the place there was in the world of our humanity for a Redeemer, the deep want of a redemption, the hopelessness and the impossibility of our nature, left simply to its own spontaneous efforts, being competent to regenerate itself.   He has shown us that all this was, over and over again, felt and witnessed to by that nature itself. He has shown us that even the greatest teachers in the schools of Athens could not shake themselves free from

---

[7] See *passim, e.g.* Cox, *Aryan Nations.* This writer does not hesitate to refer to the same hideous origin, and invest with the same foul significance, the narratives in Gen. iii. and Num. xxi. 7, 8, 9. Vol. ii. 116, *n.* 2; 114, etc.

the trammels of a corrupt nature, that they imperfectly discerned the depth of the corruption, and thereby proved themselves the subjects of it. He has thus shown us that the world by wisdom knew not God, and could not by searching find Him out.

The witness, then, of the heathen world is to the existence of sin with which it was unable to cope, and to which it was imperfectly alive; to the consciousness of a want which it was unable to supply; to the desire for light it was unable to obtain. Mankind yearned for that which it could not find, which in itself it did not possess. But every want, if a real one, argues the existence of that which will supply it. Provision is made in nature for the supply of every true and natural want, as is shown by the adaptation of one thing to another. We should infer, therefore, the abstract existence of that which would meet this want. And thus the universal testimony of the heathen world to the consciousness of the want becomes itself an unconscious anticipation of that which would supply it. The want of a redemption becomes the unconscious anticipation of a redeemer, and may be appealed to as such. The character and conditions of the want show the character and conditions he would be required to fulfil who should supply it. And they furnish, so far, a standard by which his actual character may be measured. He may be rightly estimated by his power of adaptation to the wants of humanity.

But what is the evidence which is afforded us by the study of mythology with reference to the probable origin of Christianity? If we take the more debased interpretation of it, we find it is absolutely impossible that a pure and purifying influence such as Christianity could have been evolved by a natural process from mythology. It could not have sprung from it, or have had the same origin with it. There must have been an entirely independent external and extra-natural agency at work to produce it. If, on the other hand, we suppose that the earliest ideas of religion were spontaneously developed through the influence of nature, then those ideas must have grown up and arrived at maturity in the same way; and unless we admit at some point or other the direct operation of a higher, independent and external influence, Christianity itself can have been but the ultimate result, the highest development, of these primary, self-evolved ideas. But we have seen that the actual tendency of the ideas has been to decline and to degenerate, not to become purer and more elevated; consequently here again we are met by a strong presumption that the actual origin of Christianity must be due to other causes than those suggested. That is to say, it does not seem possible to account for the higher development of the religious idea, without the admission of another influence out of, above, and beyond nature, which we can only term the direct revelation of God.

It matters not whether we can understand or define the actual operation of such an influence: if various considerations appear to converge towards and point to it, while the contrary supposition appears to be precluded absolutely, then the natural inference surely is that, in spite of ourselves, we must recognise its operation, account for it or understand it as we may.

If, therefore, the scientific investigation of the origin of religion leads us to the conclusion that it is a simply natural growth, developed naturally by the spontaneous evolution of religious germs inherent in man, we have a right to test this conclusion by the application of certain facts which are or are not consistent with it. We have seen that it is not possible to regard them as consistent with it, and therefore the inference clearly is that the proposed scientific theory fails to account for that which it professes to explain. There are certain manifest facts which are not comprehended in its induction, and which are actually fatal to it.

If, again, we cannot in any real sense *know* what is right and true without a virtual revelation to the conscience of the true and the right which consists in such knowledge, then it is clear that a path is at once opened out for us to conceive of other methods of revelation no less real, which shall approve themselves, not so much by the manner of their communication as by the subject-matter of that which they reveal. Thus, for example, given the person of Christ as an actual revelation from God, then those who beheld Him were recipients of that revelation whether they believed in Him or not: the person whom they beheld became an object to their consciousness which admitted of no dispute. The fact of the revelation, however, was antecedent to their knowledge of it. On the other hand, in the case of those who saw in Christ the manifestation of the Father, there was a yet further revelation, which was made known by other agencies that partly were and partly were not dependent on the testimony of their bodily senses ; but here also the true revelation consisted not in the method of its communication, but in the intrinsic glory of the object revealed, of which, whether through the senses or otherwise, they had become conscious. There had been a true revelation to the blind man at Jericho before with opened eyes he beheld the person of the Son of man, but he could not have *known* of this revelation except so far as it was revealed to him, and the *proof* of the revelation consisted in the object revealed. It follows then, that, just as there could be no knowledge of the person of Christ but for the fact of His manifestation to the eyes of men, so there could be no knowledge of His Divine character but for the fact of its revelation to the spirits of men. The knowledge is no proof of the revelation, but without the revelation there can be no knowledge properly so-called. We must have a

Divine revelation before we can really *know* the Divine; without it we must abide in darkness. As, however, the moral revelation of right and wrong is not of such a nature as to preclude the possibility of error, so neither is the spiritual revelation independent of the will. There ever have been, there always will be, consciences it is unable to touch.

The all-important questions, of course, arise, How can such a Divine revelation be brought home to the minds of men? and How can we recognise it when presented to us? How shall we know it when we see it, and be sure that we are not deceived? In answer to these questions we may say that the mind is prepared for the reception of a professedly Divine revelation by the combined weight of many convergent indications and the accumulated force of many independent testimonies. It is notorious that several religions appeal to a professedly Divine revelation. The Vedas of the Brahmans, the Zend-Avesta of the Parsis, the Tripi*t*aka of the Buddhists, the Kuran of the Muhammadans, all claim to be regarded, and are regarded by their respective followers, as divine. Are we called upon to admit the claim? Undoubtedly not. Every one of these collections of sacred writings rests upon a totally different basis from the Scriptures of the Old and New Testaments. No man in his senses can compare them and not perceive their essential and intrinsic difference. We have no desire to exalt our own religion at the expense of others, or to depreciate others that our own may be exalted; but our allegiance to our own religion, if we believe in it, forbids us for one moment to place it on the same level with others, as it prevents us from being blind to its generic difference and its immeasurable superiority.[b]

---

[b] "Those who would use a comparative study of religions as a means for debasing Christianity by exalting the other religions of mankind, are to my mind as dangerous allies as those who think it necessary to debase

If it could be proved that this superiority was merely a matter of opinion and of taste, and not a matter of fact, it would, of course, be worth nothing, and the sooner we allowed ourselves to be so persuaded the better it would be. But, forasmuch as the difference is demonstrably a matter of fact, it is useless to ignore it, and absurd to regard it as though it were not. What, in the eyes of the most impartial observer, are the claims of the Kuran in comparison with those of the New Testament or the Old? There is and can be no comparison. It is not that there is no truth in the Kuran, or that the truth therein is not derived from the one fountain of truth; but the evidence of revelation in it, properly so called, is simply *nil.* Or take again the Veda, as the knowledge of it has of late years been opened out to us by the unceasing and indefatigable labours of an eminent scholar of this place; where can we find in the

all other religions in order to exalt Christianity. Science wants no partisans. I make no secret that true Christianity, I mean the religion of Christ, seems to me to become more and more exalted the more we know, and the more we appreciate the treasures of truth hidden in the despised religions of the world. But no one can honestly arrive at that conviction, unless he uses honestly the same measure for all religions. It would be fatal for any religion to claim an exceptional treatment, most of all for Christianity. Christianity enjoyed no privileges and claimed no immunities when it boldly confronted and confounded the most ancient and the most powerful religions of the world. Even at present it craves no mercy, and it receives no mercy from those whom our missionaries have to meet face to face in every part of the world. Unless our religion has ceased to be what it was, its defenders should not shrink from this new trial of strength, but should encourage rather than depreciate the study of comparative theology."—Max Müller, *Science of Religion,* p. 37. All this is perfectly true when considering the claims of Christianity with a view to forming a decision; but when those claims have been considered, then, if they have not been rejected, there are other words which come into operation; namely, " He that is not with me is against me." It is strange, but no less true than strange, that a position of absolute neutrality with regard to Christ, and therefore with regard to the religion of Christ, is one that always was, and always will be, found impossible to be long maintained.

Veda, with all its beauty and with all its truth, with its vast antiquity and the glorious visions it has unfolded of the earliest dawn of human society and life—where shall we find in it the same distinctive evidence of revelation in the same conscious hold on the Divine that we cannot but acknowledge, even if we do not feel it, in the Psalms of David and in the vision of Isaiah the son of Amoz?

It is not from narrowness, or bigotry, or partiality, or want of sympathy with other religions than our own that we say this, but because the songs of a David or the burdens of an Isaiah have palpable evidences of a knowledge of God and of a mission from God that are not to be found elsewhere. If a special revelation has anywhere been vouchsafed, and the record of it exists, and if we have faculties capable of perceiving it when given, then there can be no question to which of these quarters we must turn to find it. We cannot say it is to be discovered equally in all. We may say it is to be found pre-eminently *here*, for instance, in the Scriptures of the Old Testament, and that to such an extent that the claim of the others to anything like a special or direct revelation is not for a moment to be entertained in comparison with theirs. Their witness is within.

And then, side by side with these internal marks, we have the sure and incorruptible evidence of history, which step by step can be traced backwards in its broader and more general aspects, till it leaves us in the dilemma of reading the history in the light of the prophets, and the prophets in the light of the history, or else of understanding neither. We have the stream of history flowing on contemporaneously with the stream of literature, and the phenomena presented by each constrain us to confess that they are both unique. Is this the result of accident? is it the effect of collusion, of preconcerted arrangement? or does it serve more naturally to suggest the gradual working out of a Divine plan, of which there is no second instance in the annals of the world? Doubtless this, with all that it demands, is after all the only reasonable solution of the problem. And the broad and solid results that we are able to arrive at are of a nature to be independent of the more fragmentary and partial criticisms of a philosophy that refuses to be bound by any critical canons; while they present a substantial basis of fact that must serve to correct and modify conclusions that are derived from the assumption of a uniform and dull monotony in the history and literature of the world which has never been broken. Here are the very facts which must serve to check the over-hasty generalisation. They must either be left out, or they must be tortured and perverted before they will fit in.

Thus we find, at any rate, that there is sufficient to arrest our attention in considering, for example, the claims of the Old Testament to be regarded as a special Divine revelation in a sense in which neither the Vedas nor the Kuran can pretend to be. Treating it with the strictest impartiality, as we naturally should treat any other book, we nevertheless find it to be marked with exceptional features which are very peculiar. As a matter of historic fact, it has formed the basis for another set of writings very different from its own in style and character, and that in a way that is altogether without parallel. It was the literary progenitor of the New Testament; and but for the Old Testament as a foundation the New could never have been written. And yet the relation of the New Testament to the Old is not that of a commentary, but of an independent, original, and in some sense antagonistic work. And these statements remain equally true, when the Old Testament and the New are regarded merely as human productions, as the natural growth of literature in times and circumstances very diverse. The Old Testament is a complete national literature: the

New Testament cannot in any way be regarded as a national literature, though produced for the most part by writers of the same nation as the Old, after an interval of nearly five centuries. The chief characteristic of the New Testament is that it professes to record the fulfilment and realisation of the hopes and aspirations created by the Old, and to describe the results consequent thereupon. The historic relation, therefore, of cause and effect is that which best expresses the relation subsisting between these two collections of writings, and it is one which it is impossible to deny. There may have been other causes combining to bring about the production of the New Testament, but it is impossible to eliminate altogether the influence of the Old Testament as a principal and pre-ponderating cause.

In the New Testament, however, we find the conception of the Christ fully developed, and there, if anywhere, we are to discover its ultimate form. It received no appreciable development after the latest of the New Testament books was written, or, at least, none with which we need concern ourselves. And yet this conception of the Christ as there exhibited, whether in historical narrative or in epistolary correspondence, is one that could not have arisen without adequate historical preparation and development. Even the fourfold life of Jesus, whom its several authors agree in identifying with the Christ, could not, if regarded merely as a literary production, have been written, if there had not existed previously certain ideas and notions which served as a nucleus for the crystallisation of the thought. It is hopeless to discover what these ideas and notions were, if we do not seek for them in the Old Testament. There unquestionably the germ of them existed, from thence they sprang, and by this they were nurtured and developed. And the process of their growth is capable of being historically traced. For example, in the book of

Daniel, no matter when it was written, we find a usage of the word Messiah which is unique in the Old Testament.[9] Even allowing, which I do not allow, that this book was written as late as the time of Antiochus Epiphanes, it still affords undeniable testimony to the existence at that time of the conception of a person, more or less distinct, who could be spoken of as Messiah, the word being used like a proper name without the definite article. And whether this was in the second or the sixth century B.C., it represents a development of thought, an advancement in the direction of form and substance, inasmuch as not till then is such an expression found. But on every ground there must have been some apparent reason for the conception expressed. There must have been that already existing which favoured the notion, and sufficed to create or to encourage it. Perhaps it may not be easy to determine what this was, but of its existence there can be no doubt.

To trace, then, the historic development of what we may term the Religion of the Christ will be the object of the following lectures: to follow it out in the three departments of history, poetry, and prophecy, till we arrive at the period when He who was proclaimed as the Christ appeared. The proposition with which we start is this, that there must have been a sufficient basis in the Old Testament for the New Testament doctrine of the Christ to be reared upon. That doctrine could not have rested upon nothing. It appealed to a conception it already found in existence. That conception was exclusively owing to the influence exerted by the Scriptures of the Old Testament upon the popular mind, or else to spontaneous ideas existing in the national mind, of which the only explanation and record must be sought in the Scriptures of the Old Testament. As whatever traces there are of a similar conception in other nations are apparently derived from one and the same

[9] Cf. 2 Sam. i. 21, perhaps the nearest approach to it.

source, we shall be able to compare the origin of this conception with the supposed origin of mythological conceptions, and to mark the contrast between them. That any such idea was original with the Jewish nation, and peculiar to that people, admits of no reasonable doubt. It is sufficiently clear that they laid claim to the possession of it, and there is no other nation that can dispute its possession with them. They are historically distinct from all other nations in this respect. What is the natural explanation of this fact, or does it admit of any explanation that is simply natural?

If then, by pursuing a strictly historical method, we are able to trace the growth of this idea step by step, investigating and examining the several indications of its existence, and the various circumstances that may have led to its development—the influence of natural causes, the pressure of external events, the example of surrounding nations and the like—we shall be in a better position to decide upon these questions. We shall then be able to determine what the evidence is for the first origin of this idea, whether in its rise and development it can be placed in the category of mythological conceptions that can be traced to the double meanings of words, whether there is any natural process capable of leading up to the first thought, or whether we must not consider it as a communication imparted to our humanity rather than originated by it—a communication, however, of which the importance and the value consists quite as much in its intrinsic nature as in the method employed for conveying it, and of which the character and the tendency are the highest evidence of its origin.

If again we can find in mythology no clear indications of the hope of a Redeemer, which as a matter of fact are found in the history and literature of the Jews, and if in philosophy also, which may be regarded as a protest against mythology, there is no higher indication than that afforded

by a celebrated passage in the "Republic," we may surely
arrive at the not unreasonable conclusion that these characteristics of the Jewish Scriptures, being as they are
unique, do constitute the very highest evidence of the
special revelation which they are alleged to contain. Elsewhere humanity did not cherish this hope, here it was
cherished; this is the way in which it was cherished; and
this is the reason why it was cherished. The hope professed
to be based upon a promise: a promise implies a person
promising. In this case a person promising implies an
unusual and unique operation on the part of God. The
evidence of the work done points conclusively to the doer
of it. We are led up on all hands to the confines of
the supernatural and the Divine. Mythology could give
no promise; philosophy could give no promise, human
nature itself could not have originated any promise; but
mythology, philosophy, and human nature, alike bore witness to the defect which the promise undertook to supply.
Thus far the unaided energies of man could go, but no
farther. They cried aloud unto heaven, but they could give
no answer; the only answer was the echo of their cry.

A period, however, occurred in human history when a
distinct answer was given. A note of preparation for that
answer was struck by the son of Zacharias in the wilderness, when he awoke once more the voice of the ancient
prophets. And then the answer itself came in the preaching
and the mission of Jesus. He claimed to be the Christ of
whom Moses in the law and the prophets did write. That
He advanced this claim there is not a shadow of doubt.
That His moral character must stand or fall according as
His claim was or was not just, is equally certain. His
moral and personal character were not the creation of the
Evangelists. They did not invent their Jesus, nor invent
for Him His character of the Christ. And yet His character
as depicted by them stands alone in the history and the

literature of the world. As an invention, however, it would have been little less wonderful than as a history; for there were no materials out of which to construct it, and they were not the men to use them if there had been.

We have then a promise, and a person, and a claim—a person claiming to fulfil the promise. We are all of us competent to decide how far the promise was fulfilled in Him, how far He failed to realise it. Nor is it very probable that we shall reject Him on the ground that He failed to realise the promise. If we reject Him at all, it will be on other grounds than these. And then, in that case, we shall have to face this fact, that the most silent and the most mighty revolution the world has ever known was immediately connected with the belief that the ancient promise was fulfilled in Him, so that the verdict of history will be opposed to the estimate we have formed of Jesus.

The circumstances, therefore, connected with the historic rise of a particular religion, which are of such a nature as to be independent of the perfectly free discussion of various points relating thereto, and of the particular resolution that may await the questions involved, are a valid presumptive proof that this religion was intrinsically and in its origin different from all others, inasmuch as of no other religion can the same characteristics be predicated. The indications are many and various : they are independent, cumulative, and confirmatory. They point us from many quarters to one and the same conclusion. If the several tales of several mythologies appear to be all resolvable into one original idea, which is that of the ever-recurrent decay and revival of nature, it is not so here. It is simply impossible, for example, that the record of the Jewish history, interpret it as we may, and reduce it to any extent we please, can be resolved into the mere repetition of the same idea. It stands out in marked contrast with every mythology, and furnishes the broad and solid basis in life and fact for the possible existence of other living facts, to which there is palpable evidence in literature and in history, and which but for such a basis could themselves have had no existence.

And thus the historic and literary development of the doctrine and religion of the Christ, first as it grew and gathered form before He came, and secondly as it was developed in the early Christian literature, will be the strongest evidence of its origin; and we shall find that as we cannot believe in Jesus without believing in the Christ, and cannot believe in the Christ without believing in Jesus, so neither can we disbelieve in Jesus as the Christ without rejecting an accumulation of evidence which may justly be regarded as *the record that God gave of His Son.*

LECTURE II.

THE CHRIST OF JEWISH HISTORY.

Die Gründung des jüdischen Staats durch Moses ist eine der denkwürdigsten Begeben-
heiten, welche die Geschichte aufbewahrt hat, wichtig durch die Stärke des Verstandes,
wodurch sie ins Werk gerichtet worden, wichtiger noch durch ihre Folgen auf die Welt, die
noch bis auf diesen Augenblick fortdauern. Zwei Religionen, welche den größten Theil der
bewohnten Erde beherrschen, das Christenthum und der Islamismus, stützen sich beide auf
die Religion der Hebräer, und ohne diese würde es niemals weder ein Christenthum noch
einen Koran gegeben haben.

Ja, in einem gewissen Sinne ist es unwiderleglich wahr, daß wir der Mosaischen
Religion einen großen Theil der Aufklärung danken, deren wir uns heutiges Tags
erfreuen. Denn durch sie wurde eine kostbare Wahrheit, welche die sich selbst überlassene
Vernunft erst nach einer langsamen Entwickelung würde gefunden haben, die Lehre von
dem einigen Gott, vorläufig unter dem Volke verbreitet, und als ein Gegenstand des
blinden Glaubens so lange unter demselben erhalten, bis sie endlich in den hellern Köpfen
zu einem Vernunftbegriff reifen konnte. Dadurch wurden einem großen Theil des
Menschengeschlechts alle die traurigen Irrwege erspart, worauf der Glaube an Vielgötterei
zuletzt führen muß, und die hebräische Verfassung erhielt den ausschließenden Vorzug, daß
die Religion der Weisen mit der Volksreligion nicht in directem Widerspruche stand, wie
es doch bei den aufgeklärten Zeiten der Fall war.—*Schiller.*

LECTURE II.

IF we are willing to allow that God has spoken more or less by all the religions of the world—and in proportion to the elements of truth contained in them He must have done so—then it manifestly follows that in whatever sense the Christ was His special and chosen way of revealing Himself, all other religions must in their degree bear witness unto Him. That they may directly do so is perhaps not to be expected, for in that case God must have spoken specially by them; but that they must indirectly do so is clear, for otherwise the voice of God would give an uncertain or even a discordant sound. But in point of fact there is an indirect and silent witness borne by all religions to the Christ. There is no religion which does not profess to deal with sin, and there is no religion which does not virtually confess its inability to deal with it. There is no religion which does not profess to discriminate between right and wrong, and thereby witness to the majesty of conscience. There is no religion worthy of the name which does not profess to come with a message from God, and on that ground to demand the attention of mankind. But surely thus far the testimony of all religions is in favour of, rather than opposed to, the teaching of Him who claimed to be the Christ. To insist, therefore, as there is a tendency to do now-a-days, upon the fact of God's having spoken by other religions besides our own can really have no other effect than that of exalting our own, unless it is done with the concealed intention of disparaging it.[1] If we really believe that God's message by Christ was exceptional, paramount, and final, then it must be salutary in a high degree to trace the lines of corroborative evidence as they discover themselves in the various religions of mankind, and as they converge towards Him; but if we are to arrive at the conclusion that God has not spoken by Christ in any other way than He has spoken by Confucius, by Buddha, or by Muhammad, in a higher but not in a different way, then the sooner we clearly understand this the better, because such a conclusion does not appear to be in any sense compatible with the distinct teaching of Him whom we profess to follow. As philosophers we may hold the balance evenly between all religions, and strike it in favour of none; as Christians we cannot do so, because Christ demanded nothing less than the entire surrender of the whole man, and if we refuse this we virtually reject Him. We have, however, already attempted to show that there is very strong presumptive evidence against the development of Christianity by any processes merely natural, after the manner of other religions, because of its strong and essential contrast with them; and consequently the more we study other religions, provided we study our own fairly, the more we shall be persuaded of its intrinsic difference, and of its unique superiority.

---

[1] "Many are the advantages to be derived from a careful study of other religions, but the greatest of all is that it teaches us to appreciate more truly what we possess in our own. When do we feel the blessings of our own country more warmly and truly than when we return from abroad? It is the same with regard to religion. . . . We have done so little to gain our religion, we have suffered so little in the cause of truth, that however highly we prize our own Christianity, we never prize it highly enough until we have compared it with the religions of the rest of the world."—Max Müller, *Chips*, etc., i. 183.

If, however, there was no supernatural origin, properly so called, for Christianity, it is clear that we must seek its origin among the manifold operations of nature. It must have developed itself by a process of evolution from the spontaneous energies and resources of humanity. But as a matter of fact we know its pedigree if we do not know its origin. Christianity was the historical development of Judaism, or, as it is now called, Mosaism. All the first preachers of Christianity had been notoriously disciples of Moses, and all zealous of the law. The earliest home of Christianity was Palestine, and indeed Jerusalem. And in our survey of the religions of the world, if there is none that does not bear indirect testimony to the religion of Christ, there appears to be one marked out from all the rest by the direct testimony that it bears to Him. This, however, must of course be a matter of inference, and not of proof. Still the inference may be so strong as to amount to reasonable proof. Let us look, for example, at the general tenor of Jewish history. The whole of that history, as we have it in the Old Testament, was very probably completed several centuries before Christ. It can have undergone no material alteration after it was completed. It is in the highest degree improbable that the history of Abraham, for instance, was a late addition. There can be no reasonable doubt that the lives of the patriarchs were as early as the Exodus, perhaps even earlier. But this matters not. Put the date of Genesis in its present form as late as the sixth or seventh century before Christ, or, if it is desirable, even later, monstrous as the theory may be, we find in the first thirty chapters the record of a promise given to the patriarchs no less than five times to the effect that all the families of the earth shall be blessed in them. Three times is this promise given with reference to Abraham; twice directly to him; once indirectly of him; once it is repeated to Isaac, and once again to Jacob. The first time it is made personally to Abraham, the second time it is restricted to his seed, and the form is slightly changed from " be blessed" to " bless themselves." In this changed form the promise is renewed to Isaac, while to Jacob it is repeated as before, but given to him and his seed.[2]

In whatever way, therefore, this promise is explained, there can be no doubt that it is a substantive fact of the literature, and of very ancient date. It appears, however, and this is very important, to have been overlooked, at least to a great extent, for it was imbedded in another promise which evidently took firmer hold of the popular mind, as it naturally would—the promise, namely, of the possession of the land. For it is remarkable that, whenever this promise is alluded to, as it often is subsequently,

---

[2] " ἐν σοί means 'in thee;'—that is, 'in thee as their type,' or 'in thy faith.' In the original passage it has the sense, 'by thee;'—that is, the form of their blessing shall be, by thy name. 'The Lord bless thee as He blessed Abraham and his descendants.'"—Jowett on *Galatians* iii. 8.

The passages where the promise occurs are Gen. xii. 3, *In thee shall all families of the earth be blessed,* spoken to Abraham; xviii. 18, *All the nations of the earth shall be blessed in him,* spoken of Abraham; xxii. 18, *In thy seed shall all the nations of the earth bless themselves,* spoken to Abraham; xxvi. 4, *In thy seed shall all the nations of the earth bless themselves,* spoken to Isaac; xxviii. 14, *In thee and in thy seed shall all the families of the earth be blessed,* spoken to Jacob. In the first and last cases the word used for *earth* is הָאֲדָמָה. In the other three הָאָרֶץ. The only other passages in which the reflective form " bless himself," etc., is used, are Deut. xxix. 19; Ps. lxxii. 17; Isaiah lxv. 16, *bis;* Jer. iv. 2. As in three out of the five passages in Genesis the form of the verb is a passive, and as there are certain clear instances in which the reflective form is used in a passive sense—*e.g.* Prov. xxxi. 30; Micah vi. 16; Ezek. xix. 12; Lam. iv. 1, etc.—there can be no reasonable doubt that it is at least permissible to regard the passive sense as the correct one in all; but the real import of the promise is independent of any such grammatical ambiguity. Let us suppose that the right way in which to take the words in the five cases is in the reflective sense, as the passive is sometimes reflective—*e.g.* Gen. iii. 10; Ps. lv. 13, etc.; and that the " in thee" indicates not the channel of the blessing through which it is derived but the stanit is the inheritance rather than the seed which is mentioned. This is the case, for example, in the Psalms,[3] in the Pentateuch very frequently, and in the Prophets. The oath to Abraham is commonly referred to the occupation of Canaan, and whenever there is any reference to the seed, it is the people that is meant. In fact, there is no repetition of the promise about the person or the seed, which is five times given in Genesis, throughout the whole of the Old Testament. Perhaps the nearest approach to a repetition of it is to be found in the words of Micah,[4] *Thou wilt perform the truth to Jacob and the mercy to Abraham, which thou hast sworn unto our fathers from the days of old.* This being written probably in the days of Hezekiah cannot be understood of the possession of the land, but may justly be regarded as a spiritual assurance.

dard or example of blessing according to which it is acknowledged, then we have the assertion that *all nations of the earth shall bless themselves in Abraham and his seed;* that is, all nations of the earth shall regard Abraham and his seed as the highest examples of blessing—a promise which is either significant or meaningless; if it is meaningless, here at any rate it is for any one who chooses to speculate on its possible meaning; but if it is significant, then its only meaning can be that all nations shall recognise in Abraham the most conspicuous instance of blessing, which at least implies a consciousness on the part of the writer, whoever he was, that the blessing of Abraham was to be acknowledged by the world at large; that the world at large was to sit at the feet of Abraham in admiration of the extent to which God had blessed him. This is eminently true if Abraham was the recipient of real blessings and a real covenant; eminently untrue if he had been deceived and was the possessor of no covenant. It is eminently true now to those who are partakers of the faith of Abraham; it is utterly false if the promise to Abraham was a fiction, and the supposed fulfilment of it a mistake. The particular form or manner in which St. Paul uses the promise in no way affects the inherent significance of the language, independently of all grammatical niceties, if there was any actual covenant made with Abraham, and if the claims of Jesus were valid. That significance remains even if we demur to St. Paul's argument. Its real significance was not given by him, but by the author of the promise in Genesis, whoever he was.

[3] *Eg.* Ps. cv. 9, 11.   [4] Micah vii. 20. See also Lecture iv.

But it must be observed that it is in itself conclusive evidence of the existence in Micah's time of the promise in Genesis, and that it was then very ancient.

There appears, then, on the surface of the Jewish literature, and in one of the earliest portions of it, a promise to the effect that in Abraham, Isaac, and Jacob, all the nations of the earth shall be blessed, or shall bless themselves. Whether any such promise was ever given or not, there it is; we have only now to deal with literary facts, and this apparent promise is a literary fact. Very far back in the annals of the Jewish nation we meet with this expression of a consciousness on their part that they were to be the channels or the standards of blessing to mankind; for, whatever else the promise is, it must certainly be so regarded. But what is equally strange, is that this consciousness appears to a great extent to have died away. The nation itself was isolated, and exclusive in its manners, habits, and sympathies. In the prophets, especially in Isaiah, there are indeed many passages in which this consciousness revives, and not only revives, but increases in intensity and depth. This, however, is in strong contrast to the historic development of the nation's life. While we observe that there is no distinct repetition of the promise to Abraham later than Genesis, we cannot forget that in another form it is continually repeated. To take two examples only, *Behold, thou shalt call a nation that thou knowest not, and nations that knew not thee shall run unto thee because of the Lord thy God, and for the Holy One of Israel; for He hath glorified thee.*[5] *And the Gentiles shall come to thy light, and kings to the brightness of thy rising.*[6] What is this but the same assurance given in another form? In all these cases, we must acknowledge that there is the clear expression of a deep consciousness that the mission of Israel was to be a blessing to the

<hr>

[5] Isaiah lv. 5.   [6] Isaiah lx. 3.

nations. This is manifest at the dawn of their history, and it is equally conspicuous in the palmy days of Hezekiah's reign. But there is only one way in which it can be said that the nations of the world have derived blessing from Israel, and that is, as the prophet indicates, through the knowledge of their God. We must, therefore, either acknowledge this obligation, or we must repudiate it. If we repudiate it we shall become involved in the somewhat difficult task of having to show that there was no intrinsic superiority in the sublime monotheism and pure morality of the Hebrew Scriptures over the vague and dubious conjectures of heathenism and mythology; that the Psalms, the Prophets, and the Law, are at most only on a par with the corresponding productions of other nations, if indeed they are not inferior to them. If, on the other hand, we acknowledge this obligation, then we shall have to account for the fact that, ages before it was incurred, this promise to Abraham was recorded in the national literature, answering in a remarkable way to the subsequent development of events. For in this case we have not to deal with the question of the promise being given, but with the fact of its having been recorded.

When, however, we bear in mind that Abraham's previous associations had been idolatrous, and that his father, if not he himself, had served other gods, we shall have to account for the additional circumstances of his change of faith, and to consider that the narrative in Genesis is the only narrative we possess of the first commencement of a mighty revolution of thought, which was most important and far-reaching in its consequences. As far as we know, the origin of what afterwards became Israelitish monotheism was this very episode in Abraham's life; and, according to the narrative, the form it took was that of a definite promise given by God. In other words, as it is highly improbable that Abraham should have originated this faith for himself;[7] and as, from the facts before us, it is impossible to deny that the most remarkable results flowed from it, the only natural inference is that the reality of a revelation is proved in the character and greatness of the thing revealed. The call of Abraham and the promise given to him stand out in marked contrast to all that can be explained on merely natural principles, and here if anywhere we are constrained to admit the operation of forces and influences beyond the limits of nature. If we do not postulate the existence and action of a cause which cannot be traced home to nature, we must leave unaccounted for and unaccountable great spiritual results which it is equally impossible to deny. When, however, we further take into consideration the fact that this particular promise to Abraham exists nowhere in the Old Testament[8] so plainly as it does in Genesis, till an allusion to it reappears in the first verse of St. Matthew's Gospel and in St. Paul's Epistle to the Galatians; we must then

---

[7] The words of Professor Max Müller show very strikingly that there is only one way in which the spiritual advance we perceive in Abraham is to be accounted for. "And if we are asked how this one Abraham preserved not only the primitive intuition of God as He had revealed Himself to all mankind, but passed through the denial of all other gods to the knowledge of the one God, we are content to answer that it was by a special Divine Revelation. We do not indulge in theological phraseology, but we mean every word to its fullest extent. The Father of Truth chooses His own prophets, and He speaks to them in a voice stronger than the voice of thunder. It is the same inner voice through which God speaks to all of us. That voice may dwindle away, and become hardly audible; it may lose its Divine accent, and sink into the language of worldly prudence; but it may also, from time to time, assume its real nature, with the chosen of God, and sound into their ears as a voice from heaven. A 'divine instinct' may sound more scientific and less theological; but in truth it would neither be an appropriate name for what is a gift or grace accorded to but few, nor would it be a more scientific, *i.e.* a more intelligible word than 'special revelation.'"—*Chips from a German Workshop*, i. 373.

[8] A remarkable allusion to *both* the promises is found in Joshua xxiv. 3, 13, but the first is subordinate and incidental. This narrative, how-

put over against a very ancient recorded promise, which has all the appearance of a prophecy, the no less certain historical fact of the birth of a remarkable personage who was alleged to have fulfilled it, and whose advent would have been its complete fulfilment if all or nearly all that was related of him was true.[9]

We pass on, however, to notice other points in the historic development of the national life of Israel. First, then, comes the long period of bondage in Egypt, which, according to the narrative, had been distinctly foretold to Abraham.[1] The memory of this bondage and of the redemption from it was too deeply imprinted on the national mind and on the national literature for either one or the other to be for one moment doubted. Nor, on the supposition of a *post eventum* prophecy, is it easy to understand why there should have been left upon the face of it a disagreement with the ostensible record of its fulfilment.[2] While, however, we cannot prove the actual occurrence of the prophecy, from which of course the whole supernatural character of the narrative and its Divine claims would follow, we can show that a large variety of circumstances in the history points consistently to the inference that we must make allowance for the operation of other than merely natural agencies. Abraham's actual knowledge of God is itself the strongest argument for a direct revelation, since, under the circumstances, it cannot be accounted for without; but when we have arrived thus far the antecedent improbability of certain additional features of the same narrative is to a large extent removed.

ever, not only presupposes that in Genesis, but implies familiarity with it among the people for whose benefit this was written. It is also valuable as showing the earliest interpretation of Genesis xxii. 18. Cf. Hosea i. 10 (ii. 1).

[9] For the contrast between the character of Abraham and the highest analogous Hindu conceptions, see Hardwick, *Christ and other Masters*, part ii. 164 *seq.*   [1] Gen. xv. 13.   [2] Ex. xii. 40, 41.

And so if we find a highly exceptional deliverance occurring in the history of the people, which in its substantial features cannot be questioned; as, for instance, that it was accomplished without a blow being struck on their part; that it was preceded by a variety of national calamities befalling the Egyptians, which if not entirely peculiar were at least of peculiar severity; that this deliverance was brought about by means of a person who had himself undergone a long period of probation in Egypt and in exile from Egypt; that he laid the foundation of his people's greatness and of their national peculiarities, as well as of their very national existence, by giving them a law which he succeeded in persuading them was of Divine origin, and which was undoubtedly marked by many features of exceptional prudence, not to say of Divine wisdom; that, under the circumstances, it is hard to account for the profound submission with which the Law was immediately received, if its promulgation was not accompanied with circumstances of special solemnity and awe, such as those which are recorded in the very narrative to which we are indebted for the code itself; that the position occupied by this person was entirely unique in the annals of the nation, so that, in the long roll of their kings and prophets, no second arose like him; that he claimed to stand to his people in the position of a mediator with God, and to be the bearer of a message from God; that this claim must at least in part be judged by the way in which it was advanced, and by the results which followed it, as well as by the character of the message itself; that it is equally hard to maintain the charge of imposture against Moses in the face of all the evidence which confronts us, and to acquit him of that charge if the narrative which professes, in part at any rate, to be by him, and which, if not genuine, at least claims to be authentic, is not substantially trustworthy as a narrative of fact; that from the whole tenor of the subsequent history and literature it is hardly possible to overestimate the greatness of his character and mission, and yet at the same time is not possible to estimate them duly and reject the general trustworthiness of the record; if, I say, we find all this, which we doubtless do find, it becomes a question whether an antecedent probability is not thereby created in favour of the highly exceptional significance which the record attributes to the history. We are undoubtedly dealing with a series of events which are altogether beyond the scope of ordinary human circumstance or national experience. Is it not possible that their significance in the scheme of God's providential government may be something more than ordinary? Nay, must it not be so?

Another feature altogether exceptional is to be noted in the wanderings that followed the Exodus. In the face of the corroborative evidence afforded by the Psalms and the Prophets, it is not possible to doubt the truth of their main incidents—for example, their general character and long duration.[3] In fact, so deeply did the influence of the nomad life in the wilderness imprint itself on the national character, that traces of it may be said to exist at the present day. And yet to discover any satisfactory natural causes upon which the wanderings may be adequately accounted for is not easy. How is it that a lawgiver whose energy and genius never failed him, having delivered his people from the thraldom of the then mightiest nation of the world, and having successfully maintained their independence against the tribes and kingdoms of the desert, should be unable to crown the work of his life by leading them to the goal of their common desires; but after wast-

---

[3] See, for instance, Ps. lxviii. 7, 8; lxxviii. 13 *seq.;* lxxx. 8; lxxxi. 5-10; xcv. 10; cv. 39-44; cvi. 17-19; cxxxv. cxxxvi. Hosea xi. 1; xii. 13; xiii. 4. Amos v. 25, 26. Micah vi. 4, 5; vii. 15, etc. etc.

ing forty years of fruitless lingering in the desert, should deliberately consign that work to a younger officer of his own appointment, who was not personally better fitted to accomplish it than he was himself? These things are in themselves so improbable that we must either reject them historically, which we cannot do, or else taken together they point us to the only reason for them, which is that assigned.

But, in point of fact, the same characteristics confront us at every turn. As we read page after page of the history, we are equally perplexed whether to take it with such supernatural elements as are inseparable therefrom, or to attempt, however hopelessly, to reduce it to such dimensions as may appear not to transcend the limits of the intelligible and the ordinary. For example, the main features of the occupation of Canaan are undeniable.[4] And everywhere the most conspicuous of those features is the consciousness with which the whole nation is possessed that they are about to inherit a country promised to their fathers. The reason of this persuasion is apparent on the surface of their literature. The poetry, prophecy, and history, are alike imprinted with it. If we suppose for a moment that the promise was an after-thought of the literature, then the history becomes unintelligible. If we reject the history as incredible, then the literature and history alike become unmeaning and inexplicable. If we concede the promise as an actual fact, then doubtless a sufficient impulse is discovered for the current of the history; but then, at the same time, the germ of the supernatural is conceded, and the foundation laid thereby for its occasional if not continual presence afterwards. And it is this general broad conclusion and the natural inference of this dilemma which is vastly more important than the resolution, one way or the other, of any question

---

[4] See Psalm xliv. 1–3; lxxviii. 55; cxxxv. 12; cxxxvi. 21, 22.

as to whether the earth's diurnal motion, for example, was arrested at the command of Joshua, or the like.

The promise given to Abraham, however, might be less significant if it stood alone, remarkable as it would still be in connection with the history; but it does not, and before we close the last of the books of Moses we meet with another promise in strong contrast with it—the promise, namely, that he gives the people, of a prophet who shall arise from among them like unto himself.[5] Now this promise, however it is interpreted, has the advantage of being very clear and definite, and it is furthermore distinguished by a comment which is passed upon it in the book itself. For we are distinctly told[6] that there *arose not a prophet in Israel like unto Moses* after his death. It is impossible, therefore, that the words can refer to Joshua. But it is equally impossible not to accept them as a promise or prophecy.[7] It is clear that they were intended and understood as such. The comment referred to seems to imply no less. And the later we place the date of that comment the more significant it becomes. But in point of fact we are independent of any such considerations, for down to the time of Malachi there is no name in the annals of the nation so great as that of Moses. The moral, therefore, of the promise is that the national expectation

---

[5] Deut. xviii. 15 *seq.*   [6] Deut. xxxiv. 10.

[7] It has been suggested by Eichhorn and others that the promise given by Moses was virtually and in fact the origin of the phenomenon of prophecy as it was afterwards developed in the Jewish nation. But it must be borne in mind that several centuries elapsed between the death of Moses and the era of Samuel, and a long period between the era of Samuel and that of the prophets generally, and that no one of the actual prophets bore any resemblance to Moses, so that on this supposition the promise really failed to accomplish that which is attributed to it so far as personal likeness to the lawgiver is concerned; in addition to which we should even then have to account for the bold and hazardous prediction of Moses, as well as for the ultimate consequences of it over which he could have no control.

was aroused, but the entire course of the history gives no hint of its being realised. As far as the testimony of fact goes, the last verses of Deuteronomy might have been added when the canon of the Old Testament was closed, for the Second Temple arose in its glory without witnessing the rise of any prophet who could claim to be the successor of Moses. But then, on the other hand, it is impossible to regard the promise as a later interpolation; for it is put into the lips of Moses. And if we can imagine for a moment any late writer, such as Jeremiah for example, falsely ascribing a promise like this to Moses, what possible meaning could it have had? The verdict of history had done nothing but falsify the hope expressed, and the remark at the end of the book precluded the possibility of its being interpreted of Joshua, so that we are wholly at a loss to understand it. And yet here, on the very surface of the Pentateuch, ostensibly the oldest portion of the Jewish literature, we find this clear, definite, distinct promise, to the fulfilment of which the rest of that literature bears no evidence. In the light of these facts we are doubtless at liberty to appeal to the New Testament in proof that the expectation thus aroused in the nation had not died out in the time of Christ; but to what can that expectation be referred, if not to this unique promise?

If, then, the consciousness of Abraham was that his seed should be the blessing of the world, the consciousness of Moses was that his prophetic office should give place to Another. Each of these facts on the surface of the literature is too patent to be denied. They stand written in clear and legible characters that cannot be mistaken, and they are really typical of the rest of the literature. From first to last it is marked in an extraordinary manner, if we may so say, with the consciousness of being preparatory for something yet to come. There is a fearlessness of predictive assertion about it. Deal with the several predictions one by one as we may, this general characteristic remains indestructible. It is stamped on the history no less than on those writings which are ostensibly and professedly prophetical. We meet with it as early as Abraham, and we encounter it again in the time of Moses. It is indeed possible to deny that the writer of these two passages intended them to be predictions, but it is not possible to deny that they have the form of phophecy and the appearance of being predictive. On the other hand, if we accept them as actual prophecies, we shall probably not deny that they were fulfilled in Christ.

The Jewish history, moreover, as a whole, is distinguished from all other history by its extraordinary parabolic or didactic character. This is true at whatever period we take it. The history of the wanderings, for example, is a wonderful picture of human life. The history of the occupation and of the judges is scarcely less so. The conduct of Israel is like the conduct of a wayward child, or of a person whom adversity cannot teach, and the discipline to which the nation is subjected is of a kind similar to theirs. But of no other history is this true to anything like the same extent. It is as though this nation were under the immediate guidance and the special discipline of heaven, and this is shown quite as much by the natural as by the supernatural features of the history. Leave out every incident which does not fall strictly within the limits of natural experience, and you have still in the development of the national history what may well be regarded as the result of peculiar Divine direction, and what has all the appearance of being a model national history, designed expressly for the instruction of all other nations.

After the subjugation of Canaan, the great turning-point in Israel's history is the election of a king. Under Samuel the offices of judge and prophet were combined—he was

the last of the judges, the first of the prophets after Moses.
The movement in favour of monarchy, however, did not
proceed from him, but from the people; but the first
monarch was Samuel's appointment; so that the king
was developed out of the office of the judge, and was
sanctioned by the authority of the prophet. The history
of the choice and subsequent rejection of Saul is so
remarkable that it is difficult to divest it of all supernatural elements. Why was Saul accepted by the nation
as their lawful sovereign? Mainly on account of Samuel's
appointment. Why was it afterwards understood that he
was rejected and that another was chosen in his place?
Solely because Samuel has declared it. He was the virtual
king-maker; he put down one and set up another. Was
his authority, then, a pretence merely or a shadow? Were
the whole nation duped into believing Samuel to be a
prophet of the Lord, when he was only self-deceived if he
was not imposing on them? Upon reviewing the history
calmly, it is impossible to affirm that Samuel's conduct
was that of a self-deceiver or an impostor. There must
have been truth at the bottom of it, as witnessed by its
effects. But if there was truth at the bottom of it, was it
not truth which implied a revelation? For if there was
no authoritative Divine communication, then there was
imposture or self-deception—that is to say, there was
falsehood and not truth at the bottom of Samuel's conduct,
in which case the entire framework of the subsequent
history becomes unintelligible. We cannot understand
how it was that one dynasty should have supplanted
another; that the supplanting dynasty should have been
believed, as it was believed, to be grounded solely on the
Divine word, and that this belief should have been ratified
by the event, and not subsequently created by it, as the
evidence of circumstances shows it was not, if all this
rested on the mere assertion of a professed prophet, who

claimed to speak in the name and with the direct authority of God, and whose conduct cannot be sufficiently accounted for if he did not.

Thus far, then, the history shows us in anticipation a seed, or a world-wide blessing by the seed, a prophet, and a king. As yet, however, it has given us nothing more than the hope of any one of them. As there was no prophet between Moses and Samuel, so in the case of Samuel himself, though the first of the prophets, there was no likeness to Moses. The imagination of the people was ever being disciplined into the desire of the ideal prophet through acquaintance with the actual prophets. It was so likewise with the king, but by an inverse process. Their desire for a king was spontaneous, prompted by the examples of kingly power and glory which they had around them. Their conception of the prophet was based upon recollection and experience, while it was stimulated to a yet greater ideal. No reality could surpass the conception of the prophet which was enshrined in their memory. But the ideal king never came. The hope of the nation was fixed on Saul, but Saul was rejected, and his reign was not one of glory. Then the nation's hopes were transferred to David, and in due time their allegiance became his; but it was not till the reign of Solomon that the visions of consolidated strength, peace, and prosperity, naturally associated with the thought of a king, were realised, and they were realised for a little while only to be destroyed the more irretrievably. The era of Solomon was never surpassed, and it was not repeated; for a time it once and again revived, but only to relapse into imbecility, and to result in disappointment; and with the captivity of Zedekiah the hopeful line of Judah's kings was brought to a close. On looking back over the completed list, we cannot say that the ideal king had come; and long afterwards, when the cry was heard, *We have no king but Cæsar,* it sounded as though the hope itself had been extinguished by despair.

And yet, here again, it is not possible to survey the history and investigate the foundations of the hope, and not discover that there was valid ground for it. For example, we find, according to the history, that both Saul and Jonathan are aware that David is to be the king. Can it be that such a statement was invented in order to flatter the reigning house of David? We cannot explain its invention thus. Indeed, we cannot understand the history of Saul at all, except on the supposition that he regarded David as the destined heir to his throne. But why should he have so regarded him? David had no pretensions to supplant Saul, nor any prospect or hope of supplanting him, except on the ground of a distinct promise given by Samuel. This promise was given him, according to the narrative, while he was yet young, and before his combat with the giant of Gath, which might have made him a favourite with the people.[8] Why should it have been given him? He was the youngest of his father's house, and his father's house apparently not then conspicuous.[9] Samuel does not appear to have known David, or even to have known of him when he was sent to anoint him. We can discover, therefore, no motive for his choice and no principle in his selection. Without doing unnatural violence to the whole tenor of the history, corroborated as it is by the independent evidence of many other passages,[1] it is impossible to take into account all the circumstances connected with the anointing of David, and not acknowledge that we are led up by natural and unavoidable inference to the very verge of something which we cannot explain naturally, and which has all the appearance of being a definite pro-

---

[8] 1 Sam. xvi. 1–13.

[9] See Grove's art. "Jesse" in the *Dictionary of the Bible.*

[1] Cf. Ps. lxxviii. 70; lxxxix. 19, 20, *seq.,* etc.

mise from the Unseen, but how communicated we cannot
tell. The narrative itself, no less than the promise, is
deeply imbued with these extraordinary elements, and
unless we tear it shred from shred, we cannot get rid of
them ; and yet, on the other hand, we cannot account for
them. They receive a certain elucidation from the process
of events, and if we reject that there remains no other.

If, however, we attempt to resolve the original promise
to David into an act of mere arbitrary selection on the
part of Samuel, that is not the only significant incident
we have to explain. If Samuel's choice had been sufficient
to point out David as the future king, and to excite Saul's
jealousy in consequence, would not his influence have been
sufficient to displace Saul in favour of David, seeing that
it was to the same influence that Saul himself owed his
crown ? But, instead of this, after Samuel has anointed
David, we hear no more of him, with the single exception
of the episode in Naioth,[2] till we are told of his death and
burial; on the other hand, we do hear of Jonathan, the
heir-apparent, quietly acquiescing in the career marked out
for David, as well as of his unexampled and nobly-dis-
interested friendship for him.[3] And it is impossible to
deny that, after a series of years, David not only sat on
the throne which was Jonathan's by inheritance, but was
able successfully to consolidate his throne, and to establish
his dynasty. If, then, we resolve Samuel's choice of David
into an instance of remarkable foresight, we can scarcely
account for it even on that theory without the assistance
of other than merely natural powers; and we have yet
further difficulties to contend with in the life of David
himself.

For we find that after David is securely seated on the
throne of Israel, he receives another prophetic message

[2] 1 Sam. xix. 18 ; xxv. 1. Cf. xv. 35.
[3] 1 Sam. xviii. 1 ; xxiii. 18. 2 Sam. ix.; xxi. 7.

from Nathan, which conditionally promises him the everlasting posession of the throne.[4] That such a message was delivered to him there is not a shadow of doubt; the only question is, From whom did it come? Was it nothing more than the repetition, in another form and by another prophet, of the somewhat similar act performed by Samuel? Was it nothing more than the adulation of a courtier decked out in a religious and prophetic garb? However we try to account for it, we have to face this fact, that the last king of Judah was the lineal descendant of David; and unless it can be proved that the narrative in Samuel was written subsequently to the dissolution of the monarchy, it is impossible to divest that narrative altogether of its predictive features, or to deny to them a certain correspondence in fact, which chiefly surprises us because it is not greater and more minute. The subsequent history of the kingdom, and the disastrous rent it suffered after the reign of Solomon, is itself the best evidence of the authenticity of the narrative in Samuel; because that could not have been fabricated after events had to a large extent falsified the promise it contained. And yet, if we accept it as authentic, we find ourselves unable to explain it on merely natural principles. There can be no question that the most exalted aspirations were raised in the minds of the people as to the permanence of their kingdom in the line of David.

We find, moreover, that the original promise to David is to a certain extent illustrated by the history of his great crime. If criticism has asked us to believe that the fifty-first Psalm is no record or relic of this incident, he must be a bold critic who shall seek to persuade us that the incident itself never occurred. There can be no sort of question that we have in the second book of Samuel the plain unvarnished narrative of its occurrence. But the rebuke which is given by Nathan virtually assumes the

[4] 2 Sam. vii. Cf. Ps. cxxxii. 11, etc.

main features of the previous history. No rebuke more
severe was ever administered to a king, and it was coupled
with denunciations the most terrible; and yet it was none
other than this same Nathan who had promised to David
the perpetual establishment of his kingdom. If we reject
the one event as historic, we have equal reason to reject
the other. Tremendous, however, as the rebuke was, it did
not revoke the original promise while it expressly recognised the authority by which David reigned.[5] We have to
account, then, for the unflinching boldness of the prophet,
for the deference and submission with which his message
was received, as well as for the deliberate confidence with
which both the promise and the rebuke were given. Can
these together be resolved into the mere effects of the
mental ascendency over the king which the prophet had
acquired? It must be borne in mind that in the case of
the rebuke truth and justice were at any rate on the side
of Nathan, and that the denunciations delivered were
verified in fact. Were these denunciations inserted in
order to add a mysterious import to the events which
afterwards occurred? Was the narrative of the events
framed in order to suit the mysterious character of the
denunciations? Or is the way in which the whole are
intertwined and interwoven in the narrative but one indication out of many that there are elements of supernatural
dealing in the entire transaction, which it is not possible
satisfactorily to explain? Does not the conduct of the
prophet and the king from first to last show that, understand or account for it as we may, there must have been
more in the title by which David held his throne than the
vain illusions of self-deception on either side; and that, as
we are dealing with undoubted facts, the only theory which
will adequately resolve them is the admission of the agency
of an unseen power working in natural human history in

[5] 2 Sam xii. 7 seq.

a manner highly exceptional and above nature? In other words, the narrative of the foundation of David's kingdom, which is distinctly asserted to have been Divine, is of such a character that its foundation cannot be satisfactorily regarded as merely human.

There is, however, abundant evidence to show that David's kingdom, great as it was, could only be regarded as the promise of one greater. The chief characteristic of its foundation was its hope of perpetuity and its anticipation of an endless future. Solomon was in some respects a greater sovereign than David, and he was enabled to achieve what his father was not permitted to commence. His glory, however, did not last long, and at his death it seemed as though the hopes that were cherished by and for David were about to be falsified. The kingdom of the ten tribes fell away from that of Judah; but here again, as before, not without prophetic announcements on the part of Ahijah the Shilonite, which fully recognised and ratified all that had been promised to David, though at the same time they partially revoked and modified it. The promise, which was at the first conditional, is now conditionally and to a certain extent repeated to Jeroboam, and the seed of David is *to be afflicted, but not for ever.*[6] Rehoboam was forbidden by Shemaiah to attempt to reduce the alienated tribes by force, because their defection was declared to be from God.[7] The office of the prophet, therefore, is continually asserting its authority over successive kings, and being acknowledged by them; and as the broad principles on which it is discharged are uniform, so there is no essential divergence in the definite message delivered. The original decision of Nathan is acknowledged, and the validity of David's title is confirmed. All this is the more difficult to account for if we attempt to eviscerate the original promise of its Divine element.

[6] 1 Kings xi. 34–39.   [7] 2 Kings xii. 22–24.

As, however, we proceed, we see the original stability of David's line maintaining itself. The condition implied in all the Divine promises, and expressly named to Jeroboam, was not fulfilled by him any more than it had been by Solomon; and in the second generation his dynasty was overthrown,[8] to be succeeded by others no less transient, until Jehu sat upon the throne of Israel and handed down his sceptre to his descendants of the fourth generation, who, in the person of Zachariah,[9] were finally displaced, while the monarchy itself not long after came to an end. Henceforth the dominion of the two kingdoms reverted to the representative of the house of David, under whom they were united in the person of Hezekiah, and so continued for about one hundred and thirty years till the time of the great captivity under Nebuchadnezzar.

For the history of the divided kingdom of Israel we are entirely indebted to the books of Kings, which may perhaps be suspected of partiality in favour of the kingdom of Judah; but to whatever extent this is the case, there are certain features to be observed which can hardly have been misrepresented from any such bias. For example, we find in the kingdom of Israel the development of a grander idea of the prophetic office than is ever found in Judah, and one which, in some respects, is altogether original. The prophets Elijah and Elisha are unique conceptions in the history, and their execution of their office is unique. It was, however, almost exclusively discharged in Israel. There is something very remarkable in the apostate kingdom being thus highly favoured; and the fact that the prophets' mission, though it was resisted, was nevertheless acknowledged by the kings of Israel, may surely be added to the mass of the evidence which tends to show that their mission was a reality.

The way, however, in which dynasty after dynasty is

<hr>

[8] 1 Kings xv. 28-30.   [9] 2 Kings x. 30; xv. 8-12.

set up in Israel, and removed for rebellion and idolatry, not without prophetic menaces and warnings, is also in its degree a confirmation of the authority on which the promise to David rested; because our knowledge of both is derived from the same source, and as the one could not have been invented to make the other more credible, whatever illustration either receives from the other is of real and independent value.[1] For example, the constant change of dynasty in Israel corresponds in fact with the prophetic announcement of it. We cannot suppose that the fact was arranged to suit the announcement, and scarcely less can we imagine that the announcement was recorded to embellish the fact; and yet, if not so, the agreement of the one with the other is in the highest degree significant, and shows that the power which was at work in Judah was not unknown in Israel, and because not unknown in Israel, an idolatrous and rival kingdom, is the less likely to have been unreal in Judah. At all events, He who set up and put down kings in Israel, was He who declared that He had chosen the seed of David, and would establish his throne for ever. In fact, the more we examine the history in detail, the more we see that it must be torn piecemeal and totally reconstructed before it can be reduced to the scale of ordinary history, and that, in short, it cannot be so reduced without destroying altogether its historical credibility—its value as a record.

It is, moreover, by no means unimportant to observe, that after a certain period the history itself ceases to present the same features that it formerly possessed. There is not the same conspicuous correspondence between prophetic announcement and historic incident. There are indications, not a few, that the nation was conscious that

---

[1] 1 Kings xi. 31 *seq.;* xiv. 7 *seq.;* xvi. 1-13; xx. 42, 43. 2 Kings i. 16, etc. etc.

its prophetic glory had departed.[2] No attempt even is made to reproduce the remarkable phenomena of the books of Kings and Chronicles. Just as the period of the judges was an era when the prophetic impulse was wholly in abeyance, though the ruling power was developing itself, so in the time of the monarchy the king and the prophet are found side by side in full activity; but after the close of it the office of the king is seen no more, and that of the prophet before long comes to an end. All this tends to show that the period of the prophetic development was distinct and exceptional in the life of the nation. It was a reality, and a reality that is virtually without parallel elsewhere. Still the records of the nation leave this feeling on the reader's mind, that high anticipations, both as regards kingly and prophetic power, have been raised and yet not wholly fulfilled. The book of Malachi closes not only without any manifestation of the prophet like unto Moses, but with a promise only held out of the return of Elijah, whose position and character, though very great, were at once unlike and inferior to those of Moses.

And what is true of the prophet is yet more true of the king. The distinct assurances held out of a ruler on David's throne were so far from being fulfilled that their very failure is an evidence of their reality and genuineness. They must have been given on the highest authority, because otherwise a natural jealousy for their credit and their apparent agreement with fact would have prompted the desire to suppress or to modify them. But instead of this they remain with so much of historical inconsistency as the reader may be disposed to assign to them, but at the same time with the very vivid impression produced upon him that there is something wanted to complete them— something in the future for which they still seem to wait.

---

[2] Cf. Ps. lxxiv. 9, whenever this was written. Ezra ii. 63. Neh. vii. 65. 1 Macc. iv. 46; ix. 27; xiv. 41.

It is not, therefore, nearly so much upon the literal assertions of this or that particular text or collection of texts that we dwell, as upon the general tenor of the narrative looked at as a whole, and upon the highly exceptional phenomena of the literature taken at large, which cannot with any degree of fairness be explained away, and yet cannot be truly dealt with without suggesting the very strong presumption, which accumulated evidence renders inevitable, that other forces than those merely human were at work in the history of this nation, and that there are indications of the unveiling of a will which can only be regarded as Divine. And this conclusion is proof against everything but the unwarrantable, because unscientific, *à priori* assumption that such an idea is to be rejected because of its inherent and absolute impossibility, which must simply depend upon the facts instead of being allowed to sway them.

The result, then, to which we are brought by the survey of Jewish history as a whole, is the conviction that it is singularly incomplete; that, starting with the definite and distinct promise that all the families of the earth are to be blessed in Abraham, it leaves us with no very distinct or definite notion how this has been or is to be accomplished; it awakens an anticipation which, to say the least, it barely satisfies; that, moreover, this promise, clear as it is in terms, though dark in meaning, is not more clear than the promise subsequently recorded of a great prophet who shall arise, and a king who shall rule on the throne of David, and the perpetuity which shall attend his throne—neither of which promises, however, is adequately realised within the limits of the history itself. The most natural conclusion, therefore, is that the entire history from first to last is a delusion; it is not worthy of our consideration or regard, for its conspicuous absurdities are its condemnation. But yet, on the other hand, we feel, in spite of ourselves, that this conclusion is one which we cannot adopt. This history, from first to last, is more remarkable than any other. Setting aside its supernatural features, there is no question that its broad and general character is that of substantial accuracy and truth: it is simple, concise, and graphic: it commands our confidence from its obvious impartiality. No one can say that the character of Abraham or of David is dealt with more leniently than that of Saul or Pharaoh. It is impossible to read this history and pronounce it upon internal evidence unworthy of our attention or undeserving of our belief. But the very manifest general character of the history in ordinary matters affords ground, at least so far, for a presumption in favour of its credibility in others which are not ordinary. We are forbidden to dismiss the supernatural features all at once as unworthy of credit, on account of the general character of the narrative which they mark. We are constrained either to explain them or to accept them unexplained. They do not really admit of any satisfactorily consistent natural explanation, and therefore we must accept them as they are.

And this being the case, the final impression produced by the history as a whole is that the promises contained in it, and the hopes excited by it, are in the highest degree noteworthy. And the natural inference is that, so far at any rate, a substantial foundation is laid for any claims which might hereafter be based upon these promises and hopes. It is impossible to deny that there was a *primâ facie* appearance of ground for the expectation that among the seed of Abraham there should arise a prophet and a king, in whom the kingly and prophetic character should be amply realised. And it is altogether beyond the limits of possibility that the expectation of a prophet or a king, in the form in which it appears, should have been modified in such a way as to become the groundwork of the claims which were afterwards based upon it. Put the composition of the several books, or of particular parts of them, as late as you please, and their real significance is in no degree affected thereby. In their present form they were long anterior to the first preaching of the Baptist, and yet in that form they supplied a strange and fitting, and yet altogether improbable and impossible, basis for the announcement, *There cometh one mightier than I after me, the latchet of whose shoes I am not worthy to stoop down and unloose.*[3] It was the spontaneous development of events, and in no sense the will of man, which brought about this adaptation. The character of John the Baptist is one of the greatest in Scripture, but he proclaimed the advent of one greater than himself. If that greater one should be a prophet or a king, the old promises about the king and the prophet would, to say the least, have a wonderful light thrown upon them. They would at once acquire a significance they never possessed before, and yet the capability of this significance had been there for ages. It was not created by John. And whether or not John's announcement vas verified, the ground upon which it was made was valid, for Moses had spoken of a prophet like unto himself, and Samuel had anointed David in the room of Saul to sit upon the throne of Israel, and Nathan had declared that his house and kingdom should be established for ever. Whether or not these promises were destined to ultimate failure or fulfilment, it is undeniable that there they were, and there for ages they had existed.

There is yet one other feature in which the history of Israel presents a strong contrast to that of all other nations. It was expressly declared in the law that Israel should be *a kingdom of priests, and a holy nation;*[4] and in no respect are this people more strongly marked than in their priestly and sacrificial character. The directions of the Mosaic

<hr>

[3] St. Mark i. 7.   [4] Exod. xix. 6.

ritual are minute and elaborate. From the commencement
to the close of the Old Testament, sacrifice holds a conspicuous and prominent place. Aaron and his sons, under
the legal system, are expressly set apart to minister in the
priest's office. The covenant of an everlasting priesthood
is made with Phinehas, the grandson of Aaron. And yet in
the time of Samuel we find that the priesthood has passed
out of the line of Eleazar into that of Ithamar without
any discoverable reason.[5] In the time of David it is found
distributed in both lines. (1 Chron. xxiv. 3.) At the time
of the captivity, and after the return, it is still in the line
of Eleazar, and appears to have continued so. During the
historical times, or at least during the period of the
monarchy, the high-priest's office was, comparatively
speaking, subordinate. After the captivity and later he
became the recognised head of the nation, as in a kingdom
of priests he would always have a tendency to become ;
and yet from first to last there is no one priest who stands
out very prominently as the model and pattern of priesthood, while the entire sacrificial system must have come to
an end with the destruction of the Jewish polity.

Had all this elaborate scheme of rites and ceremonies, of
priests and sacrifices, existed for no purpose whatever, or
was there a further meaning in its very existence ? because
there is no part of the Jewish constitution which can lay
anything like the claim to Divine ordinance and prescrip-
tion that the furniture and services of the tabernacle and
the functions of the priesthood can lay. These were all
ostensibly the subject of express Divine injunctions, and if
the injunctions were in any sense Divine they shed a light
upon the whole theory of sacrifice as it existed also in other

---

[5] This alone is surely an indication that the promise to Phinehas must
have been either contemporaneous with him or subsequent to the captivity;
but the former is more probable because of the manifest violation of the
promise in the time of Samuel.

nations; but if they were not—if there was no positive
and external authority for them, if they were based upon
imposture and self-deception—then they not only become
inexplicable in themselves, but the prevalence and univer-
sality of sacrifice in the world at large, as well as the very
existence of the theory of sacrifice, is a phenomenon that
we cannot account for. The origin of the institution of
sacrifice is indeed lost in obscurity, but a certain amount
of light is thrown upon its existence if in any case it was
sanctioned or adopted by Divine authority and precept—
a light which otherwise fails us altogether. And certainly,
if such a sanction is anywhere to be discovered, we must
look for it in the extant sacred writings of the Jews; but
even if we acknowledge its existence here, these writings
themselves fail to give us not only the full meaning of the
idea, but also the complete development and realisation of
the idea in history. There may never have been any such
realisation at all; but if there was the only person in whom
we can hope to find it is Christ.

In other words, the sacerdotal and sacrificial system of
the Jews, as it is expressed in their extant sacred writings,
no matter when they were written, taken in its relation to
the corresponding systems of other nations, necessarily and
naturally leads us to expect some solution of it which shall
satisfactorily account for its existence; but it is impossible to give any such account by searching the records of
history in any nation whatever. Unless the very idea of
sacrifice from first to last was a mistake, unless its essential
principle was a false one, it seems to point us not only to
a great moral truth, but also to a definite historic exhibition
and illustration of the truth, or at least to a turning-point
in history, when the human mind, which before had universally acquiesced in sacrifice, should at once and universally repudiate the repetition of the outward form, and rest
content with the realisation of the inward truth expressed

by it. Such a turning-point would really present the greatest instance of moral and mental revolution which it is possible to conceive. And such a turning-point was in fact presented by the effects and consequences of the death of Christ. The repudiation of animal sacrifice was the immediate result of the preaching of that death. Nothing else has ever operated in the same way. Nothing else can in this respect come into competition for one moment with Christ's death. The publication of the Epistle to the Hebrews, no matter who wrote it, was the evidence and the consequence of the mightiest revolution which the human mind can undergo or has ever undergone. Whether or not Jewish sacrifice led up to the Epistle to the Hebrews, and was intended to prepare for its central fact, certain it is that the central fact of that epistle was the abolition of Jewish sacrifice, and gave the signal for a total change of mind upon the subject. A revolution so mighty as the rejection of the formal expression of sacrifice, in favour of its moral signification and inward essence, is not so likely to have been occasioned by anything as by an especially high illustration of the moral truth of sacrifice.

We may declare emphatically that no historic event was adequate to produce this revolution but one, as we may likewise affirm that there is no other event which in this respect pretends to rival it. There is a direct relation of cause and effect between the death of Christ and the discontinuance of sacrifice, which is undeniable, because obvious, and which can be paralleled by nothing else in history. We may deny that the existence of sacrifice pointed prophetically and with Divine authority to the historic occurrence of the death of Christ; it is impossible to affirm that the death of Christ did not exhibit and illustrate, as nothing else ever did, the full meaning and the Divine wisdom of the law of sacrifice.

And thus it is that we find the promise of a Christ in

Jewish history. We find in that history the foundation
and the germ of all that was afterwards claimed for Christ
and advanced in His name. We find there ages before He
came or any such claims were ever advanced, the distinct
promise of a seed in which the nations should be blessed.
However we interpret that promise, whether of the seed
of Abraham or of a certain individual of his family, whether
we regard him or his family, or a certain individual of his
family, as the channel or as the standard of blessing, it is
equally true when applied to Christ. He proclaimed Himself, and was proclaimed, as the fountain of life and the
one source of blessing to mankind.

We find there the distinct promise of a great prophet,
who should stand like Moses between God and man. In
the whole cycle of history there is no name but one on
behalf of which any such claim can be advanced. Christ
may not have been that great prophet, but at least there
was none other greater than He; and in that case the promise which has existed for three thousand years, and is
still a promise, has signally failed, and though history has
revealed and confirmed its truth, it must be pronounced
a lie.

But we find there also the distinct promise of a king
whose throne is to be established for ever; and yet before
many centuries the kingdom of David is overthrown, and
in the time of Herod and Pontius Pilate we hear the
people of David crying aloud, *We have no king but Cæsar ;* [6]
while one who claimed descent from the son of Jesse was
led away to be crucified, and the superscription was written
over Him, containing the indictment upon which He suffered, *This is Jesus of Nazareth, the King of the Jews:* [7] and
before He was born, we are told that it had been said—
The Lord God shall give unto him the throne of his father

[6] St. John xix. 15.
[7] St. John xix. 19; St. Matt. xxvii. 37.

David; and he shall reign over the house of Jacob for ever, and of his kingdom there shall be no end.[8]

And, lastly, we find there from beginning to end the deep impress of a sacrificial system, which must have been unmeaning and self-imposed, and is consequently an unexplained phenomenon in history, if it did not lead upward and point onward to the perfect priesthood and sacrifice of one who should be called *not after the order of Aaron, but after the power of an endless life.*[9]

[8] St. Luke i. 32, 33.   [9] Heb. vii. 11, 16.

LECTURE III.

THE CHRIST OF THE PSALMS.

WHAT is there necessary for man to know which the Psalms are not able to teach? They are to beginners an easy and familiar introduction, a mighty augmentation of all virtue and knowledge in such as are entered before, a strong confirmation to the most perfect among others. Heroical magnanimity, exquisite justice, grave moderation, exact wisdom, repentance unfeigned, unwearied patience, the mysteries of God, the sufferings of Christ, the terrors of wrath, the comforts of grace, the works of Providence over this world, and the promised joys of that world which is to come, all good necessarily to be either known, or done, or had, this one celestial fountain yieldeth.—*Hooker.*

LECTURE III.

As it is also written in the second Psalm, Thou art my Son, this day have I begotten thee. . . . Wherefore he saith also in another Psalm, Thou shalt not suffer thine Holy One to see corruption.

ACTS xiii. 33, 35.

WE have no reasonable cause to doubt that St. Paul in his speech at Antioch in Pisidia made reference to these two Psalms, and applied them to Jesus Christ. But whether or not he did, it is at least certain that the writer of the Acts of the Apostles believed in the fitness of such an application, and desired his readers also to believe in it. If proof, therefore, were wanting, we have it here, as we have it abundantly elsewhere, that the early Church was accustomed to find in the Psalms of David much that it understood to be spoken prophetically of Jesus Christ.

But my object now is not to defend or establish the truth of any such interpretation, but rather to trace in the Psalms the growth and development of those ideas which subsequently contributed as a matter of fact to supply the basis for the Messianic conception.

We have seen already that the pattern or scheme upon which the known history of the Jewish nation developed itself was one which was eminently adapted to sustain, if it did not originate, the after-growth of the national expectation, that an illustrious Person would arise. Kingly, priestly, national, and human, that Person was to be, and blessing was to be associated with His name and office—

so much, at least, the people might have been justified in expecting from the records of their history. Let us inquire now what evidence the Psalms afford of the early rise of such an expectation, and how far they contributed to its growth.

It is not improbable that in the matter of date there are productions in the book of Psalms which range over a period of a thousand years. There are some, perhaps, as early as the Exodus, and there are others as late as the return from captivity. We do not dwell, however, so much upon the antiquity of particular Psalms, or of the evidence they may contain, as upon the testimony supplied by this branch of the national literature, which may be called its poetry or hymnology. Taking the Psalms, as represented at least by the works of David, they may be placed as a whole anterior to prophecy as a whole, and consequently may be examined first. They stand, moreover, in the position of national songs or odes, and therefore have less of that which characterises the works of an individual author than the writings of the several prophets. They may be taken, more or less, as fairly representing the spontaneous expression of national sentiment. What, then, is their evidence as to the nature of this sentiment?

The Psalms open with the description of an ideally righteous man; a description which is repeated in the 15th and 24th Psalms, becomes the expression of a strong personal resolve in the 101st, and is expanded and enlarged upon in the 112th Psalm. Two of these Psalms, the first and last, have no inscription; the others are ascribed to David. But it matters not who wrote them: they are a witness to a certain longing after an ideal standard of humanity, of which the natural tendency would be to reproduce itself in the minds of the people. The fact that they are couched in merely general language, and applied to the righteous generally, is no proof that they had not their share in tending to produce and deepen the impression that the great want of humanity was a righteous man, and that the mission of Israel would be unfulfilled till the ideal of righteousness had been produced. In proportion, therefore, as the people could grasp the promise of blessing for the nations in the seed of Abraham, they would learn from the teaching of these and similar Psalms that any one who claimed to fulfil that promise must himself be righteous to the utmost limit of their standard, of which David himself had but too conspicuously fallen short.

True, however, as this may be, the notion is too vague to be construed into any evidence of what was actually understood. Nor is it so advanced. We can only perceive here an indication of the kind of soil in which the foundation was laid for that superstructure which was afterwards to be reared, and we can determine how far it was favourable or otherwise—how far the foundation itself was solid and substantial, or insecure and sandy.

It may be well, however, to notice the more general characteristics of the Psalms first, before passing on to those which are special and personal. We cannot proceed far without discovering that the Psalms are the expression of real and continual trouble. The writer is constantly exposed to persecution. The wicked are ever oppressing and deriding him, and not seldom this appears to be on account of his integrity. *They also that render evil for good are mine adversaries; because I follow the thing that good is,*[1] may be taken as a fair sample of a large portion of the Psalms. The writer appears to be set in the very midst of the conflict between good and evil, and to bear in himself the brunt of it. Not seldom this is expressed in terms which must have transcended not only the special circumstances in which David was placed, but those also which we can conceive to have been literally true of any

---

[1] Psalm xxxviii. 20.

one; and yet they have an intense reality. If the expressions are hyperbolical, we still feel that they are true. Though the language of the 22d Psalm cannot have been warranted by the exigencies of David's case, it is too real and vivid not to be true; and in whatever sense it was true, there must have been in the mind of the writer a felt reality answering to its truth. What this was we may perhaps find it difficult to determine; but the language is its own witness, and there is only one vision, ideal or actual, in all history which can claim to have fulfilled it. We may certainly affirm of the Psalms that they first gave expression to this element of ideal suffering, and added it to those, whatever they were, which were already in existence.

Not more conspicuous, however, than the daring character of the language used, and its literal inapplicability to the writer's circumstances, is the manner in which the suffering is depicted as the writer's own. He everywhere identifies himself with the person suffering. So that the two opposite statements may be maintained with equal truth, because the maintenance of both will alone express the whole truth, that no writer whoever he was can have spoken of that which was literally verified in himself, and yet that each several writer, if there were more than one, was by sympathetic appreciation a partaker of the sufferings he so vividly described.

It was the office, then, of that portion of Jewish literature known as the Psalms to bring out in humanity, and to give expression to, the conception of righteous manhood, the experience of integrity borne down by oppression, the being persecuted for righteousness' sake, the notion of being made perfect through suffering, as well as the picture of an ideal degree of suffering, and consequently of an ideal sufferer, which men must have learnt to feel, the more they pondered it, could only wait for its complete fulfilment, if it was to be fulfilled. And inasmuch as the expression of this from first to last was everywhere cast in the form of personal experience, it became more and more impossible that the various characteristics should not group themselves round a person, and combine to form a whole, which, as it grew by constant but gradual accretion, was found to be not altogether in the likeness of David, or of any other historic character to whom it might be referred.

Another prominent feature which is seen to characterise the Psalms to even a greater degree than any other portion of the Old Testament, is the consciousness of Divine election, and of consequent trust in God, which they express. This is everywhere not the result of personal devotion to the Most High, but of the going forth of special regard on the part of God towards him who has been assured of it. There is nothing more conspicuous than this in the Psalms as a whole. So deep and abiding is this consciousness, that the sense even of intense personal guilt cannot shake it. The usurping presence of sin has only the effect of making the Psalmist cleave with the greater earnestness to God. He feels that the honour of God will be compromised if one who has trusted Him so unreservedly is left to perish. And so, with entire abandonment of soul, he throws himself upon the Lord. *Preserve thou my soul; for I am holy: my God, save thy servant that putteth his trust in thee.*[2] He never has any doubt that his cause is the cause of God. *The Lord is on my side; I will not fear: what can man do unto me?*[3] At the same time he feels that this exceptional nearness to the Divine presence has laid him under an obligation to exceptional righteousness; and it is not too much to say that this twofold consciousness of the Divine election, and of the consequent obligation to personal righteousness, is the unique characteristic of this ancient literature, and pre-eminently of the Psalms. We

---

[2] Psalm lxxxvi. 2.   [3] Psalm cxviii. 6.

have nowhere, as we have here, the picture of a man bowed down with affliction and sorrow of every kind, yet not losing his confidence in God, nor his conviction of God's righteousness; not charging God with injustice on account of what He has laid upon him, but clinging to the righteousness of God, not only as the ground of his own hope for brighter times, but as the means of raising him out of that personal sin which he feels to be so near to him. Verily, this portraiture is in itself Divine.

It is obvious, then, that the union of these several elements in the Psalms, and their combination in one and the same person—because if the writers were various their experience was uniform—shows that the election of God secures no immunity from suffering, that the righteous man is often exposed to the greatest trials, and that trial and suffering are designed to elicit faith in God, and give no occasion in themselves to distrut His goodness. All this was a distinct advance in the knowledge of God's dealings, and was itself a preparation for the advent of One who should be made perfect through suffering, and should prove Himself the righteous man by the ignominy of unmerited death He was content to endure.

Not less remarkable than the sense of personal election expressed in so many of the Psalms is the conviction of national election which continually pervades them. This is but another form of the ancient belief expressed in the promise to Abraham: *In thee shall all the families of the earth be blessed.* The ultimate confession of the psalmist is, *He hath not dealt so with any nation;*[4] but it is one which has frequently been anticipated in various ways. And yet, in spite of the intense patriotism and strong national sentiment that characterises the Psalms, there are no compositions of the Old Testament so universal in their scope, so world-wide in their human sympathy, or that

[4] Psalm cxlvii. 20.

express so deep a conviction of the future that is reserved for Israel. The assertion is distinct and emphatic that the God of Jacob is the God of the universe, and the ultimate triumph of His cause is certain. *All nations whom thou hast made shall come and worship before thee, O Lord, and shall glorify thy name; for thou art great and doest wondrous things: thou art God alone.*[5] To say the least, it is very remarkable that at a time so early a nation so obscure should have been so confident of the relation in which it stood to God, and have seen so clearly that the faith with which it was entrusted was destined to become the faith of the whole world, even as it is now recognised by the most civilised portions of mankind. If it were possible for such convictions to be justified by any result, one might plead that the known verdict of history had certainly justified these.

But then it is also manifest that the election of God, which is felt to be the distinguishing glory of the nation, is not, so to say, distributed equally over the entire mass, but is gathered up and concentrated in a single line and even in a single person. Whatever be the origin of such Psalms as the 78th, the 89th, and the 132d, there can be no question of the prominence they assign to David; and none of them, be it observed, is ascribed to him; indeed, it is not improbable that they are all later than his time. So far, therefore, they may be taken as expressing the popular opinion regarding him, and the future in store. for his line. And yet it appears in the two last of these Psalms that the hope is clung to with the greater tenacity, because the prospect of its fulfilment seems to have failed. For this reason, therefore, we cannot doubt the reality of the original hope, nor of the ground on which it was supposed to rest. Nor is there any counter-evidence deducible from other Psalms which might lead us to question

<hr>

[5] Psalm lxxxvi. 9, 10.

this. God's election of Israel, then, is clearly seen to be summed up in David and his house. On the evidence of the Psalms, there can be no question that he is the inheritor of whatever promises were made to Abraham, to Isaac, and to Jacob. If Israel as a nation inherited the promises made unto the fathers, then David, as the representative of the line of Judah, contained in himself whatever belonged to his nation. He and his family, at the time when these Psalms were written, were regarded as the most prominent possessors of whatever had been promised to the first fathers of the nation, or was believed to have been promised to them.

And it is further evident as a matter of fact that the belief in the promise to the fathers must have preceded the belief in any promise to David; because, otherwise, the effect of the promise to him would have been weakened by the subsequent invention of any wider promise which should equally include the entire mass of the nation.

We see, therefore, on the unquestionable evidence of the Psalms, that at or after the time of David, for it matters not, there was understood to be a repetition of Divine promises to him and his seed—a narrowing in of the channel of blessing originally promised to the nation at large, a concentration and limitation of it in his particular line.

We may say, indeed, that the two promises are not identical, that they are distinct and independent: that may or may not be so: the one is general the other is special; and we have to account as a literary phenomenon for their existence in the Jewish literature, and for their existence in this particular form; and we cannot deny that at no period, say between the captivity and the era of the Maccabees, would it have been possible to create the record of these two promises and the independent evidence which exists, so that their occurrence and their peculiar features should be less significant than they are at present.

That is to say, up to the period of the Maccabees, and we need not go later, no man could have foreseen that such a combination of literary phenomena as are presented in the historical books of the Old Testament and the Psalms would have been capable of supplying the groundwork for that broad and general interpretation of them to which any acceptance of the facts of Christianity, or of the ordinary doctrines of the Christian Church, must of necessity shut us up. So far then, and no farther, as these phenomena lend themselves to the interpretation which the writers of the New Testament and the Christian Church generally have passed upon them, it cannot be the result of human foresight or design, but must be regarded as a matter of simple accident if its Divine significance is rejected. We maintain, however, that the way in which these various phenomena gradually prepared themselves, if we may so say, for the reception of the burden which was afterwards to be laid upon them, is far too significant to be reputed as the work of chance, and supplies, indeed, the strongest possible moral evidence of design.

If, however, we can see in the Psalms, as a whole, a wonderful anticipation and assertion of those particular spiritual truths which are commonly regarded as more or less characteristic of Christianity; and if, looked at merely in this light, they supply the outline of that character of combined suffering and majesty, the subject at once of oppression, deliverance, and triumph, which was afterwards exhibited in full by Christ; we must not forget that in many other instances they furnish a yet higher evidence of their purpose as landmarks along the ages of a distant past to point us onwards to Him.

It is manifest that in this way they were originally understood and appealed to. But then such a use of them implies an acknowledgment of the Divine intention which they served, an intention which we would rather indicate than assume. Certain it is that the special Messianic characteristics of the Psalms, if such there are, assume altogether a different aspect if taken in connection with other features which are patent and undeniable, from that which they have when looked at by themselves, and charged with the responsibility of sustaining the entire weight of the argument to be based upon them.

The very fact, then, that certain Psalms have been termed Messianic, while many others have never' been so designated, is evidence in some degree of an essential difference between them. It proves, at least, that there are many Psalms on account of which no such claim has or can be advanced; while the zeal with which the special character of the others has been attacked and defended may seem to show that there is at any rate a *primâ facie* appearance of some marked difference in them. Is it possible to determine wherein this difference consists ?

The Psalms that have commonly been regarded as Messianic are some ten or twelve. The second Psalm depicts the dignity and permanence of the throne of Zion. The person sitting upon that throne declares, *The Lord hath said unto me, Thou art my Son ; this day have I begotten thee.* Upon His request the heathen are promised Him for His possession. Kings are to pay Him homage, and all that trust in or take refuge with Him are pronounced blessed. The writer's idea then clearly was that Zion was to be the centre of universal sovereignty. The person who rules or is to rule there is called the Anointed or the Messiah of the Lord, a term which was certainly applied to Saul and to David, but does not appear to have been used in the same way of any later king.[6] There is

<hr>

[6] The only exception is Lam. iv. 20, which probably refers to the king; other kings are said to have been anointed (1 Kings i. 34; xix. 15;

abundant evidence, then, to show that David was regarded in some special sense as the anointed of the Lord; and in view of this fact it seems more probable that the Psalm has primary reference to David himself than to any other monarch. But if this be so it is clear that he speaks of himself, or the writer speaks of him, as he has nowhere else been spoken of before. A new element, therefore, was added by this poem to the existing conception of David's throne; or, supposing the conception existed before, it was here for the first time expressed. It is quite obvious, however, that at no period of David's history was there any prospect of such a development of his kingdom as would fit in at all appropriately with the language used. Making the fullest allowance for hyperbole, there still seems to be an ideal before the writer's mind, of which the real and actual must have fallen short. And yet this ideal was embodied for ever in the form he had given to it, and supplied for his own and for all subsequent generations a standard by which the actual might be measured. Henceforth a glory was added to the throne of Zion which, if it was never fulfilled, and in proportion as it lacked fulfilment, would tend to stimulate the hope that it might be. We may truly say that a want which had never been felt before had been created by the production of this second Psalm.

And as the glory of the throne was directly connected with the term Anointed of the Lord, which the national historic records do not ascribe to any king later than David, it is probable that any longing which existed for an ideal sovereign would be associated likewise with the hope of one who should pre-eminently bear that title. This, however, will appear more fully as we proceed.[7]

2 Kings ix. 3, 6, 12, etc.), but are not called *The Lord's anointed.* Cyrus, however, is so called. (Isa. xlv. 1.)

[7] See, for example, Lecture iv.

The eighth Psalm has reference to the Mosaic narrative of the original constitution of man, and is quoted by our Lord in connection with an incident in His own career, as well as by St. Paul and in the Epistle to the Hebrews;[6] but inasmuch as it does not seem to add greatly to the definiteness of the Messianic idea in its earlier development we need not dwell upon it now. It seems, however, to associate God's highest glory in the heavens with the greater manifestation of His glory in man upon the earth, and therefore to show that it is only in man and in the nature of a man that His praise can be adequately set forth. Man is thus the fullest recipient of God's glory, which is true, whether it is understood generally or of the Incarnation. We cannot affirm that David intended to express more than the general truth, but it becomes additionally true when referred to the perfect Man.

The next Psalm which requires to be noticed is the sixteenth. In this the writer prays earnestly for preservation, and declares his unbounded and unshaken confidence in God. He feels that the reserve of wealth which he has in God will outlast the utmost trials of life, and survive even the grave itself; that in fact it is only in the immediate presence of God that there is the *fulness* of joy, and at His right hand pleasures for evermore. This is the earliest and perhaps the strongest expression in the Old Testament of that eternal life which is independent of things temporal, and superior even to death itself. It became, therefore, the permanent record of that portion in God which was the possession of the Lord's anointed or holy one, and was a perpetual witness to the delight in God, and the sense of security in and through death which he found in God. That there were other more definite elements in his hope does not appear from the language used; but here was the very essence of that hope which

6 St. Matt. xxi. 16; 1 Cor. xv. 27; Eph. i. 22; Heb. ii. 7.

was afterwards presented in a concrete form and established by the resurrection. Here was the evidence that David himself had unmistakably expressed a hope which a subsequent event, if true, had fully confirmed; a hope which could alone be proved to be valid by the manifestation of its truth in one particular and crucial instance. But when it was clear that such a hope had a thousand years before been expressed by David, there was at least a written warranty for an expectation which was then declared to have been verified. To say that David's language was intended, not by David but by the Holy Ghost, to refer to the event which verified it, could be within the power only of men who themselves spake by the Holy Ghost. If we call in question their claim to do this, we cannot prove the truth of what they affirmed; but it is not open to question that such a hope as this had been expressed by David, or by the writer of the sixteenth Psalm, whoever he was; and if we accept the fact which the apostles of Christ proclaimed, we can see not only the reasonableness of this hope, but the probability there is that the God who implanted it reserved the accomplishment of His own purposes in the language chosen to express it.

The 20th and 21st Psalms, it is generally supposed, must be taken together. They are ascribed to David, and as the first of them makes mention of the Lord's anointed, we may presume, for the reasons already given, rightly so. They occupy a remarkable position between the 16th and the 22d Psalms. The 16th Psalm expressed the writer's confidence of deliverance in and through death, the 21st Psalm speaks of his coronation and his endless life. He is also manifestly the anointed king who has been made exceeding glad with the countenance of God. Now here, whatever else there is, there is certainly the expression of a hope full of immortality. We have evidence that the Jews long afterwards interpreted this Psalm of the King

Messiah;[9] but the point I wish to observe is, that the Psalms clearly ascribe to the anointed king, whoever he may be, deliverance in death, length of days for ever and ever, and special glory in the Divine salvation. We may fairly ask, What possible meaning could David have in saying that he had asked life of the most High, and that He had given it him, even length of days for ever and ever? We may with equal fairness ask, What possible meaning could future generations attach to such language, after David had been laid unto his fathers and had seen corruption? The meaning that has been attached[1] we of course know. It is that which is derived from the familiar phrase, *O king, live for ever*, or the expression, *I will dwell in the house of the Lord for ever*, and the like; and it is plainly possible so to understand it. But it is no less certain that so to understand the language, does not exhaust its possible meaning.[2] And is there not an abiding witness in the language itself, to a fuller and further meaning, which needs only to be suggested to commend itself as at once the truest and the best? Was there not in such language another foundation-stone laid for the superstructure which was afterwards to be reared? And is it not possible that the more ardent spirits in Israel may have grasped a hope which was suggested, if it was not implied, in such words as these? Material was at any rate thus being accumulated, which, in times of great national or individual trouble, would supply the groundwork for anticipations which had not been felt before. Elements were held in solution which affliction might precipitate in a very distinct and definite form. The language itself was pregnant with hopes which

---

[9] See the Targum and Rashi.

[1] See Perowne on *l. c.* and xxiii. 6; lxi. 6; xci. 16.

[2] The proof that this was not the only meaning that it had is the fact that this and similar language became the groundwork of hopes and expectations that could not have been formed if it had been.

future circumstances might develop into being, and awaken to conscious life.

Nor must we forget that the writer of the 20th Psalm, while looking for his help from God, invokes Him as *the God of Jacob.* This is the first occasion on which the Psalmist has used this phrase. It can have had no meaning to him but the meaning which we understand by it—a meaning which is derived from our acquaintance with the facts of the Mosaic history, with which he therefore must have been familiar too. But the use of this phrase implies not only his knowledge of those facts, but his belief also that there was a special relation in which Jacob stood to God, that he was a party to a real covenant and the inheritor of a real promise. It serves therefore at once, collaterally and independently, to authenticate this portion of the Mosaic narrative, and also to give additional meaning to the Psalmist's view of his own position. God was the God of Jacob because He had chosen Jacob—because He had given him a special promise and dealt with him in a special way. As far as David represented the seed of Jacob, and gathered up in himself the blessing vouchsafed to Israel, he must have regarded that promise as, in a special sense, his own. He was the focus in which all the rays of it converged. And consequently every indication of God's dealings with himself was an indication of His dealings with the chosen seed, and his language shows us that he felt it so to be.

The next Psalm which we have to deal with is the 22d. This Psalm affords a striking instance of a feature which is characteristic of so many; namely, the abrupt transition from sorrow to joy. Two-thirds of it are taken up with the utterance of the extremest misery; but in the last ten verses the writer is as triumphant as he was before dejected. Before he has been crying from the depths of despair; now he suddenly passes into praise and becomes hopeful and confident. But neither the sorrow nor the joy can be understood as applying to David or to any other conceivable writer. We not only cannot imagine that David himself was ever the subject of the treatment here described, but that he would ever have described any personal afflictions to which he was exposed in such a way. The language becomes practically unmeaning in his case, making every possible allowance for hyperbole, and the national records furnish us with no other character to whom it is likely to have been more appropriate. The same expectation, however, of universal dominion, which was expressed in the second Psalm, finds place also here; but it is distinctly said that *the kingdom is the Lord's, and* that *He is the ruler among the heathen.* It is also said that a people yet unborn shall recognise the work of the Lord in the particular deliverance which the Psalm records—a statement entirely without meaning in the case of David, but pregnant with the fullest significance when otherwise understood. And it is plain that any one who pondered such language as this after David's time must have had perplexing inquiries stirred within him if he tried to understand it. Whatever the writer may have meant or understood, it is clear that his language was marvellously suggestive. It seemed to express and to open out anticipations which it was difficult to limit, and still more difficult to define. Hopes had manifestly centred in David's throne which were never realised; but as long as David's language remained, they could not die. It is no wonder if they gave the impulse to other hopes destined likewise to disappointment, and yet the more likely to be fulfilled the more the spirit of the language was entered into.

The 40th Psalm is, in many respects, analogous to the 22d, but it is more within the possible limits of the writer's own experience, and it closes without the same confident expressions of triumph. Like the 50th and 51st Psalms,

also, it expresses a conviction of the uselessness of sacrifices, and the far greater importance of conformity to the
Divine will. It is thus a proof that the author had risen
to a high spiritual appreciation of the law, which he
admitted to be binding on him, if we do not, with the
Septuagint and the Epistle to the Hebrews, regard it as an
evidence that he saw *in the volume of the book* prophetic
allusions to himself and his seed. But the fact is, that
this, in common with the other Psalms, becomes far more
significant when understood of Another, than it can possibly be when referred to David or to any one else, and fitly
therefore takes its place among those marvellous compositions which waited for their elucidation till the fulness of
time should come.

In vivid contrast with this is the 45th Psalm, to which
we now turn. This is manifestly and professedly a song of
love—an epithalamium, or marriage ode, in honour of some
king, whoever he may have been. But it is not a little
surprising that, in the sixth verse, his throne is identified
with the throne of God, and that he himself is addressed
as God. Taken in connection with the 2d, the 20th, and
the 21st Psalms, it shows plainly that there was in the
Psalmist's mind an eternal King and an eternal kingdom
with which the throne of David was, in some mysterious
way, not identified, but associated. Had it not been for
such an association, he could never have spoken of himself
or his kingdom as he so often did. But when we connect
this, as we are obliged to do, with the promise to the fathers,
of which David was aware, we not only see that there was
already a development, as well as a limitation, of the
original idea, but that the writer himself must have been
conscious of it. And if in any case, as apparently here in
the 45th Psalm, that writer was not David, the persistency
with which his conceptions attached themselves to David,
and centred in him, is not the less remarkable or significant.

The fact that the convictions concerning David's throne were shared by others besides himself, that they were not only personal but national, must be held to make them at least more worthy of our regard. It could have been no ordinary afflatus which, going forth, in the first instance, perhaps from David, thus extended and communicated itself to the sons of Korah, and inspired them with sentiments which, like his own, found expression in language transcending the limits of the temporal or the human, to be fulfilled and warranted only by the eternal and the Divine. Certainly, at this time, whatever hopes had been raised by the promise to Abraham, had centred in the person of a king, and in the desire for a universal and an endless kingdom.

In no Psalm, however, is this expressed so plainly as in the 72d, which is apparently ascribed to Solomon, and at all events has reference to him. Here, again, the subject is *the king* and *the king's son*. But the language is utterly unintelligible when interpreted of any temporal king. There can be as little doubt, however, that it was suggested by the actual circumstances of a living monarch; and it seems, therefore, to contain indisputable proof that, at the time of its composition, the very existence of the Davidic throne had suggested to the foremost minds of the nation the conception of a Divine kingdom, which should be established in righteousness, which should be the refuge and the security of the oppressed, which should receive the homage of, and be supreme over, all kingdoms; which should be as permanent as the sun and the moon, and be the centre and source of universal blessing. Common sense protests against the notion that the most ardent and patriotic Israelite can ever have imagined this to be literally true, or to be intended to be understood literally of the personal throne of either David or Solomon. But it is equally obvious that such ardent and enthusiastic hopes

were not only cherished, but expressed. The natural
inference therefore is, that at this time the establishment
of what promised, and was hoped, to be a permanent throne
in Israel, had given a powerful impulse in the nation to
the longing for a great and glorious dominion, which should
be superior to all other monarchies, should gather up all
into itself, and should last for ever ; while the utterance
that such longings found in the poems of David and others
was calculated to spiritualise and elevate their character, to
ennoble and direct their tendency, to raise them off the
earthly and the human, and to plant them in the heavenly
and the Divine.

The 89th Psalm, which is inscribed as a Maschil of Ethan
the Ezrahite, is highly important, because it gives an independent and poetical version of the original promise made
to David, and of which the historic record is preserved in
2 Sam. vii. At whatever period the poem was composed,
there can be no reasonable doubt that the record, in some
form or other, was already in existence. If the poem was
not based upon the record, as it is most natural to suppose,
then the record must have been suggested by the poem, or
borrowed from some earlier document no longer extant.
But in any case the poem and the narrative may be taken
as affording independent evidence to the same event. The
existing form, moreover, of the poem is almost conclusive
proof of its later origin. But the writer had so little doubt
of the reality of the original promise, that he was staggered
solely by its non-fulfilment. The reproach that he bore in
his bosom was on this account, and by such discipline his
faith in the promise was rooted and confirmed. But it is
unintelligible that a belief so deep should have taken hold
of the national mind in the way it evidently had, if no
foundation for it had existed in fact. In this respect the
poem and the history are mutually corroborative. For
some reason or other the nation had become possessed

with the idea that the permanence of David's throne was something to which the Divine faithfulness was pledged. And for the first time we find this conviction expressing itself in the terms of a forward-looking hope. The eye of the writer is turned from the contemplation of the past to the distinct anticipation of the future. His enemies have reproached him for the tardiness of the Lord's anointed. The loving-kindness that had been sworn unto David had not yet been fulfilled, but had called forth a definite longing for fulfilment. The real anointed one was yet to come. David and Saul had each borne that title, but the next that was to bear it with truth and justice was the object of hope: his footsteps were delayed; but so ardently was his advent longed for, that his very delay had become the occasion for reproach and ridicule. The writer's enemies had reproached him for his absurd and visionary hopes. An extraordinary evidence this, no matter when the Psalm was written, to the reality of an anticipation of some kind, and of the way in which it was connected in the popular mind, so far as the Psalmist was a type of it, with promises alleged to have been made to David, and commonly believed in as pertaining to him. Moreover, the whole glory of the nation is clearly regarded as centred in and represented by the occupant of David's throne and the covenant by which it was established. The national honour was in the dust because the throne of David was cast down to the ground, and because the days of his perpetual youth and the long life which had been promised him had been shortened.

The next important Psalm which requires to be noticed is the 110th. This Psalm opens with a declaration of the Lord—the revealed God of the nation—to a person whom the writer calls his lord. Disregarding the ascription,[3] or doing violence to the interpretation of it, that person may be presumed to have been David; but then the subject-

---

[3] It is inscribed *a Psalm of David.*

matter of this declaration, *Sit thou on my right hand*, becomes extravagantly inappropriate, not to say wholly unintelligible. Nor is there any evidence that a covenant of priesthood had ever been made, or was ever supposed to have been made, with David. There is no trace, anywhere in the history, of a combination of the royal and priestly functions in the person of David or of any other king, similar to that which is recorded of Melchizedec, who is the type or pattern selected. For though certain kings may have exercised certain functions more properly sacerdotal, such as blessing the people and the like, it was never said of any king that he was *the priest of the most High God*, nor does it seem at all probable that David could ever have been addressed, or have suffered himself to be addressed, in the language of the Psalm, which, in fact, if applied to him, is contradicted by the whole tenor of the existing history. Not more possible is it to regard this poem as a later production of Maccabæan times, when the functions of the priest and ruler were combined.[4] Its archaic appearance is then inexplicable, as well as the ascription which it bears and the traditional belief of its origin which had already obtained in the time of Christ. But if it is really ancient, and cannot have been addressed to David or to any descendant of David, we can only infer that it was written by David, and addressed to an unknown person whom he calls his lord. This person is described as a warrior, but a warrior for whom the Lord fights, while he sits calmly and passively at His right hand. The rod or symbol of his strength is to be sent forth by the Lord from out of Zion, and he is to rule in the midst of his enemies. His people, for he is king as well as warrior, are to be free-will offerings in the day of his power, and are to throng around him thick as the dewdrops of the dawn upon the mountains and the

4 1 Mac. xiv. 41.

plains, clad in the bright and glorious array of holiness. His own youth is to be fresh and vigorous from the fountains of the dawn. He is to be rejuvenescent like the " beam celestial"

" Which evermore makes all things new,"

according as we prefer to understand the marvellously condensed language and profuse imagery of the poet. But more conspicuous than his character as warrior and king is the fact of his priestly office. This has been the subject of the most emphatic declaration of the Almighty. *The Lord sware and will not repent, Thou art a priest for ever after the order of Melchizcdec.* As this is the only allusion in the Old Testament to the mysterious King of Salem, it is of course conclusive proof that the fourteenth chapter of Genesis was in existence at the time when this Psalm was written, whenever that was. But it is likewise proof that the writer must have contemplated another priesthood than that of Aaron, and apparently have regarded it as more complete and permanent than his. The possessor of this priesthood was the warrior king to whom his poem was addressed. So that the person he has in view combines in himself these various functions, but by far the most prominent is that of priest, for his priesthood is after a new order, or rather after an old order revived. The function of warrior also appears to be less real than figurative, for he is content to let the Lord fight for him, as indeed He continues to do throughout the Psalm, smiting kings in the day of His wrath, judging among the nations, filling their countries with the slain, and destroying the most powerful of their monarchies. And, lastly, like Gideon's warriors, this priestly king is himself to be refreshed on his way to victory by water from the brook, and so to pass on conquering and to conquer.

If, however, in order to avoid the somewhat violent and unnatural change of position assigned to this mysterious personage, who first sits on the Lord's right hand, and then fights with the Lord on his, we regard the fifth verse as addressed not to him, but to the Most High, then it is clear that in the mind of the poet he is not only king, warrior, and priest, but entitled also to the Divine and incommunicable name Adonai.[5] *The Lord* (whom before in the first verse the poet has called *my Lord*), *seated at thy right hand, O God, hath smitten through kings in the day of his wrath: he is judge among the nations, whose lands are filled with slain, while their most powerful monarchs are overthrown by him.*

In either case there is a change of imagery—in the one with regard to the position of the subject, in the other with regard to his personal action; for he who before was seated on his throne is now represented as engaged in active fight: but this matters not—the main point is that the Psalm is a witness to the conception in the mind of the writer of a person whom he called his Lord, and who was king, warrior, and priest. His cause is evidently the cause of the Most High, for it is He who fights for him. And as in the second Psalm the establishment of the king's throne was the subject of Divine appointment, so here the king's priesthood is the subject of a Divine and irrevocable oath. Dark and mysterious as these utterances must have seemed to the people of that time, and not improbably to him who wrote them, they are at least evidence as to the nature of ideas then prevalent of a person at once royal and priestly, exalted to a position of great eminence, and going forth to victory which should place the kings of the earth in subjection under him. Whatever may have been the incidents and circumstances which gave rise to such conceptions, we are not only competent to estimate their character when formed, but able likewise to see that the

---

[5] Cf. the apparent application of הָאָדוֹן to *the angel of the covenant* in Mal. iii. 1.

H

brilliancy of their colour would remain long after the aspirations which originated them had failed, and, like that of autumnal leaves on the mountain or the forest, would deepen as they decayed. And when the fortunes of the nation sunk to their lowest ebb, the permanent record of such thoughts would be precisely that around which the hopes and affections of the people would gather, and to which they would cling most tenaciously.

In illustration of this there remains one other Psalm of probably a much later period which calls for particular notice, namely, the 132d. This, like the 89th Psalm, is independent evidence of the promise that had been made to David, *Of the fruit of thy body will I set upon thy throne.* It appears also to be evidence that, whenever it was written, that promise was not considered to have been fulfilled; but it is likewise proof that such fulfilment was anxiously looked for and ardently believed in. The phenomenon, therefore, that we have to account for is the existence of this belief. If we could determine accurately the date of every psalm, we might speak with additional confidence. But the internal evidence of this particular poem is sufficient warrant for what has been said. During the lifetime of David there would have been no room for such a production, still less during that of Solomon, when the primary fulfilment of the promise was obvious. We are constrained, therefore, to refer it to a later period, when it seemed that the Lord required to be reminded of all that had been sworn in truth unto David—when, for the sake of all that had been so sworn to him, God might be entreated to turn not back the face of His anointed. In fact, the later we place the date of this Psalm the more remarkable that expression *the Lord's anointed* becomes; while, on the other hand, if we refer it to the time of David himself, it is almost needful to assume the exercise of a prophetic gift to account for its production at all. Here also we meet with the same identification of David with the anointed one (ver. 17) which has been mentioned before, and yet it is expressed in a way that seems to show that he personally was not entitled to the full significance of that name. But at all events we have here again an evidence of the belief that in the seed of David there was laid up a hope for the nation, and that the nation, so far as this writer represented them, clung to the promise of the hope.

This, then, is the nature of the evidence which is afforded by the Psalms to the development of those national anticipations that gradually, and after a long period, shaped themselves to a definite form. Although as compositions the Psalms are plainly to be referred to various ages; yet, as anonymous productions, as they often are, they have a certain claim to be regarded as a fair expression of the national thought uttering itself in popular odes and hymns. They are, in the first place, a clear proof of the way in which the people regarded themselves as inheritors of a blessing pronounced upon their fathers. It was as the seed of Jacob that they were near to God. There is no other explanation of this belief than that which is supplied by the Mosaic record of a promise attaching to the seed of Jacob. The form in which this promise is originally found is vague and general. It is the Psalms that show us a gradual limitation of the national ideas in a special direction. The promise believed to have been given originally to Abraham, and connected with his seed at large, is now found to be centered in David, and attached to the permanence of his throne. The identification of the promises in both cases needs not to be shown. We may, if we please, regard them as distinct. It is the fact that requires to be grasped, which the literature itself demonstrates, that in the time of David, and ever afterwards, his family and throne were regarded in a special manner as inheriting Divine promises and a Divine blessing; while

the additional fact of this very limitation is itself a proof
that in point of time it must have followed after, and not
preceded, a wider, less limited, and more general belief.
To have invented the notion of promises made to Abraham
after the belief had originated of blessings which centred
in David, would have been unmeaning and impossible;
while the rise and origin of this belief would still remain
to be accounted for.

The earliest traces and records of the nation which we
possess or can discover leave us in no doubt as to the way
in which they regarded themselves. The mere existence
of a character like David, and the belief which was centred
in him, would have been impossible except in a people who
believed themselves to hold the exceptional position which
their records assign to them. While, therefore, the evidence
of the hope which centred in David is patent and documentary, we cannot account for it without postulating an
earlier, more simple, and more general belief, of which we
have indeed ostensible records that on the whole may be
judged to present a trustworthy account of its origin,
inasmuch as none can be devised at once so natural, so
simple, or so complete.

And looking at the matter in this light, it is for us to
determine the relation between the promise to Abraham
and that to David, or whether they are wholly distinct
and independent. All that we can say upon the evidence
presented by the Psalms is that *they* are a very remarkable
expression of the national belief centred in David, and a
very remarkable effect arising from it.

Nor is there any similar result which can be produced
as a parallel to this from any other literature. We may
even doubt whether some confirmation of the reality and
validity of the belief is not afforded by the very productions to which it gave rise. For it is not unreasonable
to infer that effects unique and unparalleled in themselves

are indications of a unique and unparalleled cause. And consequently, as the literature produced by the Davidic promise is some evidence of the reality of the promise itself, so is the presumable reality of the Davidic promise some confirmation and evidence of an earlier promise — some proof that it must have existed, and if it existed, some proof likewise of its fulfilment.

Of course, if we assume the possibility and the actual occurrence of a Divine communication, the explanation of the whole matter is simple enough; but we desire to forego this assumption, and to arrive if possible at a result which shall be at once unbiassed and satisfactory, upon an impartial consideration of the evidence at hand. And considering the nature and amount of this evidence;—that it is in the truest sense documentary, because comprised in a national literature; that it is to be referred to many epochs and many authors; that it is consistent with itself and not contradictory, for from first to last there is no rival to dispute with David the inheritance of the promise made to him, since the case of Jeroboam is not analogous; considering that the form it assumes, whether of suffering or of triumph, whether of glory or of shame, is one that no theory of exaggeration will sufficiently account for; that this hope, while it centres in the family and seed of David, is at one time the hope of victory over death, of pleasures at God's right hand for evermore, at another of endless life and coronation with eternal felicity, at another of universal dominion and the perpetuity of his throne, of a king who is to sit at God's right hand and yet to be a priest for ever, but not like the sons of Levi; that when the nation is at its lowest, the hope is still bright and vivid that the house of David will flourish, that the Lord has ordained a lamp for His anointed;—considering all this, and even more than this, it is hard to say that the impression produced by the whole is not one that bears witness to the originating cause of all as being something more than ordinary, and more than human.

Even if we refer these literary phenomena to an intense faith in the writers, yet there must have been some cause to produce it. There must have been something to account for its origin. There is no second instance of a similar national faith producing similar national results. We cannot refer it to causes purely natural. No form of nature-worship, or development of ideas suggested by the national language, or outgrowth of previously existing heathen notions, would have sufficed to produce it. The way in which David was selected for his high office, was disiplined and prepared for it, was recognised first by the reigning family and afterwards by the people at large, all points to some external motive power such as that which is supplied by the conduct of Samuel. Here would have been an adequate cause for the effect produced, and we can find no other; but then the reality and the genuineness of this cause finds its evidence in the national literature, and in the current of the national history. Take away the cause and the effect will cease; but the effect remains permanent and indestructible, and therefore the cause was real.

It is important also to bear in mind that the occurrence of the several allusions in the Psalms, which presuppose events in the national history, is of the highest possible value; for if these allusions are genuine, they afford independent confirmation of the history, and if they are otherwise, then they can only have been produced after the history was in existence.

Moreover, it is abundantly plain that the era of David was fruitful in the production of many elements, which subsequently, and with good reason, became the foundation of national hopes that centred in an ideal personage who should be royal, priestly, national, and human. We find marked indications of these characteristic elements which were original with David, and find their first expression in the Psalms. Nothing can shake this evidence, because it is cumulative and it is obvious. It does not rest on one circumstance alone, but on many. It is not found in one Psalm, but in many. It does not depend upon the genuineness of particular Psalms, but is equally significant whether they are the productions of David or of any one else, because their uniform testimony points to David, and to the promise which centred in him. They are the perpetual record of a nation's faith, the unalterable verdict of a nation's judgment, which, being as it is entirely without parallel, requires to be accounted for, and is fully accounted for on one supposition, but on one only. If the promise to David was a fact,[6] then the Messianic Psalms are accounted for and explained. If there was in that promise no foundation of Divine reality and truth, then they are a hopeless puzzle, a phenomenon without a cause, destitute of interest and devoid of meaning; while, on the other hand, the very way in which the Psalms transcended the limitations of the original promise as the history records it, is itself an evidence of yet further development and growth, a proof that in the promise there was a germ which was destined to expand and fructify till the whole earth was covered with the shadow and the riches of it.

---

[6] It can hardly be needful to observe that David's title, as it is expressed in the Psalms, cannot be resolved into a poetic or hyperbolical expression of the truth of Prov. viii. 15: *By me kings reign, and princes decree justice,* and the like; because all the peculiar features that characterise it suggest something very much more than any such vague and general statement, and are clearly intended to do so. David's title is manifestly understood to be not ordinary but special altogether, and alike exceptional in the annals of contemporary nations and his own.

LECTURE IV.

THE CHRIST OF PROPHECY.

Sicur in citharis et hujusmodi organis musicis, non quidem omnia, quæ tanguntur, canorum aliquid resonant, sed tantum chordæ: cætera tamen in toto citharæ corpore ideo fabricata sunt, ut essent ubi vincirentur, unde et à quo tenderentur illæ, quas ad cantilenæ suavitatem modulaturus et perculsurus est artifex: Ita in his propheticis narrationibus, quæ de rebus gestis hominum prophetico spiritu deliguntur, aut aliquid jam sonant significatione futurorum: aut si nihil tale significant, ad hoc interponuntur, ut sit, unde illa significantia, tanquam sonantia connectantur.—*S. Augustinus.*

LECTURE IV.

*And beginning at Moses and all the prophets, he expounded unto them
in all the scriptures the things concerning himself.*
St. Luke xxiv. 27.

TAKING the Psalms broadly as originating in the age
of David, to which, doubtless, many of them belong,
they represent a condition of thought some two centuries
earlier than the earliest of the prophets, while there is
probably no Psalm so late as the time of Malachi.
Prophecy, moreover, was a distinct and separate development of the national life, while the writings of the
prophets, taken as a whole, are perhaps the most remarkable and original monuments of the national literature. It
is not too much to say that they are unique in the
literature of the world, and have no parallel elsewhere.
They constitute, therefore, an independent field for investigation, and exhibit generally the results of a further
advance of national thought and life.

It is also manifest that the prophets were not in the
position of absolutely new writers, who had inherited
nothing from the past. They had not only the national
history but the Psalms of David to work upon. They
were certainly familiar with, and believed in, the promise
to David. They were also undoubtedly familiar with the
history of the patriarchs, and with the promises said to
have been made to them. The writings of Hosea, one of
the earliest of the prophets, afford conclusive evidence that
he was acquainted not only with the Mosaic narrative, but

likewise with the history recorded in the books of Joshua and Judges, to which therefore we may presume he was indebted for it.[1] These facts must not be forgotten, as they cannot be denied, in dealing with the writings of the prophets.

We have got, then, at the time when the first of the prophets began to write, a deep conviction of the destiny of the people, and of the relation in which they stood to God. We have got the rooted belief that they were the depositories of Divine promises, covenants, and blessings. We have got the knowledge of the rise and establishment of David's throne, of the special covenant associated there-with, of the apparent and repeated failure of the promise made to him, inasmuch as a rival kingdom had arisen. We have got, at any rate, some of the more important Psalms, such, for example, as the 2d, the 16th, the 20th, 21st, and 22d, the 72d, and the 110th. The schools of the prophets could not have existed and the prophets themselves have been ignorant of these productions, to say nothing of the very object of those schools being the encouragement of a Divine afflatus, and the fostering of a Divine education.

The prophets, then, obviously had materials to work upon when they entered on their mission. Nothing that they wrote could have been written in ignorance of these materials, or independently of any influence which the knowledge of them may have had. It is more reasonable to suppose that some of their utterances may have been

---

[1] Hosea refers to Joshua vii. 26, in ii. 15; to Judges xix. 22, in ix. 9; and to Judges xx. in x. 9; also probably to the language of the song of Deborah, Judges v. 14, in v. 8. In him also is found the remarkable prophecy, iii. 5, *Afterward shall the children of Israel return and seek the Lord their God, and* DAVID THEIR KING; for which see a sermon by the writer in *Good Words* for April 1874. This prophecy is of the greater importance as bearing on our argument, because emanating from *Israel* and addressed to *Israel*.

suggested by them. It would be doing violence to both to dissociate altogether the one from the other.

The book of Jonah, the earliest of the prophets, no matter when it was written, is a wonderful illustration of Israel's mission to the world at large; and the conception embodied is one which at any period is marvellously significant. The mission of Jonah to Nineveh, which, so far at any rate, is unquestionable, is a marked instance of the constraining power of the prophetic impulse, and also of the way in which Israel was made to feel himself charged with a message to the nations. Moreover, the incident must be referred to a very early date, whenever the narrative of it appeared; and it supplied a running commentary on the ancient words, *In thy seed shall all the families of the earth be blessed. A prophet shall the Lord your God raise up unto you of your brethren.*

The same is equally true of Amos, who was neither a prophet nor a prophet's son, but one of the herdmen of Tekoa. He takes up the language of Joel, and proclaims the message of the Lord to Syria, Philistia, Tyre, Edom, Ammon, and Moab, as well as to the palaces of Jerusalem and the mountains of Samaria. Surely it is, under all circumstances, a remarkable phenomenon that a simple herdman and gatherer of sycamore fruit should have felt himself moved at that early age to denounce the foremost nations of his time, and to confront the most powerful monarch of his own nation; and that his mission should have been acknowledged, as it was, in an idolatrous and apostate land, and should have produced the result it did, and should have left to all time the permanent record that it has. All this becomes intelligible on the suppositions just mentioned, and, granting those suppositions, it becomes to a certain extent even natural; whereas, rejecting them, it is neither intelligible nor natural.

And it is in this ancient prophet that we meet with a

recognition of the promise made to David, which shows at once his firm belief in it, and the fact that in his time it had apparently failed: *In that day will I raise up the tabernacle of David that is fallen, and close up the breaches thereof; and I will raise up his ruins, and I will build it as in the days of old.*[2] The expression "tabernacle"[3] is remarkable, because it seems to imply the giving place to a more permanent edifice, as though the temporal throne of David was nothing more than a provisional arrangement; while the mention of "the days of old" serves to show that after the lapse of two centuries the prophet still had a sufficiently distinct remembrance of it, and of the promise on which it rested.

And if the language of Amos indicates any change from the way in which the promise had been understood by David, such change can only be regarded as a proof of development, inasmuch as the substance of the promise is still clung to, though the expected manner of its fulfilment is different. Time was gradually unfolding the essential character of the Davidic anticipations. As the husk decayed and died away, the real permanence and vitality of the kernel was more and more revealed.

Another prophet whom we must notice in passing is Micah, who flourished in what may be called the Augustan age of prophecy. The last words of his book are an obvious proof of the way in which he regarded the destiny of his nation, and may be taken as presumptive evidence that he had the record of the promises before him :—*Thou wilt perform the truth to Jacob, and the mercy to Abraham, which thou hast sworn unto our fathers from the days of old.* And it was given to Micah to add his contribution to the growing definiteness of the ancient and indefinite promise, just as it was given to him, in common with other prophets, to achieve a more spiritual conception of the Divine service;

2 Amos ix. 11.   3 סֻכַּת.   Cf. Is. xvi. 5, where the word is אֹהֶל.

for he saw that to do justly, and to love mercy, and to walk humbly before God, was more acceptable than thousands of rams, or ten thousands of rivers of oil.

He, moreover, has established his claim to be a prophet from his clear enunciation in the palmy days of Hezekiah, that *Zion should be ploughed as a field, and Jerusalem become heaps;*[4] and that *the daughter of Zion should go forth out of the city, and dwell in the field, and go even unto Babylon.*[5] But even if such declarations are resolved into the utterances of acute foresight, it is not so easy to account for or to assign any meaning to his assertion, any time during the age of Hezekiah, that the *first* or former *dominion should come to the tower of Edar,*[6] in the neighbourhood of Bethlehem, *and the kingdom to the daughter of Jerusalem.* Still less intelligible is the statement, *They shall smite the judge of Israel with a rod upon the cheek;*[7] and his yet more distinct and reiterated assertion that out of *Bethlehem Ephratah should come forth he that was to be ruler in Israel, whose goings forth had been from of old, from the days of eternity.*[8] Bearing in mind that this prophet had inherited a considerable mass of oracular and prophetic utterances, it becomes impossible to dissociate his own enunciations from them, or to suppose that he had no designed reference to them. If the throne of David was to be rebuilt after the promise of Amos, who preceded Micah, it is impossible to say that the kingdom and the first dominion of him that was to be ruler in Israel was not a repetition of the same idea, an expression running in the same channel and in the same direction. The prophets, as a matter of fact, appear to have been possessed, one and all, with a similar conception, to which they gave utterance, each in his own way, but independently, and yet in such a manner that the several elements are susceptible eventually of the most successful and significant combination. This may be

<hr>

[4] Micah iii. 12.   [5] iv. 8.   [6] iv. 8.   [7] v. 1.   [8] v. 2.

accident, and indeed its whole value consists in its not being the result of conscious design on the part of the writers, which it cannot be; but if the final and complete effect is accidental, it is hard to say what indications of the working of a conscious moral will would be sufficient to prove design. At all events there is evidence in Micah that he looked for a coming ruler in Israel at a time when actually no such ruler was wanted, inasmuch as Hezekiah was then sitting on the throne of David, and not without honour and renown that were worthy of his ancestral line.

And it is certain that in this prophet we have one or two new and original characteristics added to those already existing of the person who is the object of anticipation. He is called distinctly *the ruler and judge of Israel.* He is to be *smitten on the cheek with a rod*, which implies apparently some rejection of his claim. He is to be a person of so much dignity as to ennoble and glorify his birthplace, which is identified with Bethlehem, a town already famous alike in the annals of David and of Jacob;[9] and lastly, his goings forth are declared most mysteriously to have been from of old, from the days of eternity.

Whatever may have been originally meant or understood by all this, it is impossible not to see that this is what was written in the reign of Hezekiah, some seven centuries and more before the Christian era. And if we take it, as we are bound to do, in connection with other declarations and promises already in vogue, some light is undoubtedly thrown upon the meaning intended to have been conveyed, and not improbably understood. At all events, the meaning is susceptible of progressive illumination, and is the subject of constant but gradual development.

The shortest of the minor prophets need only detain us for a moment before passing on to him who is the greatest of all. Obadiah concludes his very brief " vision " with

[9] Gen. xxxv. 19.

the declaration, *And the kingdom shall be the Lord's,* which manifestly shows that he looked forward to the setting up of a Divine kingdom in a way that is not without its bearing upon similar and innumerable statements.

Any detailed examination of the prophet Isaiah becomes impossible here. But it is more requisite to consider his writings in a broad and general manner than to attempt to erect an argument on particular texts. There are two allusions to the throne of David in Isaiah which require notice: that in the ninth chapter, where it is said of the child that is born whose name is Wonderful, that *there shall be no end of the increase of his government and peace upon the throne of David,* but that he shall order it and establish it for ever; and that in the fifty-fifth chapter, where it is said, *I will make an everlasting covenant with you, even the sure mercies of David.* It matters not now in the slightest degree whether these two passages are by the same writer, as I believe they are, or not. If there was an interval of a century and a half, or two centuries, between them, the second is virtually the endorsement of the first. Whatever was meant by *the sure mercies of David* cannot have been very different from the hope which centred in an occupant of the throne of David who should *order and establish it for ever.* Whether such epithets as *Wonderful, Counsellor, Mighty God, Father of eternity, Prince of Peace,* can ever have been intended for any child of Ahaz, or have been appropriated by him or his people, we must determine with ourselves; but, in the face of other considerations already enumerated, it seems at least possible that they might have been otherwise understood, and at all events they do not stand alone, but are parts of a complex and elaborate whole. If the second allusion is Isaiah's own, then it has all the force of an authentic comment on the former one, and if it is not, then it still possesses an independent value as an instance of deliberate recurrence to the previous idea, of refusal to acknowledge any failure in the former promise notwithstanding its extraordinary language, and of postponement of its realisation to the yet distant and conditional future.

There is, however, yet more manifest proof that Isaiah looked for the realisation of the Davidic promises in a particular person, from the remarkable prophecy which immediately follows his denunciation of the Assyrian army in the tenth chapter, when he says that *there shall come forth a rod out of the stem of Jesse, and a branch shall grow out of his roots;* and further, that this root of Jesse *shall stand for an ensign of the people,* that *unto it shall the Gentiles seek,* and that *his rest shall be glory.* It is simply absurd to suppose that the prophet could have had in his mind any existing scion of the royal house, or that his glowing language, coupled as it was with inappropriate and unintelligible promises about the recovery of the remnant of his people, was intended to be understood of any present or actual king. The visions of returning prosperity to his afflicted land may have led him to adopt exuberant language, but that language became the soil in which a germ was imbedded that could find no adequate field for its development in existing or probable circumstances. For nothing less than the return of the condition of paradise was associated with the growth of this branch out of the roots of Jesse. It is, indeed, possible to affirm, with some show of truth, that the glowing visions of the prophet have never been fulfilled, and are only visions; but it is absurd to say that their meaning was exhausted in any anticipations he may have cherished of present or immediate prosperity. We can only decide, in accordance with reason and common sense, that another page was being added in these mysterious utterances to those declarations already in existence which spoke of a distant glory for the house of David.

In further proof also that such expressions were meant to be understood of the indefinite future and not of any actual definite present, we may refer to the 32d and the 35th chapters, the former of which speaks of a king reigning in righteousness, and describes the character of his kingdom in language that is singularly unmeaning, if interpreted of the reign of Hezekiah. The anticipations of good, however, are not unmixed with forebodings of evil, and it is not until the Spirit be poured from on high that judgment is to dwell in the wilderness and righteousness to remain in the fruitful field.

But nowhere more conspicuously than in the 35th chapter does the language of the prophet, whoever he was, transcend all possible reference to the circumstances of his own time. It can only be interpreted of that *day of the Lord*, when the good things promised to the house of David shall have been fulfilled; then it is that *the ransomed of the Lord shall return, and come to Zion with songs and everlasting joy upon their heads;* then it is that *they shall obtain joy and gladness, and sorrow and sighing shall flee away.*

Nor must we forget that if we are to discover in existing circumstances the full explanation of the prophet's language, we can only do so by depriving him of the peculiar characteristics of his office, which was certainly recognised in his own day, as we learn from the testimony of contemporary history. He was regarded as a person standing in a special relation to God, and having special access to the knowledge of His will. This estimate of his position, whether right or wrong, requires to be accounted for, and we cannot account for it on the assumption that those utterances of his which we can see to be unintelligible presented no mystery, but were clear and commonplace to the men of his own time; because, then, why should he have been reckoned as a prophet or as an exponent of the will of God ?

That the national estimate of Isaiah's mission may have been false is conceivable; but, judging from the evidence before us of the part he played, and from the works he has left behind him, we are not in a position to affirm this, and we cannot account for his prophecies on the assumption that he was no prophet, when the very feature of them which requires to be explained is their apparently prophetical character. It is impossible not to see that the natural tendency of his language must have been to arouse anticipations in the minds of the people which were certainly not realised in the present nor in the immediate future, and which in fact seemed to grow in brilliancy as the political horizon became darker.

In like manner it is not to be denied that the latter portion of the book of Isaiah, no matter when it was written, contributed certain original elements, which, taken in connection with others already in existence, may have combined to make the hope of deliverance to come yet more ardent. Here it is that we meet with the well-known phrase, *the servant of the Lord.* It is manifest that Isaiah's use of this phrase varies. Sometimes it is distinctly applied to the prophet himself;[1] sometimes it is as evidently a personification of the people at large, as in xliv. 1, *Yet now hear, O Jacob, my servant, and Israel whom I have chosen.* But there are other occasions when it is impossible that either one or the other can be meant. For example, the delineation of the Lord's servant at the commencement of chapter xlii. can only with violence be interpreted of the nation at large : *Behold my servant, whom I uphold ; mine elect, in whom my soul delighteth : I have put my Spirit upon him ; he shall bring forth judgment to the Gentiles. He shall not cry, nor lift up, nor cause his voice to be heard in the street. A bruised reed shall he not break, and the smoking flax shall he not quench :*

---

[1] Cf. xliv. 26; xlix. 5; l. 10.

he shall bring forth judgment unto truth. He shall not fail nor be discouraged, till he have set judgment in the earth : and the isles shall wait for his law. Is it possible to maintain that if this was intended to be understood of the nation at large, it was intended to be so understood apart from that clear notion of a successor to David's throne already known to be in existence? Can we suppose that the anticipations of the 32d chapter were intended to be severed from those of the 42d? If the interval of a century and a half elapsed between the production of the two, is it probable that in the mind of the people they would not be associated? Is it likely that the later writer, granting his existence, and granting also, as we must grant, his acquaintance with the materials already at hand, and his conscious participation in the same prophetic office with those who had gone before him, should have spoken as he did, and given utterance to a hope for his nation at large which he deliberately disconnected from the long-cherished hope of the promised scion of the house of David?

The known phenomena of prophecy, judging from the monuments before us, forbid the assumption of the prophetic utterances being thus isolated and independent ; or, even if they do not, the effect produced by the work as a whole, which is like that of the perspective in painting, is such as to make it difficult without violence to disregard the apparent relation of the parts.

We are, however, at all events, at liberty to assume a certain amount of unity in the latter chapters of Isaiah, which, for special reasons, we must not presuppose in the work as a whole. And thus it will probably not be denied that the figure of the Lord's servant in chapter xlii. is resumed in the 52d and 53d chapters. In the mind of the writer it was one and the same image, whatever in his own mind he may have understood, or have intended others to understand by it.   Let it, however, be granted that the idea in the prophet's own mind was that of the nation as the ideal servant of the Lord.   Then he has for the first time sketched this ideal under peculiar aspects.   He who before was to bring forth judgment to the Gentiles, while the isles were to wait for his law, is now seen in the character of one who suffers for the sake of others, who is unjustly afflicted and oppressed, who is led as a sheep to the slaughter, and whose soul is made an offering for sin ; who, while he is numbered with the transgressors, yet bears the sin of many, and makes intercession for the transgressors.   It will not be denied that this is altogether a novel and original conception.   The germ of it may possibly be found in some of the Psalms, with which the writer may have been familiar, but nowhere is the picture so elaborately drawn and so highly coloured as here.   It is not to be denied also, that, whether or not the servant of the Lord here is identical with that in chapter xlii., it is in the strongest possible contrast to the visions of royal glory that were supposed to be reserved for the house of David. The picture is altogether of another kind; and yet it is said of this man, with a strange combination of images, that he shall see his seed, and shall prolong his days, and that the pleasure of the Lord shall prosper in his hand.   So that, as the line of David was to have long life and a numerous posterity,[2] and to accomplish the purposes of God, so was it also with this servant of the Lord.   It cannot also be maintained that such a portrait as this was sketched from the life : there was no one in the nation or among the prophets who may have sat for it.   For if so, it is very singular that all memory of him should have passed away. The picture, marvellous as it is as a work of art, is evidently an ideal conception, and as such was an entirely new contribution to the gallery of ideals already in ex-

[2] Psalm lxxxix. 36.

istence, which took its place by their side, and would eventually establish its relation to them, or be rejected as an incongruous and irrelevant addition.

No sooner, however, has the prophet sketched the portrait of the Lord's servant, and drawn that picture of his ideal sorrow, which is unique in Scripture, than he bursts forth with the expression of triumphant joy, and declares that the barren woman shall become fruitful and her seed inherit the Gentiles. Indeed, it is one of the most remarkable characteristics of this writer that he distinctly declares an unlimited field for the mission of Israel. *It is a light thing that thou shouldest be my servant to raise up the tribes of Jacob, and to restore the preserved of Israel; I will also give thee for a light to the Gentiles, that thou mayest be my salvation unto the end of the earth.*[3] *And the Gentiles shall come to thy light, and kings to the brightness of thy rising.*[4] *I am sought of them that asked not for me, and I am found of them that sought me not. I said, Behold me, behold me, unto a nation that was not called by my name.*[5] Such language as this is expressive of some hope and of some conviction in the mind of the writer. What does it mean? We can only take it in connection with other hopes he has himself expressed for the house of David; in fact any hopes for the nation would, in the mind of the prophet, have centred in hopes for the national throne. However great the humiliation of the servant of the Lord, it is to be succeeded and surpassed by his exaltation and glory, whether that servant is the nation at large, or the prophet himself, or an ideal personage but dimly discerned in vision.

And thus far there can be no doubt that the writings of this prophet, whenever they were produced, contributed greatly to the development of ideas existent already in germ; and that while they by no means repudiated the ancient expectations that had been cherished for the house

<hr>

[3] Is. xlix. 6.   [4] lx. 3.   [5] lxv. 1.

of David, they originated a far more spiritual conception of the ideal servant of the Lord, who, after being chastened and afflicted as an offering for the sin of others, was to be exalted to universal and world-wide dominion. The proof of this is in every one's hands; it is patent and undeniable, and alike independent of questions arising from critical interpretation, from the date of composition, and from uncertainty of authorship. Can the phenomena presented be accounted for naturally? Do they exhibit the natural and obvious development of one idea? Is the servant of the Lord in Isaiah the natural product of the son of David in the Psalms? Admitting that the form assumed by the one was purely natural, was the later form it took in the other such as might have been expected? Is there anything analogous to this gradual development of one ideal in classical or in any other literature? Is it not peculiar to and unique in the literature of the Old Testament? And, even if the essential unity of the several ideas be called in question, their essential and distinctive character is not to be denied. We may still deal with them as separate elements, and note their historic rise at different epochs of the national history; the patriarchal idea in patriarchal times; the royal idea when the crown was brightest and most glorious; the idea of a universal law-giver when the mind of the prophet was fixed on the nation's return to the free exercise of its ancestral laws; but it will, after all, be the possible consistency of these various thoughts, their possible relation to one another, and their mutual completeness, that we shall have to account for; and in endeavouring to account for this it will not be easy to exclude the possibility of design, when it is obvious that the actual result produced is precisely that which design alone would account for.

The peculiar position of the ancient prophet receives a distinct and vivid illustration from the personal history of

Jeremiah. We see very plainly his extreme reluctance to undertake his office, the sense of deep responsibility under which he laboured, the conviction from which he was unable to escape, that the work he had to do was imposed by God. He would fain have held his peace, but the word of the Lord was unto him *as a burning fire shut up in his bones, and he was weary with forbearing, and could not stay.*[6] This sense of an imperative and inevitable mission, extra-ordinary as it was, which characterised the ancient prophets, must be allowed to lend considerable weight to what they say. Their sincerity was unimpeachable, notwithstanding the extravagance of their assumptions. People, and priest, and king, moreover, alike acknowledged their authority, even though they might combine in persecuting them.

There is no doubt as to the time that Jeremiah prophe-sied, neither is there any doubt that he distinctly assigned the duration of seventy years to the captivity at Babylon. The computation of this period may be a matter of dispute; as to the fact that it was foretold there can be none.[7] It is also certain that, living as he did at the close of the Jewish monarchy, he spoke of *a righteous branch being raised unto David, and of a king who should reign and prosper ;*[8] while he joined with that promise the assurance that Israel should be brought back out of the north country. Judging from what Jeremiah has himself told us of Zedekiah,[9] it is not probable that he should have had him in his mind when he wrote thus, though it is possible that his name may have suggested the words : *The Lord our righteousness.* But, anyhow, we see here a repetition of the familiar thought of a king being born to David. If we might assume that the writings of Isaiah, as we now have them, were in existence, then we could say without hesitation that the language of Isaiah is borrowed, and the promise he had

---

[6] Jer. xx. 9.   [7] Ezra i.; Dan. ix. 2.

[8] Jer. xxiii. 5-8.   [9] xxxvii. 2 *seq.*, and lii. 2.

given renewed; but, at all events, we have here from an independent hand a repetition, whether earlier or later, of the old idea.

And it is impossible not to say that the expectation of future good for Israel is expressly associated with that of the king who is to be born to David. The restoration of Israel is to take place in his days, and Judah and Israel are again to be one, for we must not forget that at this time Israel had no national existence. Now, the interpretation of this language may be a very difficult and doubtful matter, but as to its literal meaning there can be no doubt. This is what the prophet said, whatever his words meant. And, perhaps, the clearest and most explicit promise that yet existed in relation to the expected heir of David, was thus added to all that had gone before. Psalms like the 72d, the 89th, the 132d, and others, received a new meaning when language such as this was uttered by a man in the position of Jeremiah, who claimed and was acknowledged to be a prophet of the Lord. It is manifest that the original thought was becoming clearer and more definite; it was undergoing development; it was a growing conception, and each age and epoch contributed to its growth, each prophet added something of distinctness to the original idea. And yet, what the full idea was to be no single prophet knew, and no single age could tell what was or was not reserved for its own epoch to produce. The fulness of time alone could show whether the aggregate was complete, or whether more was still waiting to be added.

This promise also is the more remarkable from the fact that it presents a strong contrast to the other prophecies of Jeremiah, and from the circumstance of its being reiterated and expanded by him, subseqently, when he was shut up in the court of the prison.[1] His prophecies generally have more of a domestic and local character, and are concerned

---

[1] Chap. xxxiii. 15-26.

rather with the immediate destiny of his people; but here he takes a much wider range, and looks forward to the remotest future, and declares that the covenant with day and night shall be broken before David shall want a son to reign upon his throne. And yet this is in immediate connection with the promise of the branch of righteousness that is to grow up unto David, in whose days Judah shall be saved, and Jerusalem shall dwell safely. That is to say, at the very time when the throne of David was tottering to its fall, and its last occupant was passing away into captivity, a man, who felt himself compelled to declare the message of the Lord in spite of all inward reluctance and of all outward opposition, is found in the most solemn manner affirming his belief in the ancient promises, and consoling his nation with the prospect of their fulfilment, when, humanly speaking, there was none.

For the moment, then, we must hold our judgment in suspense as to the intrinsic value of such prophecies, and confine our attention to the undoubted fact of their existence as part of the literary and prophetic inheritance with which the people went into captivity. There can be no question that at that time, as far as the writings of the prophets and psalmists had influenced the nation, it was more than warranted in expecting a restoration of the throne of David in the person of some one who should unite in himself the various characteristics that had been assigned to his ideal representative and heir. And with this expectation rife among the people, the monarchy collapsed, and the nation was carried captive to Babylon.

We pass on now to the prophets of the return, beginning with Haggai, in the second year of Darius, or about fifteen years after the foundation of the second temple. With the circumstances of that foundation we are familiar, from the touching narrative in the second chapter of Ezra, which is illustrated and confirmed by the words of Haggai: *Who*

is left among you that saw this house in her first glory?
sixty-eight years before; *and how do ye see it now? is it
not in your eyes in comparison of it as nothing?*

And this comparative inferiority of the second temple
was made the basis of a very striking promise, that *the
glory of the latter house should be greater than the glory of
the former, and that in it the Lord would give peace.* We
may omit altogether the disputed words about *the desire of
all nations* coming, because, as it happens, they in no way
affect the material sense, however much to understand them
of a person rather than of material wealth may heighten it;
for here is the distinct assertion that the second house shall
surpass the former one in glory, and that apparently because
peace shall be given in it. Two points, however, must be
borne in mind—first, that the ark of the covenant, which
was the special glory of the first temple, did not exist in
the second, and consequently the declaration of the prophet
was the more daring; and secondly, that, daring as it was,
he confirmed it in the most solemn manner possible, on his
faith as a prophet, by the five-times-reiterated declaration,
Thus saith the Lord of hosts. It cannot be doubted, therefore, that this statement was made as a substantive addition
to the prophetic elements already in existence, and would
be so regarded by the people who recognised the mission
of Haggai.

About the same time arose another prophet, Zechariah,
who likewise took part in encouraging the work of Zerubbabel in building the second temple. He maintained and
illustrated the continuity of the prophetic succession after
the captivity, by reviving in his prophecies two of the
most prominent images in Isaiah and Jeremiah. For more
than two generations Jeremiah's promise of the coming
Branch had lain in abeyance, with no apparent hope of
fulfilment. And, under any view of Isaiah's epoch, his
famous prophecies and portrait of *the servant of the Lord*

must have been in existence now, and were beyond all doubt familiar to Zechariah. With these materials, then, ready to hand, he represents the Angel of the Lord saying to Joshua the high priest, *Thus saith the Lord of hosts, Behold I will bring forth* (literally, Behold me bringing in) *my servant the Branch;*[2] and describing the era of his advent as a time of ideal peace and prosperity. This promise which is first given, or apparently given by the Angel of the Lord, is subsequently repeated by the prophet himself to Joshua the high priest, in the word of the Lord, with a slight variation :—*Thus speaketh the Lord of hosts, saying, Behold the man whose name is the Branch: and he shall grow up out of his place, and he shall build the temple of the Lord,* which was now nearly finished: *Even he shall build the temple of the Lord, and he shall bear the glory, and shall sit and rule upon his throne; and he shall be a priest upon his throne, and the counsel of peace shall be between them both;*[3] that is, apparently, between the priest and the king, which twofold office this man whose name is the Branch is to unite and fulfil in his own person. It is hardly possible to doubt that such words were spoken and recorded not only with full knowledge of, but with intentional reference to, what had been said before by Jeremiah, by Isaiah, and perhaps by David in the 110th Psalm. Even if there was no conscious and designed allusion to their statements, which we cannot prove, the mere fact of the remarkable manner in which the several utterances fit into and sustain each other, is a phenomenon not a little extraordinary, and one which may be in a high degree significant.

The independent character also of Zechariah's prophecy is seen in this, that whereas the last words of Haggai were addressed to Zerubbabel, and were fraught with a blessing for him as the representative of the house of Judah, Zechariah's

---

[2] Zech. iii. 8.   [3] Zech. vi. 12, 13.

promise of the Branch was twice given to Joshua the high priest, and the first time was coupled with a personal promise to him. This circumstance is perhaps sufficient to show that the central promise in either case was intended to be kept distinct from the particular person to whom it was immediately given. Both Zerubbabel and Joshua must necessarily have had their thoughts directed to some one else. Neither could have supposed that the prophet's language ended in himself, or that the personal blessings announced were all that was declared.

The critical questions connected with the last six chapters of Zechariah are so intricate that they need not detain us here. Suffice it to say, that in these chapters, whenever they were written, there are three remarkable passages which must not altogether be passed by. The first is—*Rejoice greatly, O daughter of Zion; shout, O daughter of Jerusalem: behold, thy King cometh unto thee: he is just, and having salvation; lowly, and riding upon an ass, and upon a colt the foal of an ass. . . . . And he shall speak peace unto the heathen; and his dominion shall be from sea even to sea, and from the river even to the ends of the earth.*[4] If this was post-captivity, there was still a recurrence in it to the favourite idea of the universal kingdom, with an evident allusion to the 72d Psalm;[5] if it was earlier than the captivity, then it is impossible to refer it with propriety to any actual king; besides, the time of his dominion is to be coeval with the cessation of the chariot from Ephraim, and of the horse and the battle-bow from Jerusalem; in other words, the national power shall have ceased at the time when the rule of the national king, who is spoken of, commences.

The next passage is in the twelfth chapter: *And I will pour upon the house of David, and upon the inhabitants of Jerusalem, the spirit of grace and of supplications; and*

---

[4] Zech. ix. 9, 10.   [5] Ps. lxxii. 8, 12, etc.

they shall look upon me whom they have pierced; and they shall mourn for him, as one mourneth for his only son, and shall be in bitterness for him, as one that is in bitterness for his first-born.[6] It is impossible that the person here spoken of can have been the prophet himself, because *he* was unable to pour upon the house of David, and upon the inhabitants of Jerusalem, the spirit of grace and of supplications, an essentially Divine gift. The words, therefore, as they stand, if thus understood, appear to have no discoverable meaning.

And hardly less mysterious in any aspect are those other words in the thirteenth chapter: *Awake, O sword, against my shepherd, and against the man that is my fellow, saith the Lord of hosts: smite the shepherd, and the sheep shall be scattered: and I will turn mine hand upon the little ones.*[7] If this was post-captivity there was manifestly no one to whom it could refer; but it is no less difficult to determine to whom such language is likely to have been applied by any earlier writer. There is no instance of the rare expression, *the man that is my fellow*, being used of the reigning monarch; and even if it was so used here, we know not who he could have been, for there is no one whose history at all corresponds.

But whether these three passages are by one and the same writer or not, it is clear that they all purport to be spoken prophetically and in the name of God. They are therefore but integral elements in the whole mass of similar statements. They reproduce familiar ideas; that, namely, of dominion and glory in the person of a king, and that of exceptional suffering.

Whether we are right also in grouping these and similar statements together, it is certain that there are special characteristics common to all; for example, a peculiar obstinacy in not being readily intelligible of ordinary

<hr>

[6] Zech. xii. 10.   [7] xiii. 7.

known circumstances, and a certain facility of cohesion, which is the more remarkable, inasmuch as they are confessedly the production of various writers and of various periods.

Looking, then, at the writings of the prophets as a whole, there appear to be one, or at the most two, principal ideas, which gradually become more distinct and definite, until the conclusion is inevitable that the national literature of the Jewish people contained clearly-expressed anticipations of one who should arise in the house of David and restore his throne to more than its pristine glory, although these anticipations were at times perplexed and interwoven with others of a permanent priesthood, whether or not combined in the same person, and with obscure intimations of suffering, degradation, and death, which were to be undergone. The glory, perhaps, predominates over the suffering, but of the presence of the suffering as an element contemplated there can be no question; the only question at the time even could have been whether the suffering was an antecedent condition of the glory or a totally distinct conception.

There is, however, this feature to be observed in the latter prophecies of Zechariah, which is more consistent, perhaps, with the supposition of a later date for their origin, that the subject spoken of is found to blend with the person of the Divine being; and this also is characteristic of the latest of the prophetic utterances—that, namely, in the book of Malachi. The writer there says, speaking in the name of God: *Behold, I will send my messenger, and he shall prepare the way before me: and the Lord, whom ye seek, shall suddenly come to his temple, even the messenger of the covenant, whom ye delight in: Behold, he shall come, saith the Lord of hosts.*[8]

We must remember that this passage undoubtedly comes

[8] Mal. iii. 1.

after the entire bulk of prophetic enunciations that we have been considering was in existence. The second temple was built; Haggai's promise concerning it had been given; Malachi was no doubt familiar with it and with all the recorded sayings of Isaiah, Jeremiah Zechariah, David, and the rest. Speaking, then, late in time as he did, Malachi said: *The Lord, whom ye seek, shall suddenly come to his temple.* The expected advent of a glorious king is in abeyance. It is now the Lord himself who is to come to His temple, and fulfil the former promise of giving peace in it. He is to come as a judge. If He is not to come as a priest, He is at any rate to purify the sons of Levi, and purge them as gold and silver, that they may offer unto the Lord an offering in righteousness.

If the earlier prophetic notion of a great king is foreign to the writings of Malachi, we cannot say that his conception of the future glory is in any sense inferior to that; on the contrary, it seems even to surpass it; for the person who is to come is called the Lord,[9] and the place whither He is to come is called *His* temple. He is also apparently identified with the messenger of the covenant, a phrase which most probably contains an allusion to the Angel of His presence mentioned in Isaiah,[1] who is represented as having interposed on behalf of the nation at various critical periods of their history.

We seem, therefore, to be justified in saying that in the time of Malachi the national hope, so far as he expressed it, had become more elevated and spiritualised. The earthly metaphors were dropped; temporal power and rule were forgotten. The Lord Himself was a great king, whose name was dreadful among the heathen: the Lord Himself was the hope of His people, and to those who feared His name the Sun of righteousness would arise with healing in his wings. If this is so, the former words, *They shall*

---

[9] הָאָדוֹן.   [1] Is. lxiii. 9.

K

look on me whom they pierced, acquire a fresh significance, to say nothing of those others, *Awake, O sword, against my shepherd, and against the man that is my fellow, saith the Lord of hosts.* Whatever may have been the intention of the several writers, the combined phenomena presented by their writings cannot fail to strike us as very remarkable; and it is scarcely possible to imagine that Malachi, the latest writer of all, was not conditioned by what had gone before, and is not to be understood accordingly.

There remains, however, yet one collection of writings which must be noticed, because, whatever its date, it throws considerable light upon the interpretation of the rest, and this is the book of Daniel. Starting with the assumption that this book may be as late as the second century before Christ, we are yet led by it to certain conclusions with respect to other prophetic writings that it is difficult to set aside. For example, it is certain that in Daniel we meet with the use of a particular term which cannot be ambiguous any longer. In the second century before Christ, then, at the latest, a writer could be understood who spoke of Prince Messiah, and of Messiah being cut off.[2] It is clear, therefore, that by this time the conception of a person who should fulfil in himself the several conditions going to make up whatever was meant by Messiah was fully developed, or else that he originated its full development. This latter alternative, however, is not likely. The writer, no doubt, appealed to a condition of thought already existing. In his time the conception of a Messiah was fully formed, and any allusion to it was intelligible. But how could this be, were it not for the materials out of which such a conception could alone be formed already existing in the national literature? The term Messiah was one which had been applied to kings, prophets, and priests, in former times; but here we find an entirely different use of

<hr>

[2] Dan. ix. 25, 26.

it, as it was applied to an ideal person whose advent is yet
future.   This person is himself pre-eminently Messiah:
he is called Prince Messiah.[3]   He cannot be any one of
those persons to whom the term has been applied officially
before.   He must be one to whom it is more applicable
than to any.

The belief, then, in the advent of such a person must
have been mature and definite, but it could only have been
so because it had been fostered and inculcated by the
writings of the prophets and the national literature. There
must, therefore, have been that in the literature which was
capable of fostering it. The writings of the prophets must
have been understood in such a way that they furnished a
groundwork for the support of the notion. The matter is
not at all one of opinion; it is simply a matter of fact.
It is not a question as to the propriety of any such ideas
being derived from the writings of the prophets, but a
matter of fact that they were so derived; and of this the
evidence of the book of Daniel, whenever that book was
written, is conclusive.

Nor does the question of date materially affect the issue,
because here, a hundred and fifty years before Christ, is
the evidence that the prophets were thus understood. This
was the long result of their education of the national mind.
They had led the people up to this position. And it was
not the work of one writer, but of many. There is good
ground, then, for a strong presumption that this, which was
the combined effect produced by many writers, was more
or less nearly the particular effect which they intended to
produce. If, therefore, we find one writer deliberately
adopting the language and images of an earlier one, we
can only infer that he did it with the intention of adopting
and expanding his meaning. And when this is done by
many writers successively, and the final result is what it

מָשִׁיחַ נָגִיד. [3]

proves to be, we can only conclude that the result corresponded with the object which the writers had in view. They did intend their language to produce and cherish the hope that a deliverer would arise in the house of David; and the people were warranted in investing him with the various attributes which the several writers assigned to him. When Daniel spoke of Prince Messiah, he virtually added his endorsement to all that had been promised to the throne of David, while he gave also an unmistakable proof of the manner in which he had received and understood those promises.

The book of Daniel, then, on any supposition of its date and authorship, is a witness to the historic development of the Messianic conception. In the second century before Christ we find the notion of Messiah as a coming Prince accepted and in vogue. How much earlier it may have been, we are unable to say, but here at any rate it was then. But, in point of fact, a popular notion such as this can only have been of gradual and protracted growth. It could not have started into existence suddenly; and looking over the various stages of the national literature, as they are indicated with sufficient accuracy in the writings of the prophets, and in the Psalms, we can trace the different stages of its growth. We can see how stone by stone was added by one writer after another, till the edifice assumed the definite shape and outline which are conspicuous in the writings of Daniel.

Of course if we decide, as we very reasonably may, upon the genuineness of that book, then the considerations already mentioned receive additional weight. Then the writings of Zechariah and Malachi must have been produced in the knowledge of the prophecies of Daniel, and must be interpreted accordingly; but as all these writings were unquestionably in existence in their present form in the second century before Christ, that is more than enough

for our purpose, inasmuch as we know that then the actual
historic result produced by the various characteristics of
the prophetical writings was the anticipation in the national
mind of a person to come who could be spoken of intelli-
gibly as Messiah the Prince. It matters not whether all
the notions connected with that idea were in strict accord
and harmony; they cannot have been. The conceptions
may have been conflicting and contradictory; they could
scarcely be otherwise, if the elements that gave rise to
them were realities manifesting an historical growth, and
assignable to different epochs and to various minds.

To sum up, then, what has hitherto been said.—We have
treated the existing literature, and the several books of the
Old Testament, as we should treat any other literary
documents. We have endeavoured to estimate them only
as an honest examination of the features they present
obliges us to estimate them. We have assumed nothing
in their favour. We have conceded hypothetically almost
every, if not every, position that has been debated, which
might tend to modify the conclusion to be arrived at. And
what is the result ? It is this: that at least in the second
century before Christ, and most probably in the sixth, the
conception of a Messiah had attained so much consistency
and solidity among the Jewish nation, that we find in
writings of one period or the other, and for argument's
sake it matters not which, a usage of the word which can
only be understood of an ideal and a future person. Such
an application of the term is conclusive proof of the popular
existence of the notion. We are not concerned now with
the character of the notion, or the form it had assumed.
Here it was in actual and living reality. It was a thing
which had found expression in a word. It was a thought
which had become crystallised and formulated in speech.
What was the origin of that thought ? Taking the book
of Daniel hypothetically, as the latest expression of it, we

find it present to the national mind at a time of great national debasement. But it is far more probable that it had already been in existence for centuries. If it was not originally derived from the literature, we have no other means of tracing its origin but from the phenomena presented by the literature; and there we can see, from time to time, germs of the same thought bursting through the soil of surrounding incident. From time to time the language used is such as to be more naturally explained with reference to this latent thought than to any other accidents of the age. The recurrence of this language is to be detected in the Psalms and Prophets alone over a period of at least 500 years. Writer after writer takes it up, and deals with it in his own characteristic manner. David, Isaiah, Micah, Jeremiah, Daniel, Haggai, Zechariah, Malachi, not to mention others, are all distinguished by passages which appear to have a common allusion to this same idea, and which, if they have, are more intelligible than if they have not. In all these remarkable passages there are characteristic features in common. There is a perpetual falling back upon the throne of Judah and the house of David; and this even after the throne was at an end, and the family no longer reigning. No such feeling is ever associated with any dynasty of Israel. It cannot be resolved into mere patriotism, because the same onward-looking hope is to be found equally when the throne is illustrious and when it is fallen. It consistently disdains the present, and is continually projected into the distant future. No present glory is adequate; nothing less than endless duration and universal sovereignty is alike demanded and assured. No exaggeration of individual differences is capable of destroying the combined harmony. Each writer worked independently, but the combined effect of the whole is unity, or at least the natural semblance of consistent unity. Such an effect, however, was manifestly beyond the reach of any series or succession of writers, because the earliest were ignorant of, and could not control, the utterances of those who wrote subsequently. And the utmost that the latest could do was to revert to an earlier thought, to develop and expand it. No reason, however, can be assigned for the correspondences, any more than for the differences, between the 22d Psalm and the 53d of Isaiah. It is impossible to say that the one borrowed from the other, or that the one suggested the conception of the other. And yet, looked at together, or, if you will, in a particular light, there is an incomprehensible unity. Are we to be debarred from pronouncing this unity real simply because it is incomprehensible? The mere appearance of unity that undeniably exists cannot be accounted for by any supposed similarity of condition and circumstances in the different writers, added to which no conceivable circumstances can adequately account for the language used. No adequate reason can be assigned for the correspondences, any more than for the differences, between the 21st Psalm and the 33d of Jeremiah. It is impossible to say that the one was borrowed from or suggested the other here; and yet, after the lapse of more than four centuries, there is a certain undeniable similarity. Was this similarity, such as it is, intentional on the part of the later writer? Was he bent upon producing the kind of effect and unity which, looked at together with other productions, or in a particular aspect, his own work has produced? Was Ezekiel, when drawing his wonderful potrait of the faithful Shepherd, in his 34th and 37th chapters,[4] late in the times of the captivity, and when the throne of Judah was no more, reverting merely

---

[4] Worthy of special note in the former chapter are verses 23, 24, and in the latter, verses 24, 25. It is *my servant David* who is to reunite the divided houses of Israel and Judah: *and my servant David shall be their prince for ever.*

to a former thought? or was he not rather adding important elements of his own, the harmony and essential unity of which with the writings of other prophets he could not himself perceive, but which, after the lapse of many generations, it would be little less than wilful blindness to ignore? And are we in all these cases to reject that one particular aspect in which these independent and diverging rays are found to converge in a marvellous unity? Surely, rather, forasmuch as the unity was one which the writers confessedly could not have agreed together to produce, while we can see for ourselves how striking and significant it is, the most natural and the not unreasonable inference will be to confess in the language of the Psalmist of old: *This is the Lord's doing, and it is marvellous in our eyes.*

LECTURE V.

THE CHRIST OF THE GOSPELS.

Das Christenthum war, ehe Evangelisten und Apostel geschrieben hatten. Es verlief eine geraume Zeit, ehe der erste von ihnen schrieb und eine sehr beträchtliche, ehe der ganze Kanon zu Stande kam.

Die Religion ist nicht wahr, weil die Evangelisten und Apostel sie lehrten: sondern sie lehrten sie, weil sie wahr ist.

Auch das, was Gott lehrt, ist nicht wahr, weil es Gott lehren will, sondern Gott lehrt es, weil es wahr ist.—*Lessing*.

> Non disse Christo al suo primo convento:
> Andate e predicate al mondo ciance,
> Ma diede lor verace fondamento.
>
> *Dante*.

LECTURE V.

*The book of the generation of Jesus Christ, the son of David, the son
of Abraham.*—St. Matt. i. 1.

A RAPID survey of the literature of the Old Testament
has thus far brought us to some important conclusions
—First, to the existence, in the second century before our
era, not to put it earlier, of the doctrine or conception of a
Messiah; secondly, to the inference that that doctrine or
conception was itself a kind of commentary on the books,
inasmuch as it could only have been derived from them.
It may therefore be taken as a proof of what they were
understood to mean by the nation who were their natural
guardians, and up to a certain point as evidence of their
actual meaning. At all events, we find an impression rife
in the minds of the people, for which these books alone
can be held responsible.

From the position thus arrived at, moreover, certain
corollaries follow. If an effect like this, which was unique
in history, was produced, the cause producing it must
have been unique also. We are led therefore to the
actual existence of certain elements in the Old Testament
literature, which are not to be accounted for as we find
them. If it had not been felt with respect to these
elements that the full cause of their existence was not
supplied by the local and temporary conditions under
which they were produced, their special effect upon the
nation would not have been what it was. But, seeing

that this effect was what we know it to have been, the actual existence of these elements is thus far an evidence of the special and peculiar character of these books, a distinct and unmistakable mark of their exceptional position in literature.

Judged therefore by the effects of its teaching, and by the phenomena it presents, the Old Testament in itself is a remarkable literary monument, possessing characteristics that we cannot naturally account for. There must have been causes operating in its production to which we have no key or clue. We are compelled to postulate the existence of other forces at work than those which we recognise in the production of other and ordinary literature. Even if in such writings as Virgil's Pollio and the second book of Plato's Republic we can detect traces of somewhat similar elements, yet the clearness, the definiteness, and the extent and multiplicity of those which are found in the Old Testament, are sufficient to distinguish it very widely from the whole of classical literature. There is no doubt that the books of the Old Testament, as a whole, are distinguished from all other literature, no less by their contents than they are by their character and style. And their contents may be briefly summed up and expressed in one word by the conception or doctrine of a coming Messiah.

If, therefore, the existence and the highly exceptional features of this doctrine or conception cannot be traced back or assigned to any natural origin, it is itself an evidence so far of an origin other than natural, an indication and presumptive proof of an external and Divine communication having been made to man. For if otherwise, not only must the natural origin of this doctrine be clearly discoverable, but the actual features of its manifestation must be clearly explicable on natural principles; which they are not.

Having, however, thus far reviewed the materials from which alone the conception of a coming Messiah could have been derived, we have next to consider the way in which, as a matter of historic fact, the proclamation that He had come was spread abroad. After the completion of the books of the Old Testament, whenever that took place, it does not appear that any elements of importance were added to the existing conception of a Messiah. That conception was undoubtedly to a great degree vague and indefinite. The predominant and favourite idea was that unquestionably of a victorious king. The subject condition of the people under the Roman sway would naturally cause them to cling to that idea with fond tenacity. The foreign oppression made them long for a deliverer, made them cherish their recollections of the past of David's throne, and indulge the ancient hope of one who was to sit thereon.

But it is not to be denied that there were also vague impressions of suffering and death associated with the notion of a Messiah. The distinct assertion of Daniel that the Prince Messiah should be cut off, would alone and of itself account for these. And we can see for ourselves the kind of confirmation they would receive from other parts of the literature. The natural result of these conflicting ideas would be the notion which certainly prevailed to some extent among the people, of two Messiahs: if that was rejected, the only solution would be that the same Messiah was to suffer and to reign.

Such were the materials which were in existence when the son of Zacharias came preaching the baptism of repentance in the wilderness of Judæa, and declaring himself the forerunner of One whose shoe-latchet he was not worthy to unloose. There is no reason whatever to doubt that this was the first movement in that mighty chain of convulsive revolutions which stirred the heart of the Jewish nation towards the close of the reign of Tiberius Cæsar.

After the lapse of upwards of four centuries, a remarkable person had appeared, who seemed to aim at the restoration of the prophetic office, and to emulate in himself the traditional characteristics of Elijah. Unquestionably this was done by him with special reference to the writings of Malachi. He is said to have described himself as *the voice of one crying in the wilderness, Prepare ye the way of the Lord*, quoting words of Isaiah which were obviously in the mind of Malachi when he wrote about *the messenger of the Lord of hosts* who should prepare His way before Him, and of sending *Elijah the prophet* before the coming of the *great and dreadful day of the Lord*.

The way, then, in which John fulfilled his mission is itself a proof of the kind of anticipation which had either been created by the prophets or was capable of being created by an appeal to them. They were regarded as the bearers of a message which waited for its fulfilment. It was not supposed that the actual circumstances of their time had exhausted all the meaning of their language. It was a fact that expectations had been aroused by them, and these expectations were a reality which could be turned to account as they were by John the Baptist. While, however, this was the case, John does not seem to have encouraged the popular notion that a powerful ruler was about to appear. The key-note of his preaching was repentance ; the most conspicuous feature of his character was austerity. The movement he originated was purely moral, and in no sense political. The kingdom to which he referred was not that of Herod or Tiberius, but *the kingdom of God*. This particular phrase, also, which was characteristic of his teaching, was without doubt not original with him, but a reminiscence of the old prophetic teaching, and showed more especially a reversion to the language of Daniel, without which it is hardly to be understood. That prophet had said that *the God of Heaven* should *set up a kingdom*, which should *never be destroyed* but *stand for ever;*[1] and of the Son of man, whom he saw in the night visions, he had said that *there was given Him dominion, and glory, and a kingdom, that all people, nations, and languages should serve Him; that His dominion was an everlasting dominion, which should not pass away, and His kingdom that which should not be destroyed.*[2]

There can be no question that this figure and language was adopted by John, and that he believed his own time to be cast on the eve of the establishment of this kingdom; but he does not appear to have conceived of it as earthly or as the rival of other kingdoms already in existence. Certainly he took no steps to prepare for any such kingdom, though he believed he was preparing the way before the Lord by the preaching of the baptism of repentance for the remission of sins.

While, however, he bore his testimony to Jesus, he seems, at all events latterly, to have had misgivings about Him; and he certainly died without seeing the advent of that kingdom which he had proclaimed as near.

His career, however, had produced certain results. It must have had the effect of resuscitating the popular faith in the promises of the ancient prophets. For a long time that faith had languished; it now revived with unusual vigour, so much so that *all men mused in their hearts of John whether he were the Christ or not.*[3] He declared, however, that he was *not the Christ*, but that he was *sent before Him.* The preaching of John, then, had had the effect of raising men's minds to the very verge of immediate expectation. It had also the further effect of warning men that the kingdom which they expected could only be prepared for by a moral reformation. As it had been said of the coming Elijah that he should *turn the heart of the fathers to the children, and the heart of the*

[1] Dan. ii. 44.   [2] vii. 14.   [3] St. Luke iii. 15.

children to their fathers, so the mission of John was directed to the moral regeneration of society. This, however, he distinctly declared himself unable to complete; it was to be the work of the " one greater Man " who was to come.

I think, then, we may fairly say that the character of John the Baptist as drawn by the Evangelists is not one that could have been constructed out of the materials already existing in Isaiah and Malachi. No pondering over the obscure language of these prophets could have resulted in such a picture as the Gospel-writers have delineated. And if, availing themselves of the foundation of fact that was ready to hand, they coloured it to suit their own purposes, they did not bring it more into harmony with the original as sketched by the prophets. In fact, their own portrait of the Baptist was an original of itself. As a fabrication it was no counterpart to the shadowy outline of the prophets. It was therefore drawn from the life, or it was nothing.

But if we take the character of John as presented in the Gospels to be a true representation of an historical personage, it is not at all more easy to understand how it could have been designedly produced upon the model already existing. To suppose that John deliberately set himself down to mark out for himself a career that should have the effect of corresponding with what had been written of the messenger of the Lord, is in the highest degree improbable. Even if so, his character had all the merit of profound originality. And, therefore, as it could not have been naturally created by an effort of the personal will out of the slender materials to be gathered from the prophets, the character of John can only be regarded as an independent and spontaneous creation of history; and any correspondence it may have with the prophetical portrait of the messenger of the Lord must be judged simply on

its own merits, and cannot be ascribed, on the one hand, to
the deliberate intention of John, or, on the other, to the
constructive literary skill of the Evangelists.

And if this is true of the very first character we meet
with in the Gospel history, it becomes so in a far higher
degree of the great character of all. The only reasonable
theory of that history, if it is not accepted as a trustworthy
record of fact, is that the writers were supplied with a
remarkable character in the person of Jesus of Nazareth,
and that they designedly moulded their representation of
His character in such a way as to make it appear to be the
historical counterpart of the prophetic Messiah.

To estimate the probability of this being the case, we
must carefully remember the materials which they had
ready to hand. These were the dreams of the prophets, on
which rested the ancient but apparently the long-forgotten
hope of an heir to the house of David. As that family
was now in a very prostrate condition, it was apparently
quite hopeless that it should again emerge to power. If
David's family was ever to rule again, there was no visible
or immediate prospect of its ruling.

But on this point, if on any, the ancient prophets were
with one voice unanimous. That rule, however, was uniformly depicted in the prophetic language with the adjuncts
of worldly glory and material splendour. Kings were to be
smitten to the earth beneath the iron rod of the avenging[4]
King. Gold and silver were to be brought in abundance
to adorn the footstool of his throne.[5] All the regal gar-
ments were to smell of myrrh, aloes, and cassia, out of the
ivory palaces.[6] A very unpromising subject that of Jesus
of Nazareth out of which to construct a portrait which was
to be accepted as the counterpart of this. But these were
the materials with which the Gospel-writers had to work.
Like the Egyptian bondsmen of old, they were reduced to

---

[4] Ps. ii. 9.   [5] Is. lx. 17, 13.   [6] Ps. xlv. 8.

the necessity of making bricks without straw. But how this was to be done might have taxed a finer ingenuity than theirs.

And it must be remembered that all the knowledge we possess of the origin of that movement which is associated with the name of Jesus Christ, is comprised in the Gospels. If they are not actually the earliest Christian writings, they at least profess to deal with a time anterior to any other compositions, epistolary or narrative. Whether or not, therefore, they are to be taken exactly as we find them, they are absolutely the only sources from which we can derive our information. And while in endeavouring to form an entirely dispassionate judgment, we may justly be required to reject everything of a supernatural or miraculous character, there are certain natural features inseparable from the narrative which we are bound to accept. And among these are the claims advanced by Jesus to be the Messiah, and the way in which He advanced them, or is said to have advanced them.

It is obvious therefore that the only materials that Jesus himself or the Evangelists had to work with in advancing these claims were the writings of the prophets, the national expectations derived from them, and the movement originated by John the Baptist. There is no reason to doubt that the preaching of Jesus commenced before that of John had come to an end, or at all events before the death of John.[7] Early Christian tradition, which we need not hesitate to accept, places but a difference of six months between their respective ages. Each of the Gospels represents the ministry of Jesus as immediately connected with that of John. The fourth Gospel seems to hint at a kind of rivalry as from the first subsisting between the disciples of John and of Jesus—a rivalry, however, which

---

[7] St. John iii. 24. St. Matt. xiv. 10. St. Mark vi. 27. St. Luke iii. 20.

elicited some of the noblest features of John's character, and which was certainly not encouraged by Jesus.[8]

One of the first questions, then, which suggest themselves in considering this portion of the narrative is how far what we may call the idea of Jesus was derived from that of John. All the Evangelists agree in representing Jesus to have been baptised by John,[9] and to have had a special designation of his career given him at that moment. And they declare unanimously that John was the first to acknowledge this. It was indeed essential to the part which John may be supposed to have assumed that he should point out his great Successor. But after he had done this it was clearly open to his successor how He should determine His own career. It is not a little remarkable that He should have adopted from the first the very language of John, *Repent ye, for the kingdom of heaven is at hand.* But having begun from the same point, He had before Him a totally independent and a far more difficult course to fulfil than that of John.

But if the conception of John was original, it was also unaccountable that he should have chosen the particular character he did. With the two characters of Christ and His forerunner both before him, why should he have chosen the forerunner's instead of Christ's ? And yet there is no evidence that these two characters were ever reversed, or that the relative positions of John and Jesus were ever different. And from what we know of John it is certain that his character would never have supplied the materials for a counterpart of the prophetic Messiah, while, according to the testimony of all the Gospels, he expressly disclaimed that office.

It must be confessed, then, that Jesus when He entered on His career had before Him a task of no ordinary magni-

---

[8] St. John iii. 25 ; iv. 3.

[9] St. John implies this, i. 31, 33.

tude and difficulty, if from the first He intended to propose Himself as the Messiah. What is the evidence that he had this intention? The ministry and career of John the Baptist.

We know very little of John if he did not profess to be the forerunner of Christ, and there is sufficient evidence that Jesus regarded John and taught others to regard him in that capacity. With this evidence before us we cannot say that the distinctive character of John was one assigned to him only by the Evangelists. We must assume that he claimed to fulfil this office, and that from a very early period of his ministry Jesus acknowledged him in it. But if so, the Messianic character of Jesus was a conception present to His mind from the beginning of His ministry. It did not first dawn upon Him in consequence of unexpected success. It was not an afterthought, but He aimed at fulfilling it from the first.

For example, in the sermon on the mount He says— *Think not that I am come to destroy the law or the prophets: I am not come to destroy, but to fulfil;*[1] and at the same time announces Himself as a greater lawgiver than Moses. This from a Galilæan peasant who had been brought up in obscurity is sufficiently significant of His claims, and indicative of the office He assumed. In the same discourse He not only gives His disciples new principles of conduct, but provides for them a new model of prayer, and distinctly announces Himself as the future Judge of the world as well as the Saviour of mankind, whose doctrine is a sure foundation. Is it possible that the Man who in one of His earliest discourses made use of language such as this should have felt any hesitation in His own mind as to the career on which He was entering?

It is to be observed, also, that though His preaching

---

[1] St. Matt. v. 17; xi. 10, 14; xvii. 11, 13; xxi. 23-26. St. Mark ix. 12, 13; xi. 30-32. St. Luke vii. 27; xx. 4-6. St. John v. 32-35.

commenced with the same key-note as John's, it at once passes into a higher strain and assumes on His lips a deeper significance. John had not ventured to define what he meant by the kingdom of heaven; but no sooner does Jesus open His mouth than He says, *Blessed are the poor in spirit, for theirs is the kingdom of heaven.*[2] What a turning of things upside down was there not here for those who looked for a temporal king, and what an original conception for one who claimed to be the king for whom they looked, or of whom the prophets had spoken, but who had no other materials to work with than those which were common to the multitudes and to Him! Nor is this all, for He claims to know so well the nature of that of which He speaks, that He declares without hesitation who shall respectively be called least and first in the kingdom of heaven. At the same time He promulgates a new name for God, which fell upon men's ears like music from another world, which had never before had the same significance, and is even now but feebly apprehended and imperfectly understood after being repeated for more than eighteen centuries—that, namely, of *your Father which is in heaven;*[3] while, with an eye that sees into the very depth of truth, wisdom, and beauty, and a heart that can pass an original interpretation upon the commonest works of nature, He says of Him, that *He maketh His sun to rise on the evil and on the good, and sendeth rain on the just and on the unjust.*[4] He knows who they are whom this Father which is in heaven will reward, and who they are whom He will not forgive. He exhorts His disciples to seek first this kingdom of heaven, as though it were something already within their reach, and only required to be sought for earnestly; and to seek it even before food and clothing, because there was a higher life which God alone could supply, and because He who was mindful of the greater

---

[2] St. Matt. v. 3.   [3] v. 16.   [4] v. 45.

would assuredly not forget the less. He knows who they are that shall enter into this kingdom, and leaves it to be inferred that the determination of them rests with Him.

It is easy to see, then, that already the remarkable phrase, *the kingdom of heaven,* has assumed a very different meaning in the language of Jesus from that which it had in the teaching of John; and if one conception was original, so was the other too. Jesus cannot have derived from John the first thought of His career, the first suggestion of the character He was to personate, because the method He at once adopts is totally different. No language such as this had ever been used by John. No pretensions similar to these had ever been advanced by John. Jesus from the first enters another orbit, and the circle he describes differs from that of John as the infinite differs from the finite.

And here there are but two courses open to us. Either these were respectively the characters of John and Jesus, or else they were the invention of those who wrote the Gospels. If the characters of John and Jesus respectively were such as they are described to have been, and if the one man claimed to be the forerunner, and the other the Messiah, then we know exactly the kind of foundation upon which each had to build. And certainly, prior to the fact, no one could have ventured to predict for either the slightest prospect of success. The conception of the Messianic office as it was fulfilled by Jesus was so novel, and so unlike anything that had been or was likely to be derived from the prophets, and welcome to the popular mind, that we can only wonder at its daring originality.

If, on the other hand, these two characters were the invention of the Evangelists, and were instances of the way in which they misrepresented facts, then, as we have no means of determining what the facts were which they misrepresented, we can only estimate their misrepresentation as we find it. And not only are the two portraits of

John and Jesus, as given by the Evangelists, such as we cannot understand to have originated with men of the stamp of the disciples of Jesus, but they are also the exact opposite of what we should have expected them to construct out of the writings of the prophets and the popular anticipations based thereon.

Looking at the Gospels merely as fictitious narratives purporting to record the fulfilment of the prophets, we have to account, first of all, for the extreme and obvious dissimilarity between the prophetic ideal and the professed historic fulfilment of it. And this is equally true whether the claim to be the Messiah was advanced by Jesus Himself or by His followers on His behalf.

But, in order to see this more clearly, let us examine the method pursued by Jesus in advancing this claim. It will not be doubted that miracles were an essential part of it. That Jesus professed to work miracles there can be no question. This was a fundamental difference between the course adopted by John and that followed by Jesus. It was a conspicuous mark of the originality of the latter compared with the former. It was a distinct return to the method of the old prophets Elijah and Elisha. But though we can see that there were passages in Isaiah[5] which might have prepared men's minds for such a putting forth of the Divine power, it is not in the least degree probable that they would have suggested the anticipation of it. And yet, from the very first, the mind of Jesus seized upon this feature as an essential characteristic of the part He had assumed. And he never abandoned it to the last. It is not a question now of the reality of the miracles, but of the fact whether or not they formed a part of His conception of the Messianic office. And of this there can be no doubt. But it is hard to say whether such a conception is to be considered more probable if originating with Him

[5] Isa. xxix. 18; xxxv. 4, 5, 6; xlii. 7.

or with the writers of the Gospel narrative. Supposing
the Evangelists to have had before them the task of con-
structing the figure of a Messiah out of the materials
already existing in the Scriptures, what reason is there to
suppose that they would have performed it in this way,
and selected these particular features, by no means the
most prominent ?

The same is to be said of the method of teaching by
parable so frequently adopted by Jesus. This was a method
of which there were but few examples in the Old Testament; it was, comparatively speaking, altogether new.
And, taking the reason assigned for the choice of it by
St. Matthew,[6] we certainly cannot see either that it was
essential to the prophetic conception of the Messianic
character, or that it was a feature likely to commend itself
to men like the Evangelists, or those for whom they wrote.
And yet it was a method actually followed by Jesus, or
deliberately assigned to Him by those who wished to
represent Him as the promised Messiah.

Not less remarkable is the substance of the teaching
which was inculcated by Jesus. Bearing in mind that the
character He was to personate had to be constructed out of
materials already existing, or at all events to be conformed
naturally to them, it appears that the special prominence
given by Jesus to faith was not likely to suggest itself to
the ordinary student of the Scripture record. We probably find it difficult at times to justify to ourselves the
threefold[7] quotation of the words of Habakkuk in the
New Testament, *The just shall live by faith*, with the
superstructure that is reared upon it. Even the repeated
reference to this very passage may serve to show that the
doctrine based upon it was not the most conspicuous on
the surface of the Old Testament. But it cannot fail to
strike the most casual observer of our Lord's teaching that

----

[6] St. Matt. xiii. 35.   [7] Rom. i. 17; Gal. iii. 11; Heb. x. 38.

the inculcation of personal faith occupies perhaps the very foremost place in it. What words more common on His lips than *Thy faith hath saved thee*, and the like? while with many of His discourses it is this root-principle of faith that they seem intended to develop more than any other, or at least as frequently as any other. After we have accepted His teaching, or at any rate been instructed by it, we find it easy to discover the very same principle underlying a very large portion of the Old Testament, but it is He who has guided us to it; and from this fact we have to estimate the nature of the discovery in the first instance, and to judge of the originality of Him who made it. Surely to gather up into one root-principle the substantial teaching of a large portion both of Psalm and Prophecy was an achievement of originality and genius second only, if second, to that which could declare to professed doctors of the law, that to love the Lord with all the heart and to love one's neighbour as oneself were the two commandments on which depended all the law and the prophets.

But if such teaching as this contained in itself the marks of striking originality, how much more daring and hazardous was the undisguised attempt on the part of Jesus to identify Himself with the ultimate object of this faith! And yet it cannot be doubted that this, and nothing short of this, was in many cases the direct and expressed intention of Jesus. For what other reason was the woman with an issue of blood healed, but that her faith in *Him* had made her whole?[8] For what other reason was sight given to the two blind men in the same chapter of St. Matthew's Gospel, but that they believed *He* was able to give it? And let it be most carefully observed, that we neither assume these miracles to have been actually wrought by Jesus, nor that Jesus had the power to work them, but

<hr>

[8] St. Matt. ix. 22. St. Mark v. 34. St. Luke viii. 48.

only that He really did profess to work them; or, what the severest criticism cannot deny us, that the Evangelist represented the man whom he would have us believe to have been the Messiah as having actually wrought them, and as having wrought them under these conditions. More than this we do not ask, and thus much all are bound to concede, that these were fair samples of the way in which Jesus advanced His claim to be the Messiah, or at least of the way in which that claim was advanced for Him by the Evangelists. And we say that in either case the position to be maintained was one of which we are able to form a sufficiently correct idea. The only foundation which either the one or the other had to build upon was what had been written of old, and what was then cherished by the people in consequence of it. And it certainly does not appear that either was, or that both together were, a basis adequate to sustain the superstructure to be reared upon it. And yet we cannot doubt that it was in this manner, and in this manner only, that the earliest attempts to delineate the personal character and conduct of Jesus were made.

Again, it is perhaps legitimate to detect in the appointment of twelve apostles an indication on the part of Jesus of a claim to be the founder of a new society or kingdom, which is implied in the Messiahship. In it there was a manifest imitation of the twelve tribes, of which the nation was originally composed, and their founders. If the nation was to be reconstructed, it was certainly not unnatural that it should be so upon this scheme. But it nowhere appeared as a characteristic of the coming Messiah that He should act thus. Here, therefore, there was an original step taken which was not calculated to advance the claims put forth by Jesus, and which could only be interpreted as a parody upon the patriarchal history, if it was not accepted according to the spirit and intention of its Author. But if the act of Jesus had an anterior prejudice against it, that act becomes yet more unaccountable, not to say absurd, if regarded as the invention of the Gospel-writers. It is hard to see that their case for Jesus being the Messiah would be in any degree advanced by His being made to choose twelve men, for the most part fishermen, and sending them forth to preach. What prophecy was fulfilled by His so doing? And to suppose that the object was to give the imagined king the semblance of a court, and on that ground to commend Him as the glorious monarch spoken of by the prophets and cherished in the day-dreams of the people, is simply preposterous.

The charge, also, that was given to the twelve suggests at least one point in which the conception of Jesus and of the Evangelists appears to have been in direct opposition to the prophets. The apostles are expressly forbidden to go to the Gentiles or to the Samaritans, and on another occasion we know that our Lord refused to hear the petition of an alien on the ground that He was not sent but unto the lost sheep of the house of Israel; whereas it must have been clear to the men of that day that the promise of unlimited dominion had been given to the future king, and at least one passage, which must have been regarded both by Jesus and His disciples as Messianic, had said, *He shall speak peace unto the heathen: and his dominion shall be from sea even to sea, and from the river even to the ends of the earth.*[9] Surely, then, it was a gratuitous violation of apparent Messianic characteristics, either for Jesus to confine His attention so rigorously to the people of His own nation, or for His biographers to represent Him as doing so. And yet in this same charge to the twelve we have the spontaneous conviction breaking out that a much wider field than Palestine lay before them: *And ye shall be brought before governers and kings for my sake, for a testimony against them and the Gentiles;*[1] to-

---

[9] Zech. ix. 10.		[1] St. Matt. x. 18.

gether with a clear perception of the consequences of their teaching and of His own mission: *Think not that I am come to send peace on earth: I came not to send peace, but a sword.*[2] For *a man's foes shall be they of his own household.*[3] We may accept this as an indication that any such apparent divergence from the path prescribed to the Messiah was intentional on the part of Jesus. It was a token of conscious reserve of power. He intended His dominion to be universal, but not as it might be presumed it would be. He intended to rule over the Gentiles, but not till He had first been rejected as king of the Jews.

And all this must be reckoned as a part of the Messianic idea as it was sought to be realised by Jesus, or else as a part of that idea which His disciples attributed to Him. And in either case it does not fit in well with those materials which we know were then in existence, out of which, and of which alone, it was possible for it to have been originated.

There are, moreover, other points which appear to have been present to the mind of Jesus as an integral part of His plan, if not from the very first, at least from a very early period. The first of these was His own death. No wise man can ever be unmindful of death—and bear with me, brethren, if I pause for a moment to ask, Have not *we* here, as well as the world of science at large, been reminded but now of the ever solemn, but, to the believing Christian, the never awful nearness of death, even in the midst of ease, honour, and usefulness, by the lamentable accident of Thursday last, which has deprived this university of one of her brightest ornaments,[4] and united her in what was so recently to both an equal sorrow with the sister university[5] of this land and with the younger[6] but kindred

----

[2] St. Matt. x. 34.   [3] x. 36.   [4] John Phillips died April 24, 1874.
[5] Adam Sedgwick died Jan. 27, 1873.
[6] Louis J. R. Agassiz died Dec. 14, 1873.

institution of a distant hemisphere? Verily we have cause to pray, *So teach us to number our days that we may apply our hearts unto wisdom*, for the wise man is ever mindful of death—and therefore we need not wonder if we find allusions to His own death in the recorded words of Jesus. But the allusions we do find are of a very different character from these. Even the beatitudes in the Sermon on the Mount contained an ominous foreboding of persecution for His sake;[7] and in the charge to the twelve already mentioned we find the yet more remarkable words, *He that taketh not his cross and followeth after me is not worthy of me.*[8] Indeed, the greater portion of that address is a solemn and unambiguous warning not to be dismayed at persecution. If it was merely put into the mouth of Jesus by the writer, even then it must be reckoned as part of the writer's conception of the Messiah, and it is an indication of the consistent development of his plan from the first. He did not suddenly pause in his career and change his course, but held on steadily, knowing when he started what the goal was to be and the way to reach it. When the disciples of the imprisoned John came to Jesus to ask whether He was the Messiah, the answer given was an appeal to certain language of Isaiah, which spoke of the blind seeing, the deaf hearing, and the like, coupled with the admonitory benediction: *Blessed is he, whosoever shall not be offended in me.*[9] This not only showed the idea which Jesus had formed of the Messiah's office, but the kind of fate He anticipated for Himself. Shortly after we read of the Pharisees holding a council how they might destroy Him,[1] and of Jesus withdrawing Himself and charging the multitudes not to make Him known. This appears to the writer to be a fulfilment of other language of the prophet, but it is such as could

---

[7] St. Matt. v. 10, 11.

[8] x. 38.

[9] St. Matt. xi. 6.

[1] xii. 14.

hardly have suggested itself spontaneously to him if he were inventing his portrait of the Christ, and it would have been unlikely to commend itself to those who expected the advent of a powerful king.

It appears, however, according to him, that shortly afterwards the question was actually raised, *Is not this the son of David ?*[2]   And there can be little doubt that this question was debated in our Lord's lifetime. We may fairly ask, therefore, If it was, why was it ? For, considering the mean origin of Jesus, and the unpromising circumstances of His position, there appears to have been no adequate cause for any such question to be raised, unless the surroundings of His character were not altogether unlike those assigned to Him by the Evangelists. But if men really did ask this question, it can only have been in consequence of the teaching of John, and the teaching of Jesus about Himself, and the works wrought by Jesus : it cannot have been because of the striking external resemblance between the person of Jesus and the descriptions given by the prophets of the Messiah. Unless, therefore, we can actually disprove the fact of this question having been asked, it may surely be taken as an incidental corroboration of a considerable part of the Gospel narrative. Jesus did profess to be the Christ : He did profess to work miracles : His claims to be the Christ were advanced, and were to a certain extent admitted, notwithstanding the many outward difficulties in the way of any such admission. Surely no treatment of the Gospel history can demur to these inferences being drawn from its broad and general tenor.

There appears, however, to have been a point in the career of Jesus when His allusions to His own death became more explicit and distinct, and this was after what is called His transfiguration. According to the first Gospel,

<hr>

[2] St. Matt. xii. 14.

He had twice[3] before that event spoken of taking up the cross and following Him, so we cannot regard it as a new idea; but as the three chosen disciples came down from the mountain of vision, He said plainly, after speaking of the death of John, whom He called Elijah, *Likewise also shall the Son of man suffer of them.*[4] It is true that we are forbidden to regard any of these expressions otherwise than as natural forecastings of the future by one who could shrewdly interpret the present; but if spoken by Jesus they show clearly that He had counted the cost of the part He had chosen, and that the notion of death, and apparently of violent death, entered into His conception of that part. At all events, it is plain that this was the notion which the Evangelists had formed of the Messiah's career before they wrote.

Shortly afterwards we find Him speaking more definitely: *The Son of man shall be betrayed into the hands of men: and they shall kill him.*[5] Here then we have the two ideas of betrayal and of violent death. It is not hard to see that each of these ideas could be sustained by reference to Scripture; but the question is whether either of them, and certainly that of betrayal, was one which was likely to suggest itself, as a necessary element in the Messianic character, to any one who was bent upon finding a counterpart, imaginary or real, to that character as it existed in prophecy, or upon combining the various elements of it scattered throughout the Scriptures. And the most natural, not to say the only possible, answer, is that prior to the fact it was in the highest degree improbable.

This forewarning of betrayal and death was repeated with additional particulars on the way up to Jerusalem before the last passover, when Jesus said, *The Son of man shall be betrayed unto the chief priests and unto the scribes, and they shall condemn him to death, and shall deliver him*

---

[3] St. Matt. x. 38; xvi. 24.	[4] xvii. 12.	[5] xvii. 23.

to the Gentiles, to mock, and to scourge, and to crucify him:[6] and immediately afterwards He said to James and John that the Son of man had come *to give his life a ransom for many;*[7] declaring not only the fact, but assigning a reason for the fact. We find once or twice subsequently an indication of the same ideas of betrayal and of violent death pervading the language and the mind of Jesus; so that we are warranted in saying that if this was not His own original conception of the part He had assumed, it was at all events regarded by the Evangelists as essential to that part, not only that He should die and be betrayed, but should foretell His betrayal and His death. We lay no stress upon the prediction, except so far as it seems to have been inherent in the plan of the Evangelists.

Before, however, we can form a complete conception of their plan, there is at least one other important point which requires to be noticed, and this is the idea of resurrection, and of resurrection within a definite and given time. Following for the present St. Matthew's narrative, we find the first indication of this thought as early as the twelfth chapter, when, in answer to the Scribes and Pharisees who sought a sign of Him, Jesus said, no sign but that of the prophet Jonas should be given to the men of that generation; for as he was three days and three nights in the whale's belly, so the Son of man should be three days and three nights in the heart of the earth; and implied that His own deliverance should be greater than that of Jonas.[8] Again in the sixteenth chapter He repeats the same sign.[9] We are shortly afterwards told that from the time of Peter's confession of Him as the Christ, He began to show unto His disciples that He must suffer, and be killed, and be raised again the third day.[8] Again, after His transfiguration,

[6] St. Matt. xx. 18, 19.   [7] xx. 28.
[8] St. Matt. xii. 40, 41.   [9] xvi. 4.   [1] xvi. 21.

He charges the three disciples to *tell the vision to no man, until the Son of man be risen again from the dead;*[2] and once more, shortly afterwards, He says again, *And they shall kill him, and the third day he shall be raised again.*[3] In the twentieth chapter, as they were going up to Jerusalem, He says once more, *And the third day he shall rise again.*[4] And at the last supper He tells His disciples, *After I am risen again, I will go before you into Galilee.*[5] That is to say, according to the first Gospel, there were seven distinct references to a rising again from the dead, during the lifetime of Jesus, to which we must add, from the same source, the testimony of the two false witnesses, that He had said, *I am able to destroy the temple of God, and to build it in three days,*[6] and the taunt based on this expression with which He was reproached upon the cross, together with the application made by the chief priests and Pharisees to Pilate, *Sir, we remember that that deceiver said, while he was yet alive, After three days I will rise again.*[7] All this, it must be borne in mind, is in addition to the Evangelist's own narrative of the actual resurrection of Jesus from the dead. We are surely justified in saying, then, that, supposing the Evangelist to have sat down with the intention of representing his master as the Christ, he had conceived the notion that it was indispensable He should rise from the dead, and rise from the dead the third day, in order that His character and history might correspond the more accurately with what had been written of it in the Scriptures.

But where was there anything written of it in the Scriptures, which, prior to the invention of the story, could by any possibility have suggested the invention of it? So much so is this a fair and reasonable question, that it is not seldom, I fancy, difficult for us to harmonise

---

[2] St. Matt. xvii. 9.		[3] xvii. 23.		[4] xx. 19.
[5] xxvi. 32.			[6] xxvi. 61.		[7] xxvii. 40, 63.

our theories of Scripture and its fulfilment with what is
stated on this subject in the apostolical writings. Our
difficulty rather is to determine whether, and to what
extent, there was any properly so called fulfilment of the
several passages in the Old Testament which are applied
to the Lord's resurrection in the New. Our tendency is to
vindicate the words of David and others from any possible
direct reference to, if not from any legitimate bearing on,
the subject. We find it somewhat of an onerous task to
save the credit of the apostles in their treatment of these
Scriptures, and feel that we can only do it by an elastic
use of the Psalms and Prophets. But to whatsoever extent
this is the case—and it certainly is so sometimes and to
some extent—precisely to the same extent is it a measure
of the likelihood there was of such Scriptures becoming to
such men the suggestive origin of the story they propagated. And yet it is obvious that, short of the fact, they
not only had, but could have had, no materials out of
which to construct such a story but these very Scriptures
themselves.

The Evangelists were men who were, first of all, concerned to make their portrait of Jesus of Nazareth correspond outwardly and in detail with that which they
found in the Jewish Scriptures of the Messiah. It is not
too much to say, that if death was one of the features that
might have occurred to the minds of attentive students as
essential to that character, it was absolutely impossible
that resurrection from the dead the third day should have
done so. But this we find consistently and unvaryingly
to have been the case—notably so with the synoptical
Evangelists; manifestly so with St. John likewise. It
was indispensable to the notion they had formed of the
Messiah when they sat down to write,[8] that He should

<hr>

[8] It is hardly needful to observe that this position is independent of
the question, who may have written the Gospels—whether they were the

suffer and die, and rise again from the dead the third day. However their several narratives may vary, they do not vary in these respects. For some cause or other they had learnt to interpret the ancient Scriptures thus. There was and could be no question as to the verdict of these Scriptures. All men knew, or could ascertain with sufficient accuracy, what was written in these Scriptures. To those who agreed with and to those who differed from themselves they were a recognisable standard of appeal. If the correspondence they alleged did exist, it was at least remarkable; if it did not, the idea could be at once rejected. Every one knew and was capable of appreciating the broad merits of the case. One thing we can see and determine for ourselves—that it was absolutely impossible, or at least in the highest degree unlikely, that these existing Scriptures should have suggested the invention of the story of Jesus to the Evangelists, if it was an invention.

The next point, therefore, that we have to determine is the probability of the main features of the history of Jesus, supposing them to have occurred as they no doubt did, having suggested to the Evangelists the parallel they drew between His character and history and the prophetic portraiture. And here it must be observed, that we must leave out altogether the incident of His resurrection, because, if that was a fact, it changes at once the whole character of the argument. On this hypothesis we are bound to assume that the incident of the resurrection was the imaginary creation of the Evangelists. Whatever accident, in fact, may have suggested it, the only Messianic materials they had to work upon, with which it must be made to correspond, were a few scattered and obscure

premeditated productions of the men whose names they bear, or the spontaneous accretion of accumulated Christian tradition, as some would have us suppose. In the latter case the phenomena presented would be virtually miraculous; in the former they would be fairly open to the observations in the text, whether the actual writers were known or not.

allusions in the Psalms and Prophets. And here the improbability is precisely as great as it was before, that the narrative of the prophet Jonas should have suggested to four independent writers, or, regarding the synoptics as essentially one, to even two writers so independent as they and St. John must be considered, the story of the Lord's resurrection the third day. And yet, if we except some obscure words in the prophet Hosea,[9] there is no other Scripture authority or allusion to which its origin can possibly be referred. And yet that origin must, from the nature of the case, be distinctly traceable to Scripture as the only source from which the suggestion could have been derived.

The same may, to a great extent, be said of the triumphant entry of Jesus into Jerusalem, of His being ordained as the future judge of the world, of His being crucified with two thieves, of His raiment being parted by the soldiers, and the like, about which the several Evangelists are agreed, or at all events are not at variance. If there was not something, in fact, answering to these various circumstances, there was unquestionably not sufficient in any of the several Scriptures, or in all of them combined, to suggest the invention of the incidents to the writers. For what was there to guide them to the combination or selection of these several Scriptures ?

And certainly, in the case of Jesus Himself, it was manifestly out of and beyond His power as a man to bring about the correspondence alleged between some of these incidents and the Scriptures to which they are referred; as, for example, His triumphant entry into Jerusalem, the parting of His raiment, the piercing of His side, and the like.

We are constrained, therefore, to treat these and similar incidents as if they were the mere invention of the Gospel-

[9] Hosea vi. 2.

writers, and not part of the original plan of Jesus. And, treating them thus, we are at liberty, nay rather we are bound, to ask, Is it possible that the Scriptures alone *before*, that is to say *without* the facts, could have suggested the narrative of the facts? And is it possible that to this question there can be in the mind of any fair and unbiassed critic or student any answer but one?

If, therefore, looking at the matter in this light, we may assume the several incidents to have been facts, the further question is not unreasonable, and occurs naturally, Is it likely that, supposing the incidents to have taken place in succession, the correspondence between them and the Scriptures would have immediately suggested itself to the minds of the disciples? And I think we must answer No. St. John does indeed tell us, with reference to the resurrection, that their slowness to believe it arose from the fact that *as yet they knew not the Scripture, that He must rise again from the dead.*[1] We involuntarily ask What Scripture? and we may rest assured that a remark like this was not thrown in to give a greater appearance of consistency or of naturalness to the conduct of the disciples, but was expressive of their real attitude of mind on many similar occasions. It was not before the fact that the similarity suggested itself, it was not immediately after the fact even that it at once occurred to them. The fact, therefore, was not created by the similarity, but much more the similarity by the fact. But when the full effect of the combined whole was borne in upon their minds by the teaching of the Holy Spirit, then and then only it was seen, in the light of His presence, that there was an inexplicable harmony between the connected whole of their Master's life, the incidents of His personal history, and the majesty of His Divine character, and the portrait sketched generations and ages before by many writers in various times and under varying circum-

[1] St. John xx. 9.

stances, which forcibly brought home the conviction to their minds that the Jesus whom they had known and served and loved was in truth the promised Messiah.

Let it then be clearly understood what is the position we desire to assume, and what are the conclusions we would base upon it. There is and can be no question that at and before the time of our Lord a Christ of some kind was anticipated solely in consequence of the popular interpretation passed upon the Scriptures. Prior, however, to the fact of His appearance, not only had no such Christ been anticipated, but it was impossible to anticipate such a Christ as He is represented to have been. Either, therefore, there must have been a substantial basis of historical truth in the Gospel representation of the Christ, or else it must have been an imaginary creation. If it was an imaginary creation, then the only materials out of which it was possible for the Evangelists to create it are before us, as they were before them and before the men of their time. We know, however, that there is no trace of any such conception having been in existence, and we are competent judges of the actual impossibility there was of this conception being created out of the materials that did exist.

To take, for example, one single instance. St. Matthew alone of the Evangelists records the slaughter of the children at Bethlehem, nor is it mentioned by Josephus or any other historian of the age. We have it therefore solely on the authority of St. Matthew; but he apparently records it for the sake of pointing out the correspondence between it and a certain prophecy of Jeremiah, which is no doubt extremely slender. If, therefore, the writer invented this story, he must have done so for the sake of this very slender correspondence, and for no other imaginable reason. Surely then we are not incapable of returning an answer to the question, Was it possible, prior to the fact related, that the mere existence of these words in Jeremiah should have suggested even to the imagination of St. Matthew the invention of the story he relates? Given the occurrence of the fact, one can partly understand the application of the prophecy suggesting itself, but one cannot understand the prophecy alone giving occasion to the invention of the alleged fact. It is at least reasonable to ask, Is it more probable that the story should be true, or that it should have originated in this way? For it could have originated in no other.

And it is the same with the great bulk of the Scriptures which are alleged to have been fulfilled in the Christ of the Evangelists. We are constrained, therefore, to reject the notion that the Christ whom they depicted was an imaginary creation of their own, and are thrown back upon the conviction that there was a substantial basis of historical truth in their representation of the Christ. And, as a matter of fact, this substantial basis of historical truth cannot be doubted.

Given, then, this undeniable foundation of fact in the Evangelists, the question next arises, How much of their narrative is true? And here we must of course reject everything of a supernatural character, however we may account for it consistently with their general reputation for truth, which it is difficult to disallow. It must be granted, for example, that we know nothing of the character and life of Jesus of Nazareth except what is fairly deducible from the Gospel narrative. The teaching of Jesus Christ either was what it is represented to have been in the first three Gospels, or this is how the writers of those Gospels conceived of it. In the latter case, they must be allowed the credit of whatever estimate is formed of that teaching. On the same principle, moreover, we cannot doubt the main facts of the history of Jesus; as, for instance, His birth of humble parentage, the comparative seclusion of His early years, the brief duration of His ministry, the general character of it, the purpose and aim of His conduct, the opposition it excited, the effect it produced, the manner in which the crisis was precipitated, the circumstances of His death and burial, the incidents which were believed to have followed it. Of all this we know nothing, but what may legitimately be drawn from the Gospel narrative, just as we should arrive at a conclusion about facts from any other narrative.

It follows, therefore, that this narrative may legitimately be suffered to bear witness to itself in its unmiraculous parts, wherever coincidences can be discovered which cannot be referred to design, or whenever statements are made for which no hidden motive can be detected. And whenever, as in the case already referred to, no motive can be detected but a desire to make the narrative correspond with prophecy, we may fairly compare the antecedent improbability of the fact with the improbability of the particular fact under the circumstances having been suggested merely by the prophecy.

For example, is it more likely that Hosea's words, "I called my son out of Egypt," should have suggested to St. Matthew the narrative of the descent into Egypt, or that that descent should really have occurred? Is it more likely that St. John's narrative of the piercing of the side should have been suggested by the words in Zechariah, or that the side should really have been pierced? And then, when this comparison in isolated instances is found to preponderate largely in favour of the events related, we are in a better position to estimate rightly the cumulative effect of the whole combined. There can be no question, for example, as to the betrayal and death of Jesus Christ. There can be no question that what is alleged to have been said of those events in the Prophets was insufficient to suggest their occurrence to the minds of the Evangelists. There is no question that they could not have been brought about by any arrangement between Jesus and His disciples.

We are left therefore in this position, that we have before us the events as real historic occurrences of unquestionable authenticity, and we have also before us the passages in the Scriptures of the prophets which are known to be of far higher antiquity than the narrative of these events, and to which they are referred. We are consequently able to judge of the degree of correspondence between the two. That there is *a* correspondence is undeniable. That what correspondence there is should be the effect of previous arrangement on the part of the prophets is impossible. That it should be the result of the manipulation of facts on the part of the disciples is likewise impossible, where there is no other ground to doubt the facts, and where this correspondence is insufficient to have created them. The descent into Egypt, the murder of the innocents, the residence at Nazareth, the removal to Capernaum, the method of teaching by parables, our Lord's love of retirement, His betrayal by Judas, the circumstances of His death on the cross, the parting of His raiment, the piercing of His side,—these and a hundred other things can neither singly nor collectively have been originated by any study of the prophets, nor have derived from them any significance which they would not possess as facts apart from the narrative of the Gospels. The correspondence between them, as it was not suggested by the Prophets, so neither was it created by the Evangelists. If it exists at all, and to whatever degree it exists, its existence is independent of both.

And therefore the question, and the only question, for us to determine is, What is the correct significance and interpretation of this correspondence, being such as it is, neither more nor less? Is it a pure accident? Is it one of the freaks of chance? Is there no meaning in it whatever? Is it as purposeless and as meaningless as the formations of the hoar-frost on the window-pane, or the marvellous combinations of the kaleidoscope? Or is there a clue to its meaning? Does the Gospel narrative record the one event in history which is the interpretation of all history, and which being so, was transacted on a plan of which indications had been given in the prophets and in the history of their times? Are we right in inferring the existence of a purpose which began to be carried out of old, and which in the fulness of the times was completed? And was it that, from the nature of the case, this purpose, if it existed, could not be anticipated nor discovered till it was sufficiently matured, but that when it was adequately fulfilled it revealed itself? This is at least a theory which would appear to be consistent with the facts, if indeed there is any other by which the facts as they exist can be explained.

At all events, we are warranted in saying that unless there is a method more consonant with reason to be discovered of accounting for the broad and patent Gospel facts, the historic existence of the Christ-idea for ages before Christ came, and the alleged realisation of that idea in Him, is no slight indication of its origin, and may be used as a solid foundation on which to rear the edifice we have yet to build.

LECTURE VI.

THE CHRIST OF THE ACTS.

Πάντες οὖν ἐδοξάσθησαν καὶ ἐμεγαλύνθησαν, οὐ δἰ αὐτῶν, ἢ τῶν ἔργων αὐτῶν, ἢ τῆς δικαιοπράγιας, ἧς κατειργάσαντο, ἀλλὰ δία τοῦ θελήματος αὐτοῦ. Καὶ ἡμεῖς οὖν διὰ θελήματος αὐτοῦ ἐν Χριστῷ Ἰησοῦ κληθέντες, οὐ δἰ ἑαυτῶν δικαιούμεθα, οὐδὲ διὰ τῆς ἡμετέρας σοφίας, ἢ συνέσεως, ἢ εὐσεβείας, ἢ ἔργων, ὧν κατειργασάμεθα ἐν ὁσιότητι καρδιας· ἀλλὰ διὰ τῆς πίστεως, δἰ ἧς πάντας τοῦ ἀπ' αἰῶνος ὁ παντοκράτωρ Θεὸς ἐδικαίωσεν· ᾧ ἔστω ἡ δόξα εἰς τοὺς αἰῶνας τῶν αἰώνων. Ἀμήν.—*Clem. Rom.*

Ὑμεῖς οὖν τὴν πραϋπάθειαν ἀναλαβόντες ἀνακτίσασθε ἑαυτοὺς ἐν πίστει, ὅ ἐστιν σάρξ τοῦ κυρίου, καὶ ἐν ἀγάπῃ, ὅ ἐστιν αἷμα Ἰησοῦ Χριστοῦ.—*Ignat. ad Trall.*

LECTURE VI.

For he mightily convinced the Jews, and that publicly, shewing by the Scriptures that Jesus was Christ.—ACTS xviii. 28.

WE have thus far been led to see that there were undoubtedly anticipations of a coming Christ among the Jewish people at and long before the commencement of our era; that these anticipations were produced by the influence of the Scriptures, and by them alone; that they were more or less indefinite and probably inconsistent, but that the portrait of Jesus presented in the Gospels could not, by any possibility, have owed its origin to the scattered and fragmentary sketches of a Messiah to be found in the Old Testament, if for no other reason, at least for this, that in many cases it is not by any means clear that they referred, or were understood to refer, to a Messiah; that oftentimes, prior to the corresponding facts, there was no possibility that they should be so understood; that the facts, therefore, alleged to correspond, could not have been suggested by the particular Scriptures, or invented in order to correspond with them; that this is more especially the case in points of minute detail, as, for example, the descent into Egypt, the casting lots for the raiment, and the like; while, at the same time, though after the occurrence of these and similar incidents it is conceivable that they would make deep impression on the disciples' minds when viewed in relation to the several Scriptures, yet it is not by any means upon such minute details that the claims of Jesus must ultimately rest, but much rather upon the broad and patent facts of His history, the nature and far-sighted and deep-searching truth, and exquisite beauty of His teaching, the purity and sublimity of His moral character, the marvellous wisdom of His conduct, the unique circumstances of His death, and the cumulative evidence, when all things are considered, for His resurrection; that while, however, these features of His character may be presumed to be as much beyond the Evangelists' powers of invention as the prophetic correspondences, it is even more improbable that they should have recognised in these features the true realisation of the prophetic ideal, or that such a Jesus as they represented should have been the kind of Messiah they would have chosen to depict;—that, in fact, it is no less impossible that His character should have been the outgrowth of Scriptural study, than that the minor incidents of His history should have been suggested by the language of the prophets; and that consequently there is a presumptive reason for accepting, not only His character as historically true, but likewise the detailed incidents of His history as real occurrences; and that, having done so, we are in a position to attach what weight we please to the correspondences between the life of Jesus and the several passages of Scripture in which they have been traced; but that, as we cannot deny the prior existence of the Scriptures, so neither have we any valid ground for rejecting the incidents as real, or for doubting antecedently their possible relation to the Scriptures.

Taking, then, the Gospel portraiture of Christ as resting, to a certain extent, upon the Scriptures of the Old Testament, but as a creation which it was impossible should have grown out of them, and taking it also as representing historically the earliest conception of the actual Christ, we pass on to review another aspect of Him—that, namely, which is presented to us in the Acts of the Apostles.

And here it must be understood that we do not profess

to decide upon the relative date of this book and any one or all of the Gospels. It will probably be allowed that, whenever it was written, one Gospel at any rate was already in existence. But what we mean is this, that whenever the Acts of the Apostles and any or all of the Gospels were written, the period of time described in the book of the Acts was certainly subsequent to that depicted in the Gospels. They represented an effort to reproduce an earlier time, were intended and understood to refer to an earlier time, and so far may themselves be regarded historically as expressing an earlier conception of the Christ.

Again, we have no wish to assume the actual historic accuracy of the Acts of the Apostles. As before, we must disregard altogether its supernatural statements. But when there is no deliberate motive conceivable for misrepresentation, we may hold ourselves at liberty to acquit the writer of an intention to misrepresent.

And certainly we have a right to regard this book as the earliest and the only existing attempt to record the history of the first years of the Christian movement. All that we can ascertain of the earliest phases of Christian life must be derived from this book; so that if, in its broad features, we may not trust it, we are without the means of arriving at any certain knowledge of the earliest history of the Christian church. There is no question, however, that to this, and to a much further extent, we may fully trust it.

For example, this book professes to record the origin and earliest fortunes of a society that was gathered together, first in Palestine, and afterwards in Cyprus, Asia Minor, and Greece, in consequence of the preaching of some of the original disciples of Jesus, and their converts, who proclaimed Him as the Messiah. In the first instance, it was always the Jews to whom this proclamation was made. In some cases it was made successfully, and the Jews were baptised as believers in Jesus as the Christ, and were enrolled among the members of the new society. More frequently, however, the Jews manifested a determined opposition to the idea that Jesus was the Christ; and then the maintainers of this doctrine proclaimed it to the Gentiles, and in many cases with much greater and with conspicuous success. I think we may fairly say that there is no misrepresentation of the matter as thus stated, and not the slightest reason to doubt that the earliest known development of the Christian church took place in this manner, as the Acts of the Apostles leads us to suppose. At all events, whenever the book was written, this was the only account which the Christian church could give of its own origin, or the only account which it seemed probable would commend itself to the Christian society.

And there certainly is no doubt that the state of things not only described in but witnessed to by the existence of the Acts of the Apostles pre-supposes an earlier condition, which is either that of the Gospels or such as the Gospels have attempted to describe. That is to say, the Acts could not have been written without the previous foundation of the personal history of Jesus of Nazareth. Putting the most extreme case, that the book was a pure romance, its very existence pre-supposes the existence of another romance, which must be that of the Gospels or like that of the Gospels. It pre-supposes the existence of the romance of the life of Jesus of Nazareth.

It is, however, likewise impossible that the Acts of the Apostles can have grown out of the Gospel narrative as we now have it. Granting the existence of the four Gospels as they are now, it is beyond the power of human ingenuity to have constructed on their basis such a sequel as the history of the Acts presents to us. There was nothing in the construction or composition of these Gospels to have suggested a continuation like that supplied by the Acts of the Apostles. It expresses a conception as entirely original as they are themselves. Just as it was impossible for the Gospel portraiture of Christ to have been constructed out of the materials supplied by the prophetic Messiah, so was it impossible for the Gospel portraiture of Christ to have originated the conception expressed by the Acts of the Apostles. The book has therefore the weight and importance, so far, of an independent witness to Christ. We cannot regard the history as pure romance. No one proposes to do so. In its ordinary features it is entitled to the credit of ordinary history, and therefore its testimony to Christ is in addition to and independent of that of the Gospels, or at all events of three of them.

But if there is any statement in which we may trust the writer of the Acts, it is in the fact that the early disciples proclaimed Jesus of Nazareth as the Christ. There can be no question whatever about this. The very name Christian, which attached to the early followers of Jesus, and has continued to attach to their successors ever since, is conclusive proof that they identified Him with the promised Messiah. The very name Christianity, which is our greatest glory and our highest problem now-a-days, is an indissoluble bond between us and the early church at Antioch, as it was between that and the known anticipations of the Jewish people and the Jewish Scriptures.

As, however, the author of the third Gospel was apparently the author also of the Acts, there can be no question as to the identity of the Jesus of the Gospels with the Jesus of the Acts. And as antecedently there was no reason whatever why the history of the third Gospel should develop into the history of the Acts—as no one could have predicted or imagined beforehand, from any one of the other Gospels, or from this, that such would be its development—there is perhaps an additional presumption of general credibility attaching to the history of the

Acts and to that of the third Gospel, from the fact of the same person having been the author of both. If his history of the first years of the early church is generally trustworthy, then the greater deference is probably due to his narrative of the life of Jesus; or, at all events, we know from him the conditions under which Jesus was proclaimed and accepted as the Messiah, for they must have been substantially those under which He is presented to us in the third Gospel.

If, however, there is, as we have seen, an antecedent improbability that such a general portraiture as he has given should have been the invention of the writer, and a yet further improbability that the history he has given of Jesus should be followed by an imaginary sequel like that of the Acts, or that such a sequel as that of the Acts should have been developed out of it, then we may not unreasonably infer that his later treatise is entitled to a degree of independent consideration and deference, seeing that, if not in this way, at least in some other, as a matter of fact, the belief did gain ground and spread abroad that the Jesus of the Gospels was the Christ.

We have to take, then, the Acts of the Apostles as the earliest known record of the spread of this belief, and as a record which may in the main be trusted.

And it appears from this record that the original centre of the belief and the place where it was first propagated was Jerusalem. There is no sufficient reason to doubt this. But it is certainly very important. According to the same writer, one of the last directions given by Jesus was that those who were intrusted with His message were to preach in His name and among all nations, beginning at Jerusalem. Unexpectedly, and perhaps in a manner unintended by the speaker and unnoticed by the writer, both conditions were fulfilled at the day of Pentecost, when there were gathered together and dwelling at Jerusalem devout Jews out of every nation under heaven, as there very probably would be. It was doubtless fresh in the recollection of many that but six weeks before a notable execution of malefactors had taken place in the city, at which a young man who had achieved a remarkable notoriety in a remarkable manner had met with his death, owing to the jealousy of the priests in consequence of his extravagant pretensions. All this, according to the writer, was distinctly stated by Peter in his address on the day of Pentecost. And whether or not it was stated by Peter, the facts were unquestionably known and could not be disputed.

But the marvel is that there was no disposition to hide them. According to the writer, they were thrown in the teeth of the audience. And it must be remembered that all these people had exactly those notions of the Messiah, whatever they were, which were prevalent at that time, and none others. They had then nothing whatever to rest on but the declarations of the Scriptures, the popular anticipations based on them, and whatever change of sentiment may possibly have been produced by the preaching of John and the ministry of Jesus.

On this foundation, and on no other, any conviction of Jesus being the Christ had to be based. The outward features of His person and life were most unpromising. But there is no trace of their ever having been presented otherwise than as we ourselves know them. From the first it was that same Jesus *whom ye have crucified* . . . *whom ye slew, having hanged him on a tree,* that was proclaimed as the Christ.

Nor could there be any thought more hateful to the mind of a Jew than the notion of such a death. It was not only unwelcome but revolting. It was most opposite to all the day-dreams which they had entertained of the Messiah. It struck at the root of their fondest imaginations. And yet it is neither to be denied nor questioned that the earliest preaching of the disciples of which we have any record was of this character; and as a matter of fact it must have been, because we know nothing of Jesus Christ if we do not know that He died upon the cross.

Just, therefore, as it is impossible that the portrait of Jesus presented to us in the Gospels should have been created out of the materials supplied by the Old Testament, prior to or without the corresponding facts, so it is impossible that the early success of the disciples, so far as they were successful, should have been created by this writer's imagination, or should have been substantially other than he described it. Of its actual success we shall have abundant proof hereafter: while we may be sure that no one could have been admitted into the Christian body, or have called himself a Christian, who did not believe, or profess to believe, that the Jesus who was crucified was the Christ. By every one so calling himself He was identified with the Jewish Messiah.

We may accept, then, without a particle of discredit, the historian's statement that the Jesus who had been crucified was proclaimed as the Messiah. The first fact of which we may be certain is, that the death of Jesus on the cross was an undisguised element in the preaching which declared Him to be the Christ. No hesitation as to the historian's veracity can go far enough to warrant us in distrusting his accuracy in this respect.

But then there is another point which his narrative supplies. The principal, if not the sole argument to which the disciples appealed in their endeavours to exhibit Jesus as the Christ was the argument from Scripture. This also is a fact which it is impossible to question. The evidence from the Acts of the Apostles is cumulative and very strong. The appeal to Scripture is the staple of Peter's argument on the day of Pentecost. To the multitudes assembled in Solomon's porch he declared—*Those things which God before had shewed by the mouth of all his prophets, that Christ should suffer, he hath so fulfilled.*[1] The instruction of the Ethiopian eunuch by Philip was based upon his knowledge and belief of the prophet Isaiah. The argument from Scripture, and none other, must have been that by which Saul *confounded the Jews, which dwelt at Damascus, proving that this is very Christ.*[2] At his first interview with Cornelius, Peter affirmed of Jesus—*To him give all the prophets witness, that through his name, whosoever believeth in him shall receive remission of sins.*[3] At Antioch in Pisidia the argument from Scripture was that which was dwelt upon by Paul the convert. At Thessalonica we are told of this same Paul, that he went into the synagogue of the Jews, and for *three Sabbath days reasoned with them out of the Scriptures*[4] concerning Jesus as the Christ. The Bereans are characterised as being more noble, or of better origin, than the Thessalonians, because they not only recognised the appeal to Scripture, but *searched the Scriptures daily, whether those things were so*[5]—namely, that Jesus was the prophetic Messiah. The same argument must at least have been included among those with which the same apostle *reasoned in the synagogue every Sabbath, and persuaded the Jews* at Corinth;[6] and it is scarcely possible that the same argument should have been altogether omitted when for *a year and six months* he continued in that city *teaching the word of God,*[7] apparently among the Gentiles ; or, at all events, among a people composed of Jews and Gentiles. Nor can it have been otherwise, when he *reasoned with the Jews* at Ephesus, as it were by a dialectical process, bringing them to book out of their own Scriptures. It was manifestly so with the *Jew named Apollos, born at Alexandria, an eloquent man, and mighty in the Scriptures,* who, after being instructed

---

[1] Acts iii. 18.   [2] ix. 22.   [3] x. 43.   [4] xvii. 2.
[5] Acts xvii. 11.   [6] xviii. 4.   [7] xviii. 11.

in *the way of God more perfectly, mightily convinced the Jews, and that publicly, shewing by the Scriptures that Jesus was the Christ.*[8] And lastly, before Agrippa, Paul declared— *Having therefore obtained help of God, I continue unto this day, witnessing both to small and great, saying none other things than those which the prophets and Moses did say should come.*[9]

From this evidence, backed as it is by a mass of other evidence to which we need not now refer, there can be no question as to the fact that the argument from Scripture was that mainly employed by the early disciples of Jesus. The historian cannot have misled us here. Even if his narrative were otherwise unhistoric, we might implicitly trust it in this respect. The speeches ascribed to Peter, to Philip, and to Paul, may be more or less imaginary, but they cannot be wide of the truth as far as regards the method of argument which the speakers adopted.

And let it not be said that it follows, as a matter of course, that this would be the method adopted by men in their position when arguing with Jews, for it is precisely upon this undeniable fact that the weight of our own argument rests. Where would have been the force of such reasoning with the Jews if they could have turned round upon the disciples of Jesus and replied, We have never looked for the advent of any Messiah, nor did our Scriptures ever lead us to expect one. It was precisely because it was a fact so well known, and so confessedly incontrovertible, that the premises adopted by the disciples were actually unassailed, and were virtually unassailable. That the Jews should not have travelled with them to their conclusions is easily intelligible; but with respect to the premises assumed the disciples were on common ground with their opponents, and there was neither the wish nor the ability to drive them from it.

[8] Acts xviii. 24-28.   [9] xxvi. 22.

But it is not a little strange that the argument from Scripture was not by any means confined in its application to the Jews. In the two specimens we have of St. Paul's method of dealing with persons entirely beyond the influence of Jewish teaching, as at Lystra and Athens, there is of course no direct reference to Scripture, however much we can discover the traces of Scriptural thought and language in his addresses; but when he is dealing with a mixed assembly, or with persons who may be presumed to have had some acquaintance with the Jewish Scriptures, no matter whether they are Jews or Gentiles, he employs this argument or makes allusion to Scripture as a precious and a common possession. This is evident from his own Epistles, and it appears also from his speech before Festus and Agrippa. And in fact it was not possible that the appeal to Scripture should be omitted from any connected scheme of Christian instruction, because it was impossible to understand what such elementary terms as Christ and Christian meant, without pre-supposing the entire framework of that written record of revelation which the ancient Scriptures contained and constituted.

The preaching of Jesus Christ, wherever it went, carried with it in its train a certain unavoidable and preliminary acceptance of the Jewish Scriptures. Unless it was possible to divest Jesus of His inseparable title Christ, and to eviscerate the essential and inherent significance of the name Christian, which every believer in Jesus was proud to assume, it was not possible to do away with an implied admission that in some way or other the Scriptures pointed to and were fulfilled in Him.

Since, therefore, we cannot as a matter of fact get rid of these Messianic accidents and elements, either from the portrait of Jesus as delineated in the Gospels, or from the earliest records and traces of the original spread of the Gospel, which implied and involved belief in Jesus as the

Christ, it follows that we must recognise such belief both as a substantive part of the original movement which we call Christianity, and also as a valid and potent instrumental cause in the success of that movement. That is to say, we cannot separate the early success of the Christian movement, whatever it was, from belief in the completeness of the parallel between Jesus and the Christ of the Scriptures.

And yet there was everything in the conception of Jesus presented to us by the Acts to contradict and to do violence to those notions of the Messiah which had been previously entertained. There was nothing in the humble lot, the inglorious career, and, above all, the violent and disgraceful death of Jesus, to captivate the imagination of men who hoped for a powerful and victorious king. And if this portrait was unattractive to the Jews, it can scarcely have been less so to the Gentiles, whether they were represented on the one hand by the intellectual subtlety of Greece, or on the other by the imperial pride and power of Rome.

The position, then, at which we have now arrived is as follows :—There is in the history of the Acts, divesting it of everything miraculous and regarding it only as an expression of early Christian life, a framework of personal history pre-supposed, which is substantially that of the Gospels, and from which a death by crucifixion cannot by any possibility be eliminated. The particular development, however, of Christian life portrayed in the Acts, though it pre-supposes such an earlier history, identical in its main features with that which we possess, was by no means to have been anticipated from the Gospels. They may even be regarded as the result of an endeavour to supply a want created by the kind of movement recorded in the Acts, an attempt to gratify the not unnatural curiosity of early Christians. And even supposing that in certain details they were untrustworthy, it would still follow that in the broad and characteristic features of the personal life of Jesus they must be deserving of credit, because without such a foundation of fact not only would the incidents of the Acts of the Apostles be inconceivable, but also the kind of life of which that book must anyhow be the natural expression and result.

What we may term, then, the Christ of the Acts is a creation to a certain extent distinct from, and in some sense independent of, the Christ of the Gospels. The Christ of the Acts comes before us as a belief already in existence and operative; the Christ of the Gospels is a Person, and not a belief. But the belief is a belief in a person similar to that portrayed in the Gospels; similar, that is, in the manner of His life and death. Though one of the Gospels may be by the writer of the Acts, it matters not, because his portrait is not materially different, at least in these respects, from that of the other Evangelists ; while his later narrative, regarded only as an indication of the kind of people for whom it was written, may be considered as giving an average, or even, if you will, a favourable specimen of the life which it describes. At all events, men did at an early period of the Christian era travel about the world as Paul and Barnabas are described to have done, for the simple purpose of proclaiming the main facts of the life of Jesus, and of persuading people that He was the Christ. They were not the apostles of a political creed; they cannot be suspected of any ulterior motive; they were not the founders of a philosophy, the heralds of a scheme for social advantages or worldly advancement. They preached that a man had lived and died in Palestine, and that He was the Messiah spoken of before by the prophets.

And there is no question that wherever they were successful, and so far as they were successful, this man was everywhere and always accepted as the Messiah. Yet, in His character, as it is presented to us in the Acts and described in the Gospels, there was nothing that was calculated antecedently to win the belief that He was the prophetic Christ, for in all the most conspicuous features He was very different from what might have been, and from what actually was anticipated. This belief, however, was everywhere produced by, or was nowhere produced without, the Scriptures. It was the likeness between the Jesus who was preached and the Christ of prophecy which convinced men that the one was the fulfilment of the other. Whether or not this was what *we* should consider a valid, or satisfactory, or logical means of bringing about the particular result, there is no question whatever that it was historically *the* means by which the result was brought about. The testimony of the Acts of the Apostles is to this effect; and it is not possible in this respect to doubt its testimony.

It is plain, however, both from the Acts of the Apostles and from the nature of the case, that we have not yet taken into account all the elements at work in bringing about the result produced. It is simply impossible that the story of the life and death of Jesus alone should have wrought the conviction that He was the Messiah. There must have been, and there was, another element combined. And this was the proclamation that He had risen again from the dead. The history of the Acts may be accepted as evidence that the resurrection was proclaimed, and that its proclamation entered to a very large extent into the preaching of the disciples. While, as we have seen, it was impossible from the vague and obscure statements of Scripture to anticipate or invent beforehand the fact of the resurrection, it is easy to calculate and to understand the enormous momentum which would be added to the weight of the evidence for Jesus being the Christ, when it could be definitely announced that He had actually risen from the dead, and when the present agency of the Spirit could be appealed to in confirmation of the fact.

And we know for a certainty that it was thus that the full message of the Gospel was proclaimed. Jesus could not have been recognised as the Christ in the way He is represented to have been recognised in the Acts of the Apostles, unless we may throw in as a powerful element in the early preaching of the disciples the announcement that He had risen from the dead. It was alike impossible that, prior to the Lord's resurrection, the ingenuity of the disciples should have detected the special element that was lacking in the power and efficiency of their message, and that the conviction of Jesus being the Christ should have been produced without the declaration that He had burst the bonds of death. When that fact had been proclaimed, it swallowed up all the shame and degradation of the cross, the lowliness of the origin, the meanness and the poverty of the lot and life of Jesus. Then that life and death of shame and suffering became invested with a new, and before, impossible glory. Then the colours of the rainbow which spans the waterfall were seen in the brightness of the rising sun as it fell athwart the cloudy spray. Then a new meaning was given to the grief and triumph of the Psalmist, a new cause was revealed for the hope and longing of the Prophet, a new treasury of substance and expressiveness was added to the shadows and symbols of the Law. Then it was that the regal glories of the universal King were identified with the spiritual self-mastery of the crown of thorns, and the reed that was put into the hand was hailed as a nobler sceptre, and the title that was written by Pilate was recognised as a truer ensign of royalty than those of the mightiest kings. Then it was that the purple robe was regarded as a prouder token of majesty than the imperial vesture of the Cæsars, and the death of the Roman malefactor more glorious and heroic than the death of the warrior in the shout of victory.

But we may safely affirm that there was nothing in the incidents of the death of Jesus alone and by themselves that was capable of bringing about this change of sentiment. Neither these incidents alone, nor any combination of them, would have wrought the conviction that He was the Messiah. There was another element wanting; an element which they were incompetent to suggest, but which, when it was thrown in, was all-powerful to interpret and to glorify them. It is obviously true that we cannot argue from all this to the reality of the resurrection, but we may legitimately argue from it, that without the proclamation of the fact that Jesus of Nazareth had risen from the dead, the conviction of His being the Messiah could not have been produced; while the incidents of His life and death, apart from His resurrection, were alike as incapable of originating the story of it as they were of producing that conviction.

Not only, however, was it impossible that the doctrine of Jesus being the Messiah could have been sustained for a moment, or propagated, without the story of His resurrection, which, according to the Acts, was everywhere and always proclaimed, but there are certain characteristics of that book which we find ourselves at a loss to account for on the assumption that the story was fictitious. And it is here that we discover the greatest contrast between the Gospel history and the history of the Acts. The Gospel history is the history of Christ and the record of certain germinal principles inculcated by Him. We nowhere see any life in detailed action except His own. The glimpses that we catch of other lives serve only to throw out His into more prominent relief.

In the Acts of the Apostles it is altogether different; and necessarily and obviously so. There we have not the history of Christ, but the history of Christian life. The person of Christ is entirely withdrawn from view. The Christ that we meet with in the Acts is a Christ who lives in the persons of His followers. In the Gospels we have no such phenomenon, properly speaking, as Christian life. It is a thing unknown, and as yet not experienced. If it exists at all, it exists only in germ, and is undeveloped. The foremost of the Apostles behave very much as other men, and are not under the influence of any more powerful motive or impulse than that of personal attachment to their Master, which is scarcely distinguishable from ordinary friendship. The last chapter of the fourth Gospel has given us a picture of some of the chief disciples pursuing their ordinary avocations on the Lake of Galilee, after their Lord's resurrection. But in the Acts of the Apostles things are entirely changed. We no sooner open the first pages of that book than we find the character of the disciples transfigured. The Peter of the Acts is a totally different man from the Peter even of St. Luke's Gospel. *Depart from me, for I am a sinful man, O Lord:*[1] *Master, it is good for us to be here,*[2] on the mountain of glory : *Lo ! we have left all, and followed thee :*[3] *Woman, I know him not ;*[4] by no means represent the same man that comes before us immediately in the Acts, ready to place Himself at the head of the hundred and twenty disciples, to indicate the course of action they are to take, and to reveal the intention of the Holy Ghost by the mouth of David[5]—ready again to interpret an unusual phenomenon on the day of Pentecost as more nearly fulfilling the words of the prophet Joel than any other former event[6]—daring to confront the murderers of Jesus with the charge, *Him have ye taken, and by wicked hands have crucified and slain*[7]—and rebut-

---

[1] St. Luke v. 8.　　[2] ix. 33.　St. Matt. xvii. 4.　St. Mark ix. 5.
[3] St. Luke xviii. 28.　St. Matt. xix. 27.　St. Mark x. 28.
[4] St. Luke xxii. 57.　　[5] Acts i. 16.　　[6] ii. 16.　　[7] ii. 23.

ting the injunction not to speak at all, nor teach in the name of Jesus, with the home-thrust and matter-of-fact argument, *Whether it be right in the sight of God to hearken unto you more than unto God, judge ye; for we cannot but speak the things which we have seen and heard.*[8] Here we detect the presence of elements which are altogether absent from the Gospel history—those, namely, of Christian life and of deliberate and unshaken Christian belief; although, at the same time, there are traits enough of individual character to show the identity of the person in both cases.

But not only so, for it is manifest that this conviction of the disciples is most infectious. It spreads itself in all directions, it excites the special animosity and opposition of the Sadducees, as it naturally would, though they, with their characteristic indifference and apathy, appear to have been less prominent antagonists of Jesus during His lifetime than the Pharisees.[9] It communicates itself even to the priests, it penetrates into Samaria, and reaches as far as Damascus. The new society is found to increase to such an extent that new principles of organisation have necessarily to be adopted, and powers of deliberation and of self-government are spontaneously developed, of which the exercise may be regarded as almost if not entirely new in the history of the world. All this, if it is not distinctly traceable to the belief in the resurrection of Jesus, cannot by any possibility be separated from that belief. In fact, the belief in His resurrection was the motive power and

---

[8] Acts iv. 19, 20.

[9] This is shown in a very simple way. The Sadducees are only mentioned in the Gospel history some eight or nine times, and chiefly in St. Matthew (Mark xii. 18; Luke xx. 27): the Pharisees appear more frequently, and in each Gospel they are always mentioned first, and nearly always with disapproval expressed or implied. In the Acts the Pharisees are never unfavourable to the believers in Jesus, and even take their part (Acts v. 34; xxiii. 9); while the Sadducees, on the three occasions they are mentioned, are their strenuous opponents. (iv. 1; v. 17; xxiii. 7.)

impulse of it all, for it was involved in the conviction of His being the Messiah, for which the disciples and their followers were willing to forego everything, and to incur anything.

Such, then, is the picture of Christian life presented to us in the Acts of the Apostles. It is impossible to question its general accuracy, because it is capable of abundant corroboration from other sources. There is nothing, however, directly answering to it in the Gospel history, for the conduct of Jesus was arranged on a different plan, and the persecution of Jesus arose from a different cause. This manifestation, therefore, of Christian life was an entirely new phenomenon, possessing new and original features never exhibited before, and pointing consequently to a new and original cause. This cause we may rightly specify as the personal influence of Jesus—not the influence of His teaching, because as far as we can tell from the Acts, the disciples do not seem to have reproduced His teaching; they were concerned less with His teaching than with Him; but it was His personal influence and attachment to His person. If, however, attachment to His person while He was alive had produced no such results, why should it produce these results now He was dead? In fact, the attachment exhibited was in no sense attachment to one departed, nor to the principles for which He had died, but much rather to a person whose direct influence was still present and operative; it was devotion to a new set of principles, to new truths, and above all, to a new fact of which the full weight and significance had not been felt before, as during His lifetime it had not been possible to feel it.

In reading the Acts of the Apostles we cannot fail to see that we have entered on the stream of a new life, to which even the Gospel history offers no true parallel. We note the spontaneous action and development of a new society working on new principles and for new purposes, and the mainspring of all this is the resurrection of the Lord.

It is not, however, to be forgotten, that, as far as the history of this new life is unfolded to us in the Acts, it is not even to be referred exclusively to the Lord's resurrection. Omnipotent as that fact might be considered in itself, if a fact, it lay, comparatively speaking, dormant in the minds of the disciples for a period of fifty days. Its power was but imperfectly understood till the day of Pentecost. Then it burst forth with a sudden accession of life. Peter had indeed felt, in the interval between the ascension and Pentecost, that one must be ordained to be a witness with him and his fellows to the Lord's resurrection; he must have had, therefore, a fore-feeling of what his own mission was to be, but we read of no missionary effort whatever during the period of the fifty days. We read further in this narrative that the disciples were commanded to tarry at Jerusalem until they should be endued with power from on high. We may safely infer from this that in the opinion of the writer it was not even the bare fact of the resurrection that was sufficient to call the new society into existence, but the revelation of a new dynamical force consequent upon the resurrection and in addition to it. The writer wished it to be distinctly understood that a new energy had begun to be put forth, and that the materials with which it worked were the life and death, the resurrection and ascension, but pre-eminently the resurrection, of Jesus of Nazareth. Not these facts alone, but these facts wielded by the power of the Spirit of God, had wrought with a new influence upon men, and had produced new results in men.

And though it is possible that we may not be competent judges of the cause alleged to be in operation, we are to a certain extent competent judges of the results produced. And of these results the Acts of the Apostles is a sufficient proof. Leaving out of the question all the miraculous features of that book, the picture it has preserved to us of the early Christian society is absolutely unique in the literature of the world. What if that picture can be shown to be misrepresented or overdrawn ?—it even then remains to a very large extent a witness to the existence of a new society capable of appreciating the misrepresentation ; it is a proof of a new literary *taste* among men, for the existence and origin of which some rational account must be given. It professes itself to supply the true, and is the only extant, account. It is actually, in all substantial particulars, of unimpeachable authority, and consequently the picture it presents may be taken as a proof of the mode in which the new influence operated among men, and of the peculiar results produced by it.

And, assuredly, these results, as we see them there, can only be regarded as evidence of a new life, while the new life is itself the evidence of a new principle of life at work, and this new principle of life is the principle of deathless and eternal life revealed and exemplified in the actual resurrection of the Lord Jesus.

Nor is there any way of escaping from this or a similar conclusion but by referring the results produced, not to the fact believed, but to the belief of the fact. The marvellous phenomena of the new Christian life displayed in the Acts were simply the product of the faith of the disciples. They were the victims of their own delusions, and their own delusions produced these effects. Their own delusions, it must be remembered, were these—that Jesus was the Messiah, as proved by His life, and death, and resurrection, and as witnessed and confirmed by the gift of the Holy Ghost, to which alone, as it appeared, the rapid growth of the Christian society, in spite of all unfavourable circumstances, could be referred.

If, then, the outward circumstances of the life of Jesus were most unfavourable to His claims to be the Christ, no less so were those of the early Christian society to the diffusion of that belief; and, seeing that the cardinal fact of that belief was one which, if unreal, at once admitted of a ready and complete disproof, it appears that the most natural and rational way of accounting for the diffusion of the belief is by supposing that the fact could not be disproved. When we consider who were the first propagators of the belief, where they first propagated it, the means employed in doing so, and the success with which they did so, it appears certainly more reasonable to interpret these things as indications of an underlying element of truth, than to assume, in the face of them, that the crucial test of Jesus being the Christ was one which neither was nor could be applied, and that with the failure of that test every vestige of His claims to be regarded as the Christ of necessity came to nought.

But this is not all, for we are competent judges also of the general moral tendency and character of the new life depicted in the Acts of the Apostles. When men, without hope or prospect of temporal advantage or reward, could live, as the first disciples lived, in the fear and love of God, and suffer, as they suffered, rejoicing that they were counted worthy to suffer shame for the name of Jesus, we are constrained, in spite of ourselves, to decide whether the fruits produced were those of the good tree or the bad; whether they were worthier of the spirit of evil or of the Holy Spirit; and conscience itself seems to determine that it is not possible to reject these things as the special manifestations of the Holy Spirit's working. To do so would but too nearly resemble what is spoken of in the Gospels as the unpardonable sin against the Holy Ghost.

We point, then, not to the miraculous features of the Acts of the Apostles, as commonly understood, but to the far greater miracle of the new and Divine life which that book exhibits in operation, as the irresistible proof of the new and Divine energy at work in the world; and we say that it would be a libel on the truth to suppose that such results could be sufficiently accounted for on the supposition that they were created by a belief which, if not literally and virtually true, was entirely and absolutely false.

The results referred to were the direct consequence of faith in Jesus as the Messiah. To His being the Messiah, not only faith in His resurrection was essential, but much more the fact that He had truly risen from the dead. If He was merely believed to have risen, but had not risen from the dead, then He could in no sense be the Messiah —the belief in His Messiahship was based upon a falsehood, and to that falsehood must be attributed, as the sole and direct cause, all the marvellous phenomena of moral regeneration and of new spiritual life to which the Acts of the Apostles is an undeniable witness.

There is and can be no manner of question, that faith in Jesus as the Christ came upon men with the force of a new and Divine principle of life, producing results most opposite to the naturally selfish and unloving tendencies of the human heart, and purifying the springs of individual and social existence to a degree with which nothing can compare. Nor has this original impulse ever spent itself. Nowhere in history do we find it so pure and strong as in the Acts of the Apostles. There we see it bubbling up from the fountain-head clear, and bright, and sparkling as it is destined never to be again; but the stream that issues from the fountain has never failed to this hour, nor can it ever fail. The fountain is perennial as the source of truth itself, and the head of that fountain is Jesus as the Christ.

In the historic development, then, of the doctrine of

the Christ, the Acts of the Apostles has its place. It shows us the earliest known phases of belief in Jesus as the Christ. It exhibits a belief in the entire framework of the Gospel history concerning Him as in vogue among men:—His life of persevering goodness, His wonderful works,[1] His betrayal,[2] His rejection in favour of Barabbas,[3] the share of Pilate in His execution,[4] His violent death by crucifixion,[5] His burial,[6] His resurrection from the dead the third day,[7] His frequent appearance during forty days after His resurrection,[8] His ascension into heaven,[9] His session on the right hand of God,[10] His return to judgment,[11] His Divine Sonship,[12] His office as the appointed channel of forgiveness,[13] and of baptism by the Holy Ghost,[14] His being made *both Lord and Christ,*[15] *a Prince and a Saviour,*[16] to give repentance to Israel, and to be a light of the Gentiles.[17] We cannot question that all this was a part of the earliest known belief of those people who were called Christians first in Antioch.

But, furthermore, we find these people from the first baptising believers in the name of the Lord Jesus,[18] or of Jesus as the Lord, and of their breaking bread[19] in token of their fellowship with one another and with the Lord. Now, the former of these customs, namely baptism, is not to be accounted for by the Gospel of St. Luke. There is no reference in it to any such command by Jesus; and yet, on the testimony of the Acts, the universal prevalence of the custom is not to be denied. The prevalence of the custom, then, from the first, is a presumptive witness to some injunction having been given respecting it. The only possible inference is, that the injunction was given by Jesus; but there are few more striking phenomena in

---

[1] Acts x. 38.　[2] i. 16; vii. 52.　[3] ii. 14.　[4] ii. 13.　[5] ii. 23; v. 30.
[6] xiii. 29.　[7] x. 40.　[8] i. 3; x. 41.　[9] ii. 34.　[10] v. 31.　[11] x. 42.
[12] iii. 13; iv. 27, etc.　[13] x. 43.　[14] ii. 38.　[15] ii. 36.　[16] v. 31.
[17] xiii. 47.　[18] ii. 38; viii. 16, etc.　[19] ii. 42, 46; xx. 7.

the records of the early church than the silence of St. Luke's Gospel on the matter of baptism, and the prominence of the rite in his history of the Acts. The latter book is an unimpeachable witness to the early prevalence of the custom; but the custom is itself a witness to a prior belief in Jesus, and a belief in Jesus as the Christ. What manner of man the Jesus believed in was we have already seen;—one who was betrayed, crucified, dead, and buried; one who had risen from the dead and ascended into heaven. It was impossible that one who was crucified and buried merely should have been the Christ, or have been supposed to be the Christ. The only means by which his death could become not simply glorified, but divested of its inherent shame, was by a belief in that which, prior to the fact, it was not possible to anticipate from the scanty and obscure allusions in the Scriptures, and which, after the proclamation of the fact, had nothing to rest on but those obscure allusions, unless it was the reality of the fact proclaimed.

We may, therefore, take the prevalence of baptism and the breaking of bread as a clear indication of the personal influence, the personal command, and consequently of the personal life, of Jesus. We have nothing to which to refer these customs, unless it be the direct command of Jesus, to which in three of the Gospels the breaking of bread is referred, and to which in St. Matthew and St. Mark the practice of baptism is referred.

Thus the history of the Acts is a direct witness to a previously existing life, and to a belief that the person so existing was the Christ of prophecy. The principal agency employed in producing the belief was that of the Scriptures of the Old Testament. By them the Jews were confounded, or were mightily convinced that Jesus was the Christ.

And so the history may be taken as a proof of the

historic reality both of the person and of the Messianic office which He claimed to fill. Men could not have been called Christians had that office been an unreality, an idea which had no existence, or which rested on no ostensible foundation. Jesus could not have been believed in as the fullest realisation of that idea if His life had been a shadow and not an historic existence. Shadows do not originate customs so definite and so persistent as those of baptism and the breaking of bread. The Christ of the Acts is a phenomenon which cannot be accounted for but on the supposition of the prior existence of the Christ of the Gospels. The Christ of the Gospels, however, is a conception entirely distinct from the Christ of the Acts, and cannot have been originated in order to account for the phenomena presented by that book. Without the foundation of a human life similar to that of Jesus, the history of the Acts, containing such a substantial frame-work of truth as we know it must contain, could not have been written.

But just as it was impossible that the Christ of the Gospels should have been constructed out of the Messianic materials previously existing in the Scriptures, so is it even more clearly impossible that the Christ of the Acts should have been constructed out of those materials. And, in fact, the apparent and conspicuous unlikeness between the Christ of the Acts and the Christ of prophecy affords a strong presumptive argument that the belief in Jesus as the Christ could not have obtained to the extent it did but for the underlying fact of the resurrection. It was that fact alone, and not the belief in the fact, which gave whatever semblance of probability there was to the statement that He was the Christ. That such a statement should have been to a large extent discredited, being as it was contrary to all experience, is in no way surprising; that it should have been believed so firmly, so widely, and with such results as it was, affords the strongest possible presumption that the faith had been created by the fact, and not the fact invented by the faith. For every individual who believed the fact did so with precisely the same reason for disbelieving which they had who rejected it.

The picture of Christian life, then, presented in the Acts, is the necessary and natural result of the picture of the life of Christ presented in the Gospels: the necessary and natural result, if that life was a reality, but by no means natural or necessary if it was not: by no means an obvious result if that life was an invention; by all means an unnatural and an impossible result if that life was unreal or was other than it professed to be.

The history of the Acts was the most vivid illustration of the words—*Because I live, ye shall live also.* The Gospels contained the narrative of all that Jesus *began* both to do and teach. The Acts contained the record of what He still taught and did after His visible presence was withdrawn. It was not the spirit of His teaching which produced these results, but the power of His unseen personal presence and influence. The evidence of His life was in the life and action of His followers. There was a new development or manifestation of His existence, a development which would have been impossible had His existence been unreal.

Of the historic existence of this new development there can be no doubt: the Acts of the Apostles is not the only, though it may be the oldest and most original, monument —a monument which is a permanent illustration of the truth that Christian life is an evidence of the life of Christ. It is impossible to account for the phenomena of Christian life when displayed in their simplest and purest forms, as they are in the Acts of the Apostles, except on the supposition of the unseen life of Christ.

The pulses of spiritual life are to be felt in all ages and in every clime, but the heart from which they are derived is in heaven. If the pulse of regenerate life is felt to beat within ourselves, we shall not question the source from whence it is derived. We shall know that it can have no origin but one, and that origin the living person of the Lord. If we are strangers to the reality of His life in our own hearts, we may well question its reality in Him, for we shall lack the highest evidence which can be offered to the world or to ourselves—the only evidence, in fact, which can ever be complete, the evidence of life derived from life. If we are conscious of a new life within, we shall know that it cannot be referred to nature, or to self, or to our fellow-men—that it is not of the earth earthy, but to be referred only to the Lord from heaven.

As many as received him, to them gave he power to become the sons of God, even to them that believe on his name; which were born not of blood, nor of the will of the flesh, nor of the will of man, but of God.[1] This is the simplest and the only true explanation which can be given of the phenomenon of Christian life. It is a life which Christ gives to as many as receive Him, and believe on His name. It is a life which is unique in the history of the world—unique as it was seen in germ in the manifested life of Christ, and unique as it was displayed in its earliest efforts at development in the life and action of His first disciples. If the stream of its existence had come to an end we might hesitate to decide about its origin; but as every Christian has within himself a life which answers to that of the first believers, and which he cannot but recognise as identical, or at least as cognate with it, he knows that the stream is flowing still, and is destined to flow on for ever; and, consequently, we cannot consider it premature to adopt the inference suggested by Gamaliel eighteen

[1] St. John i. 12, 13.

centuries ago, and to decide that a stream which has flowed with a volume so deep, and broad, and strong, must have its fountain-head with God.

We might indeed tremble for the future of Christianity if God had left Himself utterly without witness in the present, and we were thrown back only on the past, which is ever receding farther and farther from the recognition of experience; but, forasmuch as the power of awakening a sympathetic response in the individual heart is unquestionably the endowment of this religion in a way that no other can boast, we may point to this characteristic of it as at once a sufficient and abiding indication of its true origin, and as being also the special feature to which St. John appealed, in saying, *This is the record, that God hath given to us eternal life, and this life is in His Son.*[2]

It was no development of man's natural instincts of religion which produced such a manifestation of it as that of the Acts of the Apostles; but the Christian life of the first disciples was itself a supernatural production, pointing to the existence of one who had been proved to be the Christ, not because He had died upon the cross and been buried, but because He had risen from the dead and ascended into heaven, and had shed forth gifts of spiritual grace upon the whole body of believers, showing Himself thus the fulfilment of psalm and prophecy more than if He had restored again the kingdom to Israel, and had gathered in subjection to the throne of David all the kingdoms of the world and the glory of them.

<hr>

[2] 1 John v. 11.

LECTURE VII.

THE CHRIST OF THE PAULINE EPISTLES.

Πολλῶν δ' ἀνθρώπων ἴδεν ἄστεα, καὶ νόον ἔγνω.
Hom. Od.

—— pues creo
De la clemencia divina,
Que no hay luces en el cielo,
Que no hay en el mar arenas,
No hay átomos en el viento,
Que, sumados todos juntos,
No sean número pequeño
De los pecados que sabe
Dios perdonar.
Calderon.

LECTURE VII.

THE next stage in the development of that conception of the Christ which is derived, or to be derived, from the New Testament, is supplied by the Epistles of St. Paul. The Acts of the Apostles gave us the picture of a work in progress; the Epistles of St. Paul give us the picture of a work done. No one would hesitate to place the Acts, as it stands in the New Testament, before any of the Epistles, whatever the actual relative dates of composition may be, because for the most part it has reference to a period of time which must have preceded those events which made it necessary for the Epistles to be written. It professes to supply us with an earlier link in the chain of circumstances reaching from the human life of Jesus to the latest utterances of the Christian mind in the New Testament. The Christian life depicted is Christian life at an earlier stage. Nor is it possible to doubt the general accuracy of the portrait sketched.

When, however, we come to the Pauline Epistles, we at once enter upon ground even more certain and clearly undeniable still. Here we are able, in the case at least of the most important letters, to fix the actual date within a year or two. And, in fact, we may safely say that the bulk of the Pauline writings was in existence within thirty years after the death of Christ, and that in all probability the four great and undisputed Epistles were written within five-and-twenty years of that time.

Here, then, at all events, we have firm and solid ground to tread upon. The letters to Rome, Corinth, and Galatia, are undoubted; they were written by St. Paul, and they were sent to the Christians at those places, and sent within the time specified. No reasonable doubt as to authorship attaches to any of the other letters to which the apostle's name is affixed, but here at least we are secure. We have in the greatest of St. Paul's writings undoubted genuine productions of the early Christian mind, and probably the very earliest productions. These productions, moreover, are in the form of letters, and their testimony is therefore the more valuable from this fact. A narrative or history is always more or less open to the suspicion of being written with a bias, but a genuine letter presupposes a second witness to the writer in the person to whom it is written. Putting aside the imaginary case, inapplicable to St. Paul's Epistles, of a letter being written to a second person for the purpose of conveying a false impression to a third, it is not possible to reject the evidence supplied incidentally in the letters written by St. Paul to his various correspondents.

For example, they one and all assume and establish beyond dispute the existence of a Christian society in the places to which they were sent. They tell us something about the constitution of this society, something about its character and life, and a great deal about the nature of its belief. We are able, at all events, to gather from St. Paul's Epistles a very fair notion of the kind of teaching which the several persons addressed had received from him. What is written is no doubt in agreement with what had been taught. Within five-and-twenty years, therefore, after the death of Christ, there was a considerable society, in centres so far separated as Rome and

Galatia, of persons who believed in Jesus. All these persons had been baptised: they were baptised in the name of Jesus, or at least in baptism they were considered to have put on Christ.[1] All these persons were unquestionably in the habit of breaking bread in commemoration of the death of Jesus. If there is no allusion to this latter practice in the letters to Rome and Galatia, there is abundant reference to it in the first of those to the Corinthians,[2] who occupied geographically a middle position between the Romans and Galatians, and are therefore an additional instance of the extension of the new society.

It is evident, moreover, from these Epistles, that the societies in question were bound together by faith in one and the same person, who is called Jesus Christ; and it is certain that this was the same Jesus of whom we read in the Acts, and whose life is recorded in the Gospels. From the Epistles of St. Paul we have all the principal facts of the life of Jesus, and these correspond with what we know of it from the Gospels and the Acts.

For example, we have His descent from the family of Abraham and from the family of David;[3] we have His supernatural birth implied;[4] we have His sufferings,[5] His betrayal,[6] His rejection by Pilate and Herod,[7] His death upon the cross,[8] His burial,[9] His resurrection from the dead the third day,[10] five of His manifestations after His resurrection,[11] His ascension into glory,[12] His session at the right hand of God,[13] His return to judgment.[14]

It is impossible, therefore, to doubt that the person to whom St. Paul refers as Jesus Christ is the same Jesus of whom we read in the Gospels and the Acts. All the

---

[1] Gal. iii 27; Rom. vi. 3.   [2] 1 Cor. xi. 20-34.   [3] Gal. iii. 16; Rom. i. 3.
[4] Gal. iv. 4; Rom. i. 3.   [5] 2 Cor. i. 5.   [6] 1 Cor. xi. 23.
[7] 1 Cor. ii. 8.   [8] Gal. vi. 14.   [9] 1 Cor. xv. 4.
[10] Rom. vi. 4; 1 Cor. xv. 4.   [11] 1 Cor. xv. 5-7.   [12] Rom. viii. 17, 29.
[13] Rom. viii. 34.   [14] 1 Cor. i. 7, 8.

main features of His history correspond with them as there given.` It is clear, moreover, that the writer implicitly believed these facts in His history, and that the persons to whom he wrote believed them too. It is certain, moreover, that both he and they identified Jesus with the Christ, and did so on account of the remarkable character of His history. So manifestly is this the case, that the two names Jesus and Christ frequently appear conjoined in the writings of St. Paul as the single appellation of one and the same person. It is a foregone conclusion both with him and those to whom he writes that Jesus is the Christ. The Acts of the Apostles gave us some account of the process by which men were brought to this conclusion. In the Epistles of St. Paul the conclusion is a thing of the past.

And we must bear in mind that it was so certainly with many people at Rome, Corinth, and Galatia, five-and-twenty years after the death of Christ. It is manifest also, from the mere mention of these places, that it must have been so not only with the Jews, but even to a larger extent with the Gentiles also. Though there may have been Jews among the converts in all these places, the larger portion must have been composed of Gentiles. The names of the persons saluted in the Epistle to the Romans are all of them Greek or Roman, only one is Jewish.[1] It is impossible to compute the aggregate numbers of these several churches, but they must have been many thousands. Among all these people the conviction was firmly established that Jesus was the Christ. Frequently He is spoken of by no other name than Christ or the Christ.

But everywhere there are traces of this persuasion having been wrought by means of the Jewish Scriptures. A foundation of Scriptural teaching is implied wherever the term Christ is used, and the references to Scripture

---

[1] Rom. xvi. 6. *Greet Mary, who bestowed much labour on us.*

statements are frequent. The persons addressed must have been very familiar with the books of the Old Testament. They must have accepted it as an elemental principle that the Scriptures spoke of a Christ to come. Otherwise, their baptism in the name of Jesus, and their belief in Him, would have meant nothing. They would have been strangers to the import of the new name they bore, and had so gladly adopted. The Romans are told that the Gospel had been *promised before by the prophets in the Holy Scriptures*,[2] that Jesus Christ *was made of the seed of David according to the flesh.*[3] Abraham and David are quoted as instances of persons who were accounted righteous without the law, and knew the blessedness of being so.[4] Everywhere the writer speaks as *to them that know the law.*[5] The Corinthians are reminded that whatsoever things happened unto Israel, *happened unto them for ensamples: and they are written*, he says, *for our admonition, upon whom the ends of the world are come.*[6] They are taught that Christ died for our sins *according to the Scriptures*, that He was buried, and rose again the third day *according to the Scriptures.*[7] The Galatians are instructed from the allegories of the Law[8] the greater excellence of the way of faith which they had forsaken. All this is evidence of a marvellous revolution of thought, but it is a revolution which is presupposed in their condition as Christians.

The Epistles of St. Paul, then, are evidence (1) that in all the churches to which they were addressed the same conclusion had been arrived at of which we found traces in the Acts of the Apostles and in the Gospels—namely that a Jesus who had been crucified was the Christ; and (2) that it had been arrived at principally, or in part through the influence of the Scriptures.

---

[2] Rom. i. 2.   [3] i. 3.   [4] Gal. iii. 6; Rom. iv. 6.
[5] Rom. vii. 1.   [6] 1 Cor. x. 11.   [7] xv. 3, 4.   [8] Gal. iv. 24.

It is surely remarkable that in persons whose intellectual and moral peculiarities must have been so different as those of the Romans, Corinthians, and Galatians, not only the same result should have been obtained, but that it should have been obtained by the same logical process —namely, that the Scriptures of the Old Testament spoke of a Christ, and that Jesus was the Christ of whom they spoke. It cannot be regarded as an idiosyncrasy of particular cases, for it was the universal and unvarying characteristic of the faith in Jesus, wherever it was spread abroad. The moral lever by which the early heathen world was converted to what we call Christianity, was the complete fulfilment in the person of Jesus of the prophetic ideal of the Christ. And of the extent to which this conversion had spread within thirty years after the death of Christ, the Epistles to Thessalonica, Rome, Corinth, Galatia, Philippi, Colossæ, Ephesus, are sufficient and conclusive evidence. They are the historic proof of the development and acceptance of the doctrine or religion of the Christ at that time, and to that extent, and to that degree.

Furthermore, the Epistles of St. Paul, as we have them, are evidence to a large extent, as has long ago been shown,[9] of the generally trustworthy and authentic character of the history of the Acts;[1] and they would be evidence, even if that book did not exist, of a period and condition somewhat similar to those therein described having preceded the acceptance of the Gospel in the various centres to which they were addressed. The condition of implanted and established faith to which they

---

[9] By Paley in the *Horæ Paulinæ.*

[1] So Professor Jowett says, speaking of the First Epistle to the Thessalonians: "The statements of the Epistle are a real confirmation of the narrative of the Acts; and the degree of coincidence in the narrative of the Acts is a sufficient evidence that the Epistle must have been written on the second Apostolical journey."—*Epistles of St. Paul,* vol i. p. 36.

witness could only have been brought about, as indeed they themselves show it was, by a long-continued course of itinerant and missionary effort, such as that which the Acts ascribe to Paul and Barnabas, and the other early preachers of the faith.   Even if the Acts could be shown, which they cannot, to be unhistoric,[2] the Epistles which are undeniably genuine would show that the state of things to which they witness must have been preceded by an historic period not altogether dissimilar from that which the Acts had fictitiously described.   Indeed, the Epistles themselves are abundant evidence to the " Acts " manner of life, and habitual conduct of one at least of the apostles, namely Paul himself.   He has left on permanent record, in the Second Epistle to the Corinthians,[3] the kind of life which he and his fellow-disciples had voluntarily undertaken, in the long catalogue of sufferings by which he proved himself the minister of Christ.   He must have been a madman, or a fool, to have acted in such a way for no conceivable end, unless the end for which he acted was so plainly set before him, that as a wise man he could not refuse to suffer gladly the loss of all things for it.   And to the end of time his life and character, as portrayed in his own writings, will be an unsolved and insoluble enigma

[2] " Whatever may be the reason, the amount of discrepancy between the earlier chapters of the Acts and the Epistle to the Galatians contrasts with the precise agreement of the later chapters with the Epistles to the Romans and Corinthians, as well as with the internal consistency of the Epistle to the Galatians itself. In inquiries of this sort it is often supposed that, if the evidence of the genuineness of a single book of Scripture be weakened, or the credit of a single chapter shaken, the whole is over-thrown. Sometimes the danger of losing the whole is made an argument against criticism of any part. Much more true it is that, in short portions or single verses of Scripture the whole is contained. Had we but one discourse of Christ, one Epistle of Paul, more than half would have been preserved.";—Jowett, *Epistles of St. Paul*, vol. i. p. 400. It is precisely in this belief that the object of the present lectures has been to show how much virtually remains as a solid basis for faith after the largest critical concessions have been made.   [3] Chaps. vi. and xi.

to all who are ignorant of or who reject the key to it, which participation in the faith and hope and love of the writer, and that alone, supplies.

But again, as the Epistles of St. Paul are a witness to the marvellous progress of faith in Jesus, within thirty years after the crucifixion, so they are clear evidence likewise to the general character of that faith as it was embraced by the writer himself. They contain the record of his mind probably for the last ten or a dozen years of his life. It is impossible that in that period he should not have been subject to the modification and growth of wider experience and of longer life.[4] But the substantial framework of his belief is as manifest in the First Epistle to the Thessalonians as it is in the Second Epistle to Timothy. It is still the same Jesus who was *killed*[5] by the Jews about twenty years before, who is acknowledged as both Lord and Christ; it is He who is to return to judgment, who therefore hath ascended up on high.[6] There can be no question whatever as to the reality of the person spoken of, or as to His identity. It was no dream, it could have been no impersonation of a vague idea, no concrete embodiment of a mere notion or set of notions. The Thessalonians had been taught *to wait for the Son of the living and true God from heaven, whom he raised from the dead, even Jesus.*[7] Here was the entire foundation assumed of facts which must have taken place but little more than

---

[4] "There is a growth in the Epistles of St. Paul, it is true; but it is the growth of Christian life, not of intellectual progress—the growth not of reflection, but of spiritual experience, enlarging as the world widens before the Apostle's eyes, passing from life to death, or from strife to peace, with the changes in the Apostle's own life, or the circumstances of his converts. There is a rest also in the Epistles of St. Paul, discernible not in forms of thought or types of doctrine, but in the person of Christ Himself, who is his centre in every Epistle, however various may be his modes of expression, or his treatment of controversial questions."— Jowett, *Epistles of St. Paul,* vol. i. p. 3.

[5] 1 Thess. ii. 15, 19.   [6] i. 10.   [7] i. 9, 10.

twenty years before they had been proclaimed to the Thessalonians:[8] the natural human life, the death, the resurrection, the ascension of a person who is called Jesus, and is acknowledged as the Christ, and to such an extent, and for so long, that the two names have become incorporated into one, Jesus Christ, expressing at once both the office and the person filling the office. When we remember that this same Epistle makes mention of *the churches of God which in Judæa were in Christ Jesus,*[9] and implies both that they had undergone persecution and that the Thessalonians were partakers with them of a common faith, and of a similar persecution for the sake of Jesus, we see at once that a considerable portion of this twenty years is virtually bridged over by the period of time requisite for the transmission of the faith from Palestine to Macedonia, from Asia to Europe, and for that personal change in the writer himself, which we know from other sources had taken place, and to which he alludes here when he says, he was *allowed of God to be put in trust with the Gospel.*[1]

It becomes then morally and absolutely impossible, that in the brief space of a dozen or fifteen years, which is the utmost that remains unaccounted for after the known historic death of the person called Christ, and the rise of the *churches* here mentioned *in Judæa,* there should have

[8] If we place the date of the crucifixion March 27, A.D. 31, and the founding of the church at Thessalonica, A.D. 52, the actual interval would have been about one-and-twenty years, but it can hardly have been more. Some with less probability place the date of the crucifixion, April 7, A.D. 30. Even if the preaching of Paul at Thessalonica is brought down to A.D. 53, the greatest possible interval is three-and-twenty years, which is virtually lessened by the considerations mentioned in the text. We have a genuine letter of A.D. 53, containing incidental reference to sundry events, which, on the evidence of the same letter, had been well known for several years before in the country where they occurred, and which, from the collateral and independent evidence of another letter (the Epistle to the Galatians), written not later than A.D. 58, must have been familiar to the writer for a period of nearly twenty years when it was written.

[9] 1 Thess. ii. 14.   [1] ii. 4.

gathered any haze of uncertainty as to the actual character of the events alluded to as the death and resurrection of the Lord Jesus in the First Epistle to the Thessalonians. We have what amounts practically to an unbroken chain of corroborative testimony, extending from the crucifixion of Jesus to the time, twenty years later, when, in an important maritime city of Macedonia, He was implicitly believed in as the Christ, and multitudes were prepared to submit to persecution rather than surrender that belief. Is there anything but the actual historic reality of the main events recorded in the Gospels to which a revolution so momentous can satisfactorily be referred? This is a question which irresistibly suggests itself to us, and there does not seem to be any reasonable answer to it but one.

It is important, however, to observe, that whatever we may regard as the ultimate drift of the First Epistle to the Thessalonians, it is impossible to be unconscious of the basis of historic fact underlying it which we everywhere encounter. No less than four times is the death[2] of Jesus spoken of; twice His resurrection from the dead[3] is distinctly declared as an article of the common faith; five times allusion is made to His future return.[4] It is true that, for the most part, this reference is incidental, but it is all the more worthy of our attention from that circumstance. The substratum of solid fact is broad and deep, or else we should not so often come upon it.

We see, moreover, that the teaching which had been imparted to the Thessalonians is spoken of as *the Gospel.* It is *our Gospel; the Gospel of God; the Gospel of Christ.* It is called the *word of God.* It is said to have come to them *in power and in the Holy Ghost;* to have been received *with joy, not as the word of men, but as the word of God, which wrought effectually in them that believed.* It

---

[2] 1 Thess. i. 10; ii. 15; iv. 14; v. 10.   [3] i. 10; iv. 14.
[4] 1 Thess. i. 10; ii. 19; iii. 13; iv. 16; v. 23.

was recognised apparently as the Gospel of *salvation by our Lord Jesus Christ.* It was a Gospel which required holiness of life, and the Thessalonians had been charged to *walk worthy of God, who had called them unto his kingdom and glory.* All this reminds us vividly of that *gospel of the kingdom* which had been the one theme of Christ's preaching. The alternate and concurrent affliction and joy with which it had been received at Thessalonica corresponds exactly with the account of its reception everywhere, as recorded in the Acts. If in Asia Minor the disciples had been reminded that *we must through much tribulation enter into the kingdom of God,*[5] we read in the letter to Thessalonica, *Verily, when we were with you, we told you before that we should suffer tribulation; even as it came to pass, and ye know.*[6] If the mission of Philip to Samaria had caused *great joy in that city,*[7] the Thessalonians are not only exhorted to *rejoice evermore,*[8] but their first entrance into the Gospel was *with joy of the Holy Ghost.*[9] On the other hand, the message of the Gospel had found them in a state of idolatry; it was *from idols* that they had *turned to serve the living and true God, and to wait for his Son from heaven.*[1] It is impossible not to accept all this as a literal and accurate statement of the condition of the church at Thessalonica. But it implies as certainly, in the disciples there, a knowledge of all the main facts of the life of Jesus; a belief in the Old Testament Scriptures as documents which had been fulfilled in Him, for otherwise He would not have been received as Christ; a recognition of Him as the Son of God, who within, perhaps, the last twenty years, had lived and died on earth, and had ascended into heaven; a conviction that, in some way or other, they were partakers of the Holy Ghost in consequence of their faith in Jesus, which reminds us of

<hr>

[5] Acts xiv. 22. [6] 1 Thess. iii. 4. [7] Acts viii. 8.
[8] 1 Thess. v. 16. [9] i. 6. [1] i. 9, 10.

various accounts in the Acts describing the gift of the Holy Ghost, as well as of the promise ascribed to John the Baptist,—*he shall baptize you with the Holy Ghost.*[2]

A revolution of thought more remarkable than that which is thus implied it is impossible to conceive; but of the fact the Epistles to the Thessalonians are the abiding monument, and, being in all probability the very earliest Christian writings extant, they are invaluable as an index of Christian faith at that time, of the progress it had made, and of the means by which it had been diffused. The faith of the Thessalonian church was substantially the faith of the Gospels and the Acts. The Jesus of the one was the Jesus of the others, and undistinguishable from the person who is known to us in history as having suffered death in the reign of Tiberius Cæsar.[3] Within about twenty years after that event the story of His death had penetrated, at all events, as far as Macedonia, and had produced the peculiar results of which the apostle's writings are proof, in a body of men who had renounced idolatry, and given evidence of a moral reformation, and become so attached, not to the memory, but to the person of Jesus, that they were willing to endure persecution for His name's sake. The comparatively brief space of time which had elapsed between the known occurrence of the life and death of Jesus, and the prevalence of belief in Him as the Christ and the Son of God, which must have obtained for several years before Paul preached at Thessalonica, precludes the possibility of the events proclaimed being cunningly devised

---

[2] St. Matt. iii. 11 ; St. Luke iii. 16.

[3] Tac. *Ann.* xv. 44. The words cannot be too often quoted :—"Ergo abolendo rumori Nero subdidit reos, quæsitissimis pœnis adfecit, quos, per flagitia invisos, vulgus Christianos adpellabat. Auctor nominis ejus Christus, Tiberio imperitante, per Procuratorem Pontium Pilatum supplicio adfectus erat; repressaque in præsens exitiabilis superstitio rursus erumpebat, non modo per Judæam, originem ejus mali, sed per urbem etiam, quo cuncta undique atrocia aut pudenda confluunt celebranturque."

fables, as far at least as the circumstances of His life and death are concerned; and that life and death alone would have been insufficient to suggest the notion that He was the Christ, or to produce the results which we know to have been produced. Here again then, as before, everything turns upon the testimony which was borne to Jesus as the Christ. The desire to represent Him as the Christ would have occurred to no one, had not the events which followed His death suggested it; and certainly the results which everywhere followed the proclamation of Him as the Christ are more intelligible, on the supposition that those events were realities, than they are upon the alternative supposition that they were not.

And this becomes even more evident when we take into account the means by which the results were brought about. The Epistles to Thessalonica bear the names of three men of whom we know scarcely anything but what is told us in the Acts. It is plain that they were the authors of the revolution. These itinerant preachers had carried the proclamation that Jesus was the Christ through Palestine and Asia Minor into Macedonia, so as to work conviction and moral reformation in men who had before been idolaters. This had not been done with flattering words nor for the hope of gain; their exhortation had not been *of deceit, nor of uncleanness, nor in guile*, but as before God which trieth the hearts, so that they could say, *Ye are witnesses, and God also, how holily and justly and unblameably we behaved ourselves among you that believe.*[4]

Results so remarkable, which become more remarkable when we consider the agency which produced them, cannot be separated from the fundamental assertion by which they were preceded and accompanied, that Jesus was the Christ. This assertion, like a thread of different colour, runs through the tissue and texture, not only of this but of

<hr>

[4] 1 Thess. ii. 10,

every Epistle. It is the foundation corner-stone which lies at the bottom of the whole edifice of Pauline teaching. It is the stout knotted gnarled root which bears up the trunk and branches of the tree. All the ethical precepts, and the wise moral exhortation so abundant everywhere and so conspicuously excellent are but the flowers and fruit of this fair and wide-spreading tree. It was because believers were engrafted into Jesus Christ, who was declared to be the Son of God with power according to the Spirit of holiness by the resurrection from the dead, that they were not only required and exhorted to be holy as He was holy, but had likewise themselves received an impulse to holiness to which they had before been strangers. It was because the disciples at Colossæ had been taught and believed that they were dead and risen with Christ that the appeal could reach them, to *set their affections on things above, and not on things on the earth.* We may fairly claim the high, novel, and unexampled moral tone everywhere pervading these early Christian writings as the most satisfactory and conclusive evidence of the reality of that operation and influence of the Holy Spirit of which they speak so much. If ever the tree is known by his fruits whether it is good or bad, we can have no hesitation in pronouncing on the character of these fruits. And if they were the undeniable and unique production of a tree which specially claimed to be of the Divine planting, then certainly, so far as the fruits could be evidence of it, the claim was made good. Before the tree could be shown to be one which the Lord had not planted, it would be requisite, not only to call in question the evidence upon which that one fact rested which declared Jesus to be the Christ, and which, as far as the senses are concerned, could never be conclusive; but likewise to disprove, which was not possible, the abiding testimony of those living fruits which ever accompanied the recognition of Jesus as the

Christ, and of which the Epistles of St. Paul are the true measure, as they are the unalterable expression.

These early writings, then, may be taken as original and genuine exponents of the doctrine or religion of the Christ as it was declared and accepted within a quarter of a century after Jesus had been crucified. The writings themselves contain internal and incidental evidence that substantially the same belief had been in vogue for a period of at least twelve or fifteen years previously. (The Epistle to the Galatians alone shows this.) Consequently we are carried back by undeniable and documentary evidence to a time distant by about ten years only from the principal events upon which the belief as it was received was based.

For we cannot separate the earliest expressions of that belief from the historic event of the death of Jesus. The same Epistle to the Galatians speaks of the death and resurrection of Jesus Christ in terms which leave no doubt upon the mind that the events referred to were the actual crucifixion of Jesus and the resurrection which was declared to have succeeded it. What the Apostle's faith was at the time of writing this letter, that it had been certainly for fourteen, possibly for seventeen, years before, and possibly even for a yet longer period.[5] He bears

---

[5] It is plain that St. Paul identifies the Gospel which he preached to the Galatians (i. 11.) with that which he had received at his conversion. (i. 12–16.) There can have been no material change in his own belief during that interval, or he would not have spoken as he does in the first chapter. It would also seem that all the events alluded to in Galatians i. and ii. had preceded the first preaching in Galatia, and therefore the period virtually covered by this Epistle must be much greater than that given in the text. At all events, it carries us back to the time of St. Paul's conversion. Professor Jowett places " an interval of four or five years " between the Epistles to the Thessalonians and that to the Galatians.— *Epistles,* i. 281. I cannot accept the inference drawn by him that in Galatians v. 11 and 2 Cor. v. 16 (vol. i. p. 8 *seq.*) we have indications of what would have been a natural change of belief in St. Paul himself

implicit and emphatic witness that it had and could have undergone no material change. So that when he first became possessed by the conviction that the crucified and risen Jesus was the Christ, there had elapsed but an interval of time since His death which was fairly and accurately within the grasp of memory. What is a period of ten or even fifteen years for any man in middle life to look back upon? Not seldom casual words, fragments of conversations, and the most commonplace incidents which happened at that distance of time, retain their hold upon the memory with unrelaxed tenacity, and remain engraven on the imagination with indelible clearness. And how much more is it so with public events of prominent and of stirring import! Let any one of us seek to recall events, personal or public, which happened ten years ago. Is it possible that we can be deceived about them? The haze of distance may indeed invest them at times with indistinctness, and give them all the appearance of unreality, no matter how vivid our recollection of them may be; and not unfrequently it may seem hard to believe that circumstances actually occurred through which we are conscious that we ourselves have passed. But does the converse ever happen? Does any man in his senses ever believe that events actually took place ten years ago which exist only in his own imagination? Is it possible that internal impressions of his own should be able to project themselves on the outer world so vividly as to beget the belief that they had a veritable existence in the world of fact? And is it possible for impressions so projected to

after his conversion. Much more in accordance with the truth, as it seems to me, is the remark of Alford on 2 Cor v. 16—"The fact alluded to in the concessive clause, is, not any personal knowledge of the Lord Jesus while He was on earth, but that view of Him which Paul took *before his conversion*, when he knew Him only according to His outward apparent standing in this world, *only as Jesus of Nazareth.*" The italics are his.

have a conspicuous and remarkable influence on his whole after life ?   And is it possible that the writer, when the Son of God was revealed in him, when that revelation of Jesus Christ of which he speaks[6] had become a spiritual fact to his consciousness, should, out of the consciousness so influenced, have projected into the world of fact a life, death, and resurrection, which had no existence, which were but the offspring of his own perverted imagination and distempered fancy—it being all the while a known fact that a life and death under similar circumstances had taken place in Jerusalem about ten years[7] before, and that it was this person so living and dying whom he believed to be the Christ ?   Surely the question is one which forthwith answers itself.

On the other hand, however, it must not be forgotten that there are many events which have happened, whether to ourselves or to the world at large, which we have not adequately understood till long after they have happened. It is not always easy to recognise the full significance of events at the time when they occur.   The life and death of Jesus Christ were events of which St. Paul can hardly have been unconscious at the time when they took place. His own determined opposition to the faith which he afterwards preached, is proof, at all events, of the identity of the Jesus whom he preached with the Jesus whom he had opposed.   And even if his faith could be accounted for as a thing devoid of historic foundation, the same could not be said for his vehement opposition.   If it was an imaginary or unreal Jesus in whom he believed, it must have been a real historic Jesus whom he persecuted, and the same Jesus whose life and death we have recorded in the Gospels, and mentioned in the Acts.

[6] Gal. i. 15, 16.

[7] The real interval was probably much less. Saul's conversion is placed by Alford in A.D. 37. It may have been earlier.

While, therefore, the Epistle to the Galatians virtually carries us back, as a witness to the historic reality of the events implied, to a very short period after the death of Christ, and to events contemporaneous with the early manhood of the writer, it is also a permanent witness to the changed aspect in which he had learnt to regard these events. A name which had once been hateful to him, and to which he had offered strenuous and bitter opposition, had now for more than fourteen years been the object of devoted and affectionate regard. He had himself been the principal agent in making known that name. He had been taught the meaning of an event which had happened within his own recollection, and which was unquestionable ; and he could now say, *I am crucified with Christ : nevertheless I live ; yet not I, but Christ liveth in me : and the life which I now live in the flesh I live by the faith of the Son of God, who loved me, and gave himself for me.*[8]

And the whole point of the change which had passed upon him was involved in that word Christ. About the death of Jesus there was and could be no question; the only question was, Who was He that had died ? It was not about the reality of certain facts, without which the persecution of St. Paul was as unintelligible as his conversion, but about the meaning and import of those facts. Had Jesus died for Himself or for others ? Was His death the one event anticipated in the Scriptures and fulfilling them, or was it not ? If His death was but the natural culmination of His life, did not His life and death together show that the story of His resurrection which Paul himself had before rejected, might after all be possibly not untrue ? And if His resurrection was a fact, did not that event, together with His life and death, combine to throw a flood of light upon the whole of the Old Testament, which nothing else could throw ?

[8] Gal. ii. 20.

We indeed may reason thus upon the facts before us, but we cannot thus reproduce the line of reasoning in the Apostle's mind. To him there was a yet more cogent argument, to which he is himself a witness. The persecuted and risen Jesus had revealed Himself in him. He had given that revelation of Himself to the inner world of his spiritual consciousness of which he speaks in the opening of his letter to the Galatian church. To resist that revelation would have been to resist the Holy Ghost: to resist the force of inevitable moral conviction. He could not resist it. He was constrained to surrender himself from henceforth a willing and obedient servant to the Jesus whom he had persecuted. And his life remains to this day an indestructible monument to the vitality and significance of those events, whose historic reality it is impossible to deny.

We are led, then, by these considerations to the further question, which can hardly fail to suggest itself to every one, and of which so much has oftentimes been made: How is it that the Epistles of St. Paul are so different in their character from the Gospels? Is it possible that the Christ of the Gospels can be the Christ of the Pauline Epistles? If we take St. Paul for our guide in his representation of Christianity, do we not necessarily reject that conception of it which has been embodied in the Gospels?

In attempting to deal with this question we must remember that St. Paul's Epistles may be taken as the accurate record of the effect produced upon his own mind by the events of the life of Jesus, as those events interpreted themselves to him. They are also, no doubt, an accurate record of the Gospel which he preached among the several churches which he founded, or with which he was brought in contact. They are therefore, so far, an accurate record of the form which Christianity had assumed in those various churches within thirty years after the death of Christ.   Whether or not there was any other form prevalent elsewhere, or what that form was, we are unable to determine, except from indications in the letters themselves, and so far as the Gospels or the Acts may be supposed to show it.   The Acts of the Apostles, moreover, as a matter of fact, whether the book was written with that design or not, serves as an intermediate and connecting link between the Epistles and the Gospels.   Not only does the history of it bridge over the interval of time, but the book itself supplies the inevitable transition.   The Acts recorded the preaching of Jesus as the Christ, the Epistles imply the existence of various churches which had so accepted Him, and give us a more detailed picture of the effect and influence of so accepting Him.   But the tone of thought expressed in the Acts is virtually far nearer to the Epistles than it is to the Gospels; and the history is a clear witness that Jesus was proclaimed as the Christ, and that there was no faith in Him where He was not so acknowledged.   It can, however, scarcely be doubted that the writer of the Acts was also the writer of the third Gospel, which does not differ materially in its exhibition of the life of Jesus from the other synoptics.   We may presume, therefore, that the writer was not himself conscious of any material or substantial divergence between the picture of Jesus he had given in the Gospel and the conception of Him embodied or implied in the Acts.   And if he was, as we may reasonably suppose, the friend and companion of St. Paul, we can hardly imagine that he was conscious of any real divergence between the Epistle to the Galatians, for example, and his own evangelical narrative.   Not making these assumptions absolutely, we may at all events infer that the early traditions on which they rest are so far in favour of the conclusions we have drawn from them; and may tend to show that the differences some have supposed may, after all, be more imaginary than real.

And certainly, the Gospels, the Acts, and the Epistles, have at any rate this feature in common, that they represent Jesus to have been the Christ. They all of them agree that the Jesus whom they thus represent was crucified, dead, and buried; they are unanimous in affirming that He rose from the dead the third day, that He was several times seen of His disciples during a period (according to St. Luke or the writer of the Acts) of forty days after His death, but was never so seen afterwards; they one and all declare or imply that He ascended into heaven at the end of that time, and that His personal return, under whatever circumstances, is an event to be ever anticipated till it comes. Lastly, they all agree that this same Jesus is the Son of God, the Messiah promised of old, and the ultimate judge of the world. The framework of fact, then, is unquestionably the same in all, and so also in these last particulars is the framework of doctrine. But the central, fundamental, and essential point of the doctrine, which was based upon the facts and presupposed them, which is everywhere implied, and never omitted or lost sight of, is the declaration that Jesus is the Christ.

We have, then, this circumstance to deal with, that there is no known document of an earlier date than the earliest of St. Paul's Epistles, in which the doctrine of Jesus being the Christ is found. But it is found stated there in all its clearness and integrity. The doctrine was at that time fully developed, the belief mature; and whatever Christian literature came into existence afterwards, whether Gospels, Acts, or Epistles, did not add materially to its essential features. But the doctrine or belief already existing in this form was necessarily the product of two factors, an effect produced by the combined operation of two causes—the Old Testament Scriptures and the life of Jesus. Neither of these causes alone was sufficient to produce the result which as a matter of fact we know was produced. The life of Jesus alone could not have given existence to the first Epistle to the Thessalonians, or the Epistle to the Galatians. The study of the Old Testament alone could not have produced either of them. They were in no sense a reproduction of the ancient prophets. They were new and original creations, necessarily presupposing the human life of Jesus and the Scriptures of the prophets. Of the historic reality of either of these factors at that time—namely, of the Scriptures of the Old Testament or of the human life of Jesus—there is not the slightest doubt.

But, further, it could not by human ingenuity have been foreseen that what we may call the fusion of these two principles, the combined operation of these two factors, would have produced these results any more than, prior to experience, it could have been foreseen that the combination of oxygen and hydrogen would produce water. The results, however, as we know them for a certainty from the writings of St. Paul, and as we see them in those writings themselves, were produced. But, as a matter of fact, we could not have had the belief that Jesus was the Christ, nor the results which followed the proclamation of that belief, without the previous existence and combined operation of the two causes specified. Is not then the known effect an evidence of the inherent vitality of the causes producing it, and a corroboration of the soundness of the principle which governed their union? Experience justified the application because it proved the truth of the principle.

For it cannot be too carefully noted that the effects of which the Pauline Epistles are evidence were not produced by any mere abstract admiration for the character of Jesus, but by belief in Him as the Christ; and it is this which guides us to a just appreciation of the necessary difference between the Epistles and the Gospels. The one aim at giving us the presentation of a life, the other record the influence of that life. It is natural that in an early and unconscious age of the Church the record of the influence of the life, occurring in the form it does, should be older than and different from the portrait of the life, and that it should have preceded the portrait of the life. The influence registered itself spontaneously in the form of letters; the life could only be recalled in the form of history. It would be the colossal framework of the life, and not its minute detail, to which the influence would be mainly due. And this influence, within certain broad and comprehensive limits, would be the same everywhere. There would be an outward difference of expression, but an internal identity of operation, wherever the same vital principles were received, just as the expression of the First Epistle to the Thessalonians may differ from that of the Second Epistle to Timothy; but the motive spiritual influence implied and at work in both is the same.

Thus the Epistles of St. Paul are the record of the effect or influence of the life of Jesus, but of the life of Jesus as the Christ; not as a philosopher, or a teacher of morality, or a legislator of rules of life; but as the Christ or anointed one of God, who was in Himself the fountain and channel of all spiritual life; the giver of the Holy Ghost; the one mediator between God and man, who was in Himself the bond of union between man and God, the reconciler of the two divided and antagonistic natures, because the revelation under a new and unprecedented aspect of the character of God, and therefore the last and fullest exponent of the will of God.

All this if Jesus was the Christ He would be, for it was implied and signified in His being the Christ, that is the chosen and appointed human channel of approach to God.

Consequently, if Jesus were declared to be the Christ, there would be no action of his life which would not be fraught with the deepest possible meaning for man. He would be the representative of every man before God and in his approach to God. His life would be man's perfect life, His death would be man's death as a sinner, His resurrection would be man's resurrection in righteousness and His full and free absolution and release from sin, His ascension would be man's spiritual ascension to the presence of God, and His continual session in the heavenly places.

That He should be so recognised and accepted implied, indeed, and involved the teaching of the Holy Spirit; but to this agency and influence continual reference is made in the Apostle's writings, as we see it at work in the Acts and find it was promised in the Gospels. It was in demonstration of the spirit and of power that his speech had been to the Corinthians.[9] It was by the hearing of faith that the Galatians had received the Spirit;[1] it was in the Holy Ghost, and therefore in much assurance or certainty of conviction that the Gospel had come to the Thessalonians.[2] And therefore it was that the life of Jesus was recognised and accepted as the typical or symbolic life of man when He was acknowledged as the Christ. But inasmuch as the Gospels dealt with the life of Christ not in its effects but in its historic unfolding, as it was in itself and not as it was destined to influence others, it was not possible that they should present the same phenomena, however much the germ of that influence may have been embodied in the words of Jesus as it was of necessity contained in His acts.

Moreover, the Gospels themselves give us to understand that mightier results than any as yet witnessed were at hand; if not, why should the command to go into all the

[9] 1 Cor. ii. 4.   [1] Gal. iii. 2.   [2] 1 Thess. i. 5.

world have been given to men who as yet had never passed the confines of Palestine ?[3]

While, therefore, the manifest difference between the Gospels and Epistles is itself a proof that these Epistles could not have been originated as the natural and proper sequel to the facts which the Gospels record, the Epistles themselves are likewise evidence to the prior existence of certain facts which were substantially those of the Gospels. If Jesus was the Christ, as the Gospels uniformly declare Him to have been, then the Epistles are the record and abiding evidence of certain results, not indeed such as we might beforehand have expected the Gospels to produce, but such as could not have been produced but for the reality of the facts they record, and the belief they are written to proclaim, that Jesus was the Christ.

The Pauline Epistles, then, are evidence, first, of certain facts, such as the life and death of Jesus Christ, which, as long as these writings last, cannot be resolved into myth or fiction; and, secondly, they are evidence of the very widespread acceptance of a particular belief, and of the results which followed its acceptance. This was the conviction or belief that Jesus was the Christ. The Epistles, moreover, are evidence, conclusive and undeniable, of the acceptance of this belief, which was based upon facts, within a short space of time after the occurrence of the facts upon which it was based. It is certain also that the widespread acceptance of this belief, and the rapid growth of the religion involving it, cannot be accounted for on the assumption that it was due solely to the influence of the life and teaching of Jesus, because, if so, it is presumable that there would not have been the marked difference there is between the only records we possess of that life and teaching, and the effects of its influence as we see them in the Epistles. Consequently, in order to

[3] Cf. St. Matt. xxvi. 13; St. Mark xiv. 9, etc.

account for its acceptance, we must throw in the operation of another element, without which it is not possible that Jesus should have been the Christ, or that the declaration that He was should have met with any widespread acceptance, and this element is the bestowal of new life which is implied in His resurrection and in the gift of the Holy Spirit which followed it.

Not only is the statement of the resurrection as a fact implied in every one of the Epistles, but the evidence of its effect and operation as a new principle of life is present and conspicuous everywhere. And it is the presence of this element which at once accounts for and explains not only the existence of the Epistles themselves, but also the fact of the marked difference which exists between them and the Gospels. The Gospels are ostensibly the records of certain facts and teaching, and of certain facts and teaching which ostensibly lead on and up to another great and transcendent fact which is supposed to rest upon them, while the effect that the whole together are intended to produce is the conviction that Jesus is the Christ. The Epistles, on the other hand, are the expression of the results which followed this conviction. The Gospels show us how Jesus claimed to be and was the giver of new life ; the Epistles show us the operation and reality of that new life He gave. The Gospels, therefore, one and all, stop short exactly there where the Epistles begin. The Gospels declare and disclose to us a great fact; the Epistles show us the operation and consequence of that fact. It is impossible that the outward aspect of the two should be identical. The teaching of Jesus, marvellous and novel as it was, as a motive power was and could be nothing in comparison of His resurrection, if that resurrection was a fact. The Epistles themselves, regarded as mere literary productions, are evidence that it was a fact. For they could not have been produced at the time and under the circumstances they were produced, and by the man who produced them, and with the essential features that characterise them, unless it had been a fact. They are not merely the transcript of certain personal opinions, but evidence to the reality of a fact producing them. For, otherwise, we must admit that the phenomena presented by the Pauline Epistles, and by the early Christian churches to which they were sent, were the product of deception and delusion, which is verily absurd.

Although, then, it is true that the Gospels have drawn the portrait of the human life of Christ, while the Epistles have presented us with the contrast of internal conception, and although the record of the latter is undoubtedly earlier in point of time, as it naturally would be, there is no essential antagonism or difference between them. If we know anything of the teaching of Jesus, one prominent and inseparable feature of it must have been that He was Himself the Christ, for otherwise the continual proclamation of the kingdom of heaven, as from the first it was proclaimed, and the appointment of the twelve and of the seventy to proclaim it, would have been unmeaning.

But it is precisely this truth which is the kernel of the Epistles of St. Paul. He has himself accepted Jesus as the Christ, and his writings are the monument of his acceptance and the record of all that it implied. To have such a record as this so early in point of time is a proof that the leaven had begun to work, while it is itself an indication of the manner in which it worked. But just as the leaven is distinct from the meal in which it works, and from the effect produced by its mode of working, so also necessarily is the record of the human life of Christ distinct and different from the picture of that new life to which it had given the impulse.

Nor is it otherwise than natural that traces of the existence and operation of this new life, while carrying us back inevitably to a cause producing it, should have come into existence as they did in the letters of St. Paul, before, possibly, any detailed record of the life of Christ had been committed to writing.[4]   This, indeed, it may not be given us to decide, but all that we are concerned to show is that the unquestionable testimony of St Paul's Epistles, assuming as they do the framework of the Gospel narrative and the essence of the Gospel teaching, is in no way contradicted, and is not necessarily modified by the possibly subsequent attempts to present in detail a record of the human life and teaching of Jesus Christ. The consistency of the various extant narratives among themselves is altogether a different matter, upon which we need not now touch; but it may be safely affirmed that the utmost that can be made of their alleged contradictions and inconsistencies is as nothing compared with the weight and significance of their combined testimony, confirmed and corroborated as it is by the wholly independent and necessarily unconscious witness of the writings of St. Paul, to the main central and essential facts of the history.

In the face, then, of the various considerations which we have had in review before us, it appears that we cannot set aside the evidence afforded by the Pauline writings to the nature and origin of the earliest Christian belief, and of the first Christian society. However numerous and interesting the questions that may arise on these matters which we cannot answer, they are really inconsiderable when compared with the amount of positive and satisfac-

---

[4] This would naturally be the case in a society as yet hardly conscious of its own existence; and the fact that it historically was so is no slight indication of the reality and genuineness of the causes at work. There could hardly be a greater proof of the historic origin of Christianity than the known existence of writings like the Pauline Epistles within a quarter of a century after that event which was alike the foundation of them and of the religion from which they sprang—the death of Christ.

tory evidence that is fairly within our reach. We see that
the same foundation of belief is virtually implied in all
the Apostle's letters,—and that this is a foundation of fact.
He could not have appealed to the Colossians, as he did,
to set their affections on things above, and not on things
on the earth, because they were dead, and their life was
hid with Christ in God, unless the resurrection and ascension of Jesus had been proclaimed at Colossæ, unless
Jesus had been accepted as the Christ accordingly, and
unless the acceptance of that truth had been followed, in
those to whom he wrote, by the answer of their own conscience to it in the personal experience of the gift of the
Holy Ghost. They were themselves conscious and independent witnesses to the fact that the teaching of the
Apostle had wrought in them, as truth alone could work.
They knew that, as they were not the victims of delusion
on the part of the Apostle, so they were not acting in collusion with him, but were free, responsible, and independent witnesses to the truth which he proclaimed, as well
as to the tendency of that truth to act upon their lives.
This, which is alike the grand result of one and all his
letters, and a result about which we may be quite sure, is
at once superior to and independent of a multitude of
minor and subordinate questions about which we must for
ever be content to remain in ignorance.

There are then, from what has been said, certain broad
conclusions which we may safely draw. The body of the
New Testament writings, but peculiarly the Epistles of St.
Paul, both from their manifest character and their known
origin, afford irresistible and conclusive evidence to the
operation of a new principle in the world to which there
is no parallel in secular literature. This principle openly
declared itself as the influence of the Holy Spirit. As
to its novelty there can be no doubt, for the only instance
of a similar agency at work, and this is but a partial

parallel, is to be found in the Scriptures of the Old Testament. As to its tendency, also, there can be no doubt, unless we are prepared to assert that the moral tendency of the Pauline writings is pernicious, and the principles inculcated bad. As to its origin, therefore, there can alone be any doubt, whether it was righteous and true, or whether it was virtually unrighteous because inherently and radically false. And this is practically determined by the former consideration; for *by their fruits ye shall know them.*

But further, this gift of the Holy Spirit, which was continually appealed to and claimed by the first preachers of the Gospel, and implied and evidenced in the early Christian correspondence of St. Paul, was ever promised and bestowed in confirmation of the truth which was embraced when Jesus was acknowledged as the Christ. As a matter of fact there is no evidence of a principle at work analogous to that of which the writings of the New Testament, regarded merely as writings, are the abiding monument, outside the limits of the early Christian society. This is simply a question of literature, and not at all an assertion of dogma. *These are written that ye might believe,* may fairly and conclusively be taken as the motto of the New Testament Scriptures. We do not assume inspiration in order to exalt those Scriptures; but we take those Scriptures as they are, and deduce from their existence and their highly exceptional phenomena, the necessary postulate of a special and unique inspiration. As a matter of fact the confession of the name of Jesus as the Christ was followed by results new and unparalleled in the history of the world. If the Gospels and the Acts were lost to us, the measure of those results would be preserved imperishably in the known and undoubted Epistles of St. Paul. As they could not have been written but for the conviction and confession that Jesus was the Christ, so neither are the phenomena they present and imply to be accounted for on the supposition, that Jesus was not the Christ: on the supposition, that is, either that the facts which proved Him to be the Christ were fallacious and unreal, or that there was something essentially hollow and unsound in the conception of that office, and those hopes which He was declared to have fulfilled. For Jesus was proclaimed as the Christ, not to the Jews only, but to the Gentiles also. Jesus was accepted as the Christ, not by the Jews only who believed, but by the Gentiles also.

There is therefore, in the Christ-office of Jesus, that which is alike independent of nationality and of time. We, in the present day, cannot afford to surrender the claim advanced for Jesus to be the Christ, for, in so doing, we shall renounce our title to the name of Christian. It was to the validity of this claim, no less than to the historic reality of the person advancing and fulfilling it, that the gift of the Holy Ghost was promised and bestowed as an attesting witness. His testimony would have been invalidated, and God, in the language of St. John, have been made a liar, had there been any flaw in the cardinal facts of the life of Jesus, or in the reality of that office which He claimed to fill.

And thus, lastly, the fact of Jesus being the Christ, which is witnessed to by the historic gift of the Holy Ghost, which alone will enable us adequately and satisfactorily to account for the essential and characteristic features of the earliest Christian literature, as we find them in the writings of St. Paul, becomes the effectual and conclusive seal of the substantial and essential truth of the Old Testament Scriptures as a whole. There was a hope embodied in those Scriptures, which was not of man's discovery or conception, which was Divinely-inspired, and based on a promise which was God-given. It was a hope which grew brighter and brighter as the time of its fulfilment drew near. It was a hope of which we can clearly trace the development, and yet a hope to which, neither in its origin nor in its development, can we assign a sufficient natural cause. It has never been given to any nation but one to indulge instinctively an irrepressible hope like that of the Messiah, which the progress of the ages has fulfilled. It has never been given to any literature but one to express this hope in a thousand forms, unconsciously to conceive, to nurture, and to develop it, in manifold parts and in divers manners, till it became a substantial and consistent whole, and to leave this expression for centuries as an heirloom to mankind, the significance and preciousness of which time alone would declare and history conclusively reveal. But to this nation and to this literature it was given. The national mind of Israel was pregnant with a mighty thought, a thought which we cannot fail to detect from the earliest to the latest monuments of its literature. As it was impossible that this thought should be self-originated, we can only recognise it as the fruit of the nation's exceptional nearness and dearness to God, the offspring of God's covenant and union with the nation; and when the life of Jesus could be looked back upon and regarded as a whole, then it was found, and not before, that that life was the fullest and the complete realisation of the mighty thought. When He was recognised as the man-child whom Zion travailed to bring forth, the fulness of the hope which, for long ages, patriarchs, prophets, and poets had cherished, and the law itself had foreshadowed and symbólised,—when He was accepted as the Christ and the Prophet that should come into the world, then it was seen that the hope of the fathers was not a dream, and that He who had spoken by the prophets was none other than the Holy Spirit of truth.

LECTURE VIII.

THE CHRIST OF THE OTHER BOOKS.

LECTURE VIII.

THAT which we know as the doctrine or conception of the Christ is only to be gathered from the New Testament as a whole. The writings which by accident or design are comprised in that collection present us with a certain idea which is completely contained in them, and which cannot be added to by anything outside of them from the rest of Christian literature. This is, first, the conception of the human life of Jesus as it is recorded in the Gospels, and secondly, the idea that He was the Christ or Messiah promised of old, which is common to every book of the New Testament, the early progress of which we read in the Acts of the Apostles, and the various expressions of which we find in the several Epistles and in the book of the Revelation.

The substantive result of this aggregate of writings is the doctrine or religion of the Christ which is presented to us under various aspects and by various minds. It is quite open to us, then, to regard this conception or idea, contained as it is in the New Testament, as a positive fact of literature produced approximately within the first century of our era.

And it is to be observed that there is no other literary phenomenon answering to this fact since its appearance eighteen centuries ago. Neither was there any strict parallel to it before its appearance. For, wonderful as the phenomena presented by the Scriptures of the Old Testament really are, and supplying as they do the foundation upon which those of the New Testament are based, they nevertheless offer no true parallel to them.

For the doctrine or conception of the Christ as we have it, which is the essential and necessary basis of the religion which we call Christianity, is unquestionably the product of a human life. In whatever aspect we regard the Gospels, every one of them leads us up to a human life as the ultimate reason of its existence. Even if the narrative is overlaid with unhistoric details, it is impossible but that there must be an historic foundation for the main events of it. And the fourfold testimony of the existing Gospels is probably to be regarded as corroborative of this conclusion. The history of the Acts, trustworthy as it undoubtedly is in its general tenor, is likewise impossible without supposing the previous existence of the life of Jesus. And when we come to the Pauline Epistles, written as some of them probably were before any of the other books, and leading us up, as we have seen they do, to a much earlier period in the life of the writer, who must himself have been contemporary with the Person whom he first persecuted and afterwards preached, it is abundantly evident that the human life of that Person is not only the corner-stone of every epistle that he wrote, but the indispensable foundation of his after history, without which almost all that we know of him remains inexplicable.

So far then as the Christ idea or the doctrine of the Christ is connected with the person of Jesus, the reality of His human life is established beyond a doubt, for the existing phenomena of the literature, as we have it, would be impossible otherwise.

It remains then to notice other aspects of the same idea presented to us in the New Testament, and to inquire what their relation is to those we have already considered. These are principally three; those, namely, of the Epistle of St. James, the First Epistle of St. John, and the Revelation. The Epistles of St. Peter and the Epistle of St. Jude do not present the same marked contrast to the other writings that these do; and the Epistle to the Hebrews is mainly the development of one idea, that, namely, of the priesthood of Jesus Christ, which, though not foreign to some of the other writers, is worthy of separate and independent consideration, but not for our present object.

The Epistle of St. James naturally comes first, because of its supposed antagonism to the writings of St. Paul, to which our attention was last directed. The writer calls himself *a servant of God and of the Lord Jesus Christ,*[1] thereby implying not only that Jesus was the Christ, but that in some way He was unexceptionally near to God. He speaks afterwards of *the faith of our Lord Jesus Christ, the Lord of glory,*[2] which it seems hardly possible to understand unless He had in some way been glorified. And His resurrection and ascension to glory after His death of shame are virtually implied when he speaks of *the coming of the Lord.*[3] Moreover, the *poor* who are *rich in faith, the faith of our Lord Jesus Christ, and heirs of the kingdom* which God *hath promised to them that love Him,* are said to be the *chosen* of God;[4] which recalls the preaching of Jesus, *Repent ye and believe the Gospel;*[5] the *Gospel of the kingdom;*[6] *many be called but few chosen,*[7] and the like. His reference to *the engrafted word,* which is to be received *with meekness,* and is *able to save the soul,*[8] brings back to us very forcibly the parable of the sower, as also does *the fruit of righteousness, which is sown in peace of them that make peace.*[9] The earnest exhortation to be *doers of the word and not hearers only,*[10] reminds us of the conclusion

---

[1] St. James i. 1.   [2] ii. 1.   [3] v. 8.   [4] ii. 5.
[5] St. Mark i. 15.   [6] St. Matt. xxiv. 14.   [7] xx. 16.
[8] St. James i. 21.   [9] iii. 18.   [10] i. 22.

of the sermon on the mount; and the injunction to *ask in faith, nothing wavering*,[1] recalls the promise of the Lord, *Ask, and it shall be given you*.[2]   Such admonitions as, *Let patience have her perfect work, that ye may be perfect*,[3] and *Take, my brethren, the prophets who have spoken in the name of the Lord for an example of suffering affliction and of patience*,[4] so frequently repeated as they are, follow on wonderfully from *Rejoice and be exceeding glad, for so persecuted they the prophets which were before you*,[5] and *be ye therefore perfect*.[6]   *The worthy name by which ye are called*[7] can hardly be other than the name of Christ in baptism.

And though there is no direct allusion to the sufferings of Christ, yet as a time of persecution and suffering is implied, and patience is continually enjoined, we must presuppose His death who had given so conspicuous an example of patience and was now exalted to glory : while, *Behold we count them happy which endure*[8] is borrowed from the words of Jesus, *Blessed are they which are persecuted for righteousness' sake, for theirs is the kingdom of heaven*,[9] and *He that endureth unto the end, the same shall be saved*,[10] as also is, *Blessed is the man that endureth temptation, for when he is tried he shall receive the crown of life which the Lord hath promised to them that love him*.[11] In fact there is probably no document of the New Testament that has so many points of contact with the synoptical Gospels as the Epistle of St. James ; clearly showing that, whatever was his conception of the Christ, the person in whom he so believed was none other than the Jesus whose history they record.   We have then as a common framework in this Epistle, the Fatherhood of God,[12] the exaltation of Jesus who is acknowledged as the

---

[1] St. James i. 6.   [2] St. Matt. vii. 7.   [3] St. James i. 4.
[4] St. James v. 10.   [5] St. Matt. v. 12.   [6] v. 48.
[7] St. James ii. 7.   [8] v. 11.   [9] St. Matt. v. 10.
[10] St Matt. xxiv. 13.   [11] St. James i. 12.   [12] St. James i. 17, 27.

Christ,[1] His return to judgment,[2] and manifold allusions to His recorded teaching.[3] The conception embodied in it is that rather of a glorified than a suffering Christ, and yet the aspect of Christian life which is most prominent is that of fellowship with His sufferings in unceasing patience, and imitation of His example in the consistency of righteous conversation. The clear and emphatic recognition of Jesus as the Christ is sufficient, at all events, to add this Epistle to the number of those early writings which the doctrine and religion of the Christ originated, however various its testimony may be.

But there are certain points in which it approximates with remarkable closeness to the Pauline teaching, notwithstanding its apparent difference. For example, when the writer says, *Of his own will begat he us with the word of truth, that we should be a kind of firstfruits of his creatures,*[4] he virtually implies that the Gospel had acted with a regenerating influence on himself and his converts, as the effect of it is so frequently described by St. Paul. It had come with a new power, and had given them new life, even as the Apostle of the Gentiles had said, *You hath he quickened who were dead in trespasses and sins.*[5] The spiritual operation which is thus implied is a clear proof that to the minds of both writers the same effect was present. The word or message of Jesus Christ, which was the word of truth, was no dead formal precept of morality, or repetition of a mere historical statement, but a living energetic principle capable of begetting and imparting life. A confession like this is invaluable as coming from St. James, because the common-sense ethical character of his Epistle is apt to blind us to the necessary foundation of spiritual life which is pre-supposed in it. And this spiritual life was as much the gift of Jesus

---

[1] St. James ii. 1.   [2] v. 8.   [3] v. 12; St. Matt. v. 34, etc.
[4] St. James i. 18.   [5] Ephes. ii. 1.

Christ, and the effect of belief in His word, to him, as it was to St. Paul.

This assertion on his part is evidence, therefore, not only of a common basis of facts which each writer assumed, but of a common method of operation implied as being inherent in the facts. The belief that Jesus risen and glorified was the Christ, is acknowledged by St. James to have had the same quickening and reviving power in obedience to the will of God, which is affirmed by the great Apostle of the Divine election, who says that *the gift of God is eternal life through Jesus Christ our Lord, who was delivered for our offences and raised again for our justification ;*[1] that *it is not of him that willeth, nor of him that runneth, but of God that showeth mercy.*[2]

Nor is there the same hopeless divergence between these two writers on the question as to how man can be just before God, which is frequently supposed, and as at first sight appears. It is impossible to resist the cogency of the trenchant practical arguments of St. James on the worthlessness of faith which has no influence on works. They are obviously conclusive. Whatever may have been their historic relation to the teaching of St. Paul, there can be no question that they form a wholesome ethical complement to that teaching ; one, however, which is virtually implied in every Epistle of St. Paul himself. But just as the practical conclusions of St. James are implied and expressed in St. Paul, so likewise are the principles of St. Paul implied and virtually expressed in St. James. For what is the foundation principle of St. Paul, but that all the world must become guilty before God if judged according to the strict letter of the Law.[3] Therefore it is that God hath set forth in the Gospel a more excellent way whereby the guilty may be accounted

[1] Rom. vi. 23; iv. 25.   [2] ix. 16.
[3] Rom. iii. 19, 20.

righteous in Jesus Christ.[4] This is the very word of truth which quickens and saves the soul. But since, as we have seen, this latter truth has already been stated by St. James, so also is the previous foundation principle established by him. For when he says, *Whosoever shall keep the whole law, and yet offend in one point, he is guilty of all,*[5] what does he do virtually, but bring in the whole world guilty before God, as St. Paul has already done ? Judged by the strict letter of the Law, there is no man living who sinneth not. This was alike the teaching of Solomon[6] and of David,[7] and consequently St. James can neither have been ignorant of nor have run counter to it; but when he asserts this foundation principle in the way he does, we are able to see precisely where the operation of that word of truth comes in, which being *received with meekness* and *engrafted* in the heart *is able to save the soul.*

Surely, therefore, we may fairly say that St. Paul and St. James represent two aspects of Christian truth, but only two aspects of the same Christian truth. The same Divine light fell upon minds of different hue and colour, and the effect produced differed accordingly; but as we can detect evidence of the same operation in both, so likewise have we conclusive proof that the origin of the light was the same to both, for it streamed forth from the glorified Jesus who was by both acknowledged as the Christ, the chosen of God.

We pass on next to the Epistles of St. John, which we treat as documents falling perhaps within the first century, and valuable for our purpose for the evidence only which they furnish as to the writer's conception of the doctrine and religion of the Christ. In the opening of the First Epistle we have the emphatic assertion that the writer was an eyewitness of the human life which had been manifested

----

[4] Rom. iii. 21.   [5] St. James ii. 10.

[6] 1 Kings viii. 46.   [7] Ps. cxliii. 2.

and had come forth from the Father. This was the human life of His Son Jesus Christ.[1] Nor is there any doubt as to the identity of this person with the historic Jesus who lived and *died,* because the writer says that *the blood of Jesus Christ his Son cleanseth us from all sin.*[2] Here is the recognition of that idea of the high priesthood of Jesus Christ which is the main subject of the Epistle to the Hebrews. The cleansing is a spiritual cleansing, but it is the inward analogue of the ceremonial purification and atonement for sin typified under the Law. As the fact of our Lord's death is not expressly alluded to in the Epistle of St. James, so neither is the fact of His resurrection in the Epistles of St. John, but is continually implied. For He is recognised as the advocate with the Father, and as being Himself the source of life, which involves therefore His resurrection and ascension. In the Epistle of St. James, the writer's mind was chiefly filled with the glorified condition of Jesus, and the necessity of a life conformable to it in the brethren; but St. John seems mainly occupied with the thought of the *death* of Christ, and of the life which is centred in Him. As St. James also presupposed without alluding in terms to the work of the Spirit, so St. John, on the other hand, not only presupposes but expressly refers to that work; for, says he, *ye have an unction from the Holy One, and ye know all things.*[3]

But that which will at once be recognised as the most characteristic feature of the teaching of St. John's Epistles is the prominence he assigns to love. The bent of St. James's character was moral righteousness and integrity, that of St. John's is devout and fervent love. It was a love borrowed from the love of Him who laid down His life for sinners. It is this love whereby we are to *have boldness in the day of judgment,*[4] in the expectation of which

---

[1] 1 John i. 1–3. [2] i. 7.
[3] 1 John ii. 20. Cf. also iii. 24; iv. 13. [4] iv. 17.

day of His appearing we detect another point of contact
with St. James, as likewise with St. Paul. The notion of
a death for sin, the effect of which has been to put away
sin and to cleanse from sin,[5] is so common in St. Paul that
we need not dwell upon it; and the notion of a love
derived from the love of Christ cannot be foreign to him
who has drawn for us the famous picture of love in his
First Epistle to Corinth.

It is clear, then, that these various writings are so many
illustrations of the effect produced upon individual minds
by the facts of the 'life of Jesus and the belief that He
was the Christ. It is not upon their authority that we
dwell, so much as upon the undeniable evidence they afford
of the operation of a particular belief, based upon a series
of facts which are manifestly common to all the writers.
That this belief and these facts would operate variously
on various minds was only natural and to be expected.
The differences, however, are plainly differences of individual character, and the identity of operation and the
sameness of results produced, which are recognisable in
all, are the more remarkable from this necessary contrast
of individual character. And it is the general and broad
result thus produced in a variety of minds manifestly so
independent as to be capable of being not seldom represented as antagonistic, that we call the doctrine, or conception, or religion of the Christ. The unity and completeness
of the full idea are to be gathered only from a survey of
all the records. One part of the conception is more
prominent in some writings than it is in others. But as
a matter of fact, all are requisite for the expression of
the complete conception before we can deal with it as a
substantive whole.

With a view to this, the Epistles of St. Peter and St.
Jude may be briefly mentioned next. In the First Epistle

<hr>

[5] 2 Cor. v. 21, etc.

of St. Peter, it matters not now who wrote it, we have in the opening verses the sufferings, death, resurrection, and future appearing of *our Lord Jesus Christ.*[1] "The strangers" to whom it is written are addressed as *elect according to the foreknowledge of God the Father*, and they are characterised as having been *born again, not of corruptible seed, but of incorruptible, by the word* or reason *of God, who liveth and abideth for ever.*[2] Furthermore, we have mention made of *sanctification of the Spirit*, which is the *spirit of Christ*, through which the disciples have *purified* their *souls in obeying the truth ;*[3] and the Gospel, which is identified with the spoken word of the Lord,[4] is said to have been preached *with the Holy Ghost sent down from heaven.*[5] The redemption of believers is said to be *with the precious blood of Christ, as of a lamb without blemish and without spot*,[6] showing that the writer recognised in the death of Jesus the complete fulfilment of the types of the law. The Epistle is evidence also that many Gentiles, *which in time past were not a people*, had now become *the people of God ;*[7] that they willingly regarded themselves as spiritual heirs of the promises made to Israel ; and that this change in their position had been brought about by their acknowledgment of Jesus as the Christ.[8] It is clear, also, that times of trouble were at hand, and that some had begun to be reproached for the name of Christ, and to suffer for being called Christian ;[9] but the day of Christ's glory was about to be revealed, when they would be glad with exceeding joy.[10] The practice of baptism as a common rite[11] is also spoken of in this Epistle, and the responsibility of godly conversation is strongly insisted upon.[12]

The Second Epistle of St. Peter is chiefly remarkable

---

[1] 1 Peter i. 1–11.   [2] i. 23.   [3] i. 2, 11, 22.
[4] 1 Peter i. 25.   [5] i. 12.   [6] i. 19.
[7] 1 Peter ii. 10.   [8] ii. 7.   [9] iv. 12, 14, 16.
[10] 1 Peter iv. 13.   [11] iii. 21.   [12] i. 15, etc.

for its vivid anticipation of judgment, for its strenuous inculcation of holiness and denunciation of ungodliness, and for the additional title of Saviour,[1] which it frequently assigns to our Lord Jesus Christ. Familiarity with the Scriptures of the Old Testament, and frequent allusion to them, are characteristic of both these Epistles.

Passing on to St. Jude, we find that his Epistle is addressed to them that are sanctified by God the Father and preserved in or reserved for *Jesus Christ*, and called.[2] The writer speaks of the common salvation, which he implies was obtained through the *grace of God* and *our Lord Jesus Christ*.[3] He exhorts his disciples, by confirmation in the faith and prayer in the Holy Ghost, to keep themselves *in the love of God, looking for the mercy of our Lord Jesus Christ unto eternal life*.[4] He makes mention of certain feasts of charity,[5] and speaks of the apostles of our Lord Jesus Christ, whose spoken words must have been fresh in the memory of those to whom he wrote.[6] We are here, then, as it were, brought face to face with men who had listened to the teaching of those who had received their commission from the Lord himself, and we have collateral evidence of the general tenor of their teaching.

The opening of the Revelation of St. John bears witness to belief in Jesus as one who had died and risen again;[7] who was to come with clouds, when *every eye should see him, and they also which pierced him*.[8] His death had not only been a priestly expiation for sin, but it had conferred a priesthood upon believers,[9] even as St. Peter had called them a *royal priesthood*.[10] The offices of king and priest, which were united in Jesus Christ, were united also in believers. The sublime vision of the Son of Man in glory is the most remarkable feature of this part of the

---

[1] 2 Peter i. 1, 11; ii. 20; iii. 2, 18.   [2] Jude 1.   [3] Jude 4.
[4] Jude 21.   [5] 12.   [6] 17.   [7] Rev. i. 18.
[8] Rev. i. 7.   [9] i. 6.   [10] 1 Peter ii. 9.

Apocalypse, the whole of which book is itself an exhibition of the glorified Jesus in His character of judge. The Epistles to the Seven Churches of Asia recognise Him as *the Son of God;*[1] as *he which searcheth the hearts and reins, and will give to every one according to his works.*[2] Each of these Epistles ends with the remarkable words,—*He that hath an ear, let him hear what the Spirit saith unto the churches,*—the Spirit being clearly the Spirit of Christ or of Him which *hath the seven Spirits of God.*[3] Jesus Christ is further represented in the Apocalypse as *the Lion of the tribe of Judah,*[4] *the root and offspring of David,*[5] *the Lamb slain from the foundation of the world,*[6] who hath *redeemed us to God by his blood out of every kindred, and tongue, and people, and nation.*[7] The saints arrayed in white robes are said to be they *which came out of great tribulation, and had washed their robes and made them white in the blood of the Lamb.*[8] When the seventh angel sounded, there were great voices in heaven, saying,—*The kingdoms of this world are become the kingdoms of our Lord and of his Christ; and he shall reign for-ever and ever.*[9] *The testimony of Jesus* is declared to be *the spirit of prophecy;*[10] and finally, He is Himself called *The Word of God,* and is said to have *on his vesture and on his thigh a name written, King of kings, and Lord of lords.*[11]

Such is a brief summary of the Apocalyptic conception of Jesus as the Christ. Whatever may be the date of the Revelation, it expresses, perhaps, the fullest development of the Messianic character and glories of Jesus, and it is unquestionably the work of a man who had been nurtured in Judaism. It represents, moreover, the fullest effect produced by turning the many-coloured light of prophecy upon the personal history of Jesus. The writer sees in all

---

[1] Rev. ii. 18. [2] ii. 23. [3] iii. 1. [4] v. 5.
[5] Rev. xxii. 16. [6] xiii. 8. [7] v. 9. [8] vii. 13, 14.
[9] Rev. xi. 15. [10] xix. 10. [11] xix. 16.

prophecy, from Genesis to Daniel, a testimony bearing witness to Jesus. It is plain, moreover, that the two features of the Godhead and of the priesthood of the Messiah, which are more especially wrought out in the Epistle to the Hebrews, are contained in form and essence in the Revelation, as they were implied in the First Epistle of St. Peter and in many of those of St. Paul. Though this last great anonymous Epistle has expanded more fully the priesthood of Jesus, it has not, in doing so, added any new feature to His character.

We are, therefore, now in a position to survey as a whole the doctrine or religion of the Christ, as it is contained in the earliest Christian writings we possess, and developed by them out of materials previously existing in the sacred writings of the Jews.

And first, there is the clear fact, not only attested by history but which we must also postulate in order to account for the phenomena presented in these writings, of the human life and death of Jesus. That human life and death is the corner-stone of their existence, which, without it, would have been impossible. Secondly, there is the fact, equally certain, that this same Jesus was proclaimed by men of various minds and characters as the Christ, for without it also the Christian literature could have had no existence. Thirdly, there is the necessary inference that the Christ-character which He was declared to have fulfilled was a substantive reality, not only in the minds of those who received Him, but of those also who rejected Him in that character, and consequently that this ideal conception had been, as a matter of fact, produced by the Scriptures of the Old Testament. Fourthly, there is the no less necessary inference that it was impossible for Jesus to have been thus accepted in consequence of the effect produced only by His life and death. We must postulate other influences, which are mainly two,—first, the reality of

His resurrection; and secondly, the reality of the effects which accompanied and followed His recognition as the Christ in the gift of the Holy Spirit. The evidence of the reality of this gift is in our own hands, and consists in the existence of the earliest Christian literature embodied in the New Testament. There is irresistible and conclusive evidence there of the operation of a new power, to which there is no complete analogy in the history or literature of the world, but to which corroborative witness is borne even in the linguistic phenomena of these writings.

For example, there is no phrase in the Old Testament directly answering to the Holy Spirit of the New. We have of course such phrases as, *the Spirit of God, the Spirit of the Lord, my Spirit,* and the like. We have *thy Holy Spirit* once in the fifty-first Psalm, and *his Holy Spirit* twice in the sixty-third of Isaiah,—but even these phrases nowhere else; but *the Holy Spirit* never occurs.[1] No sooner, however, do we open these pages, than we encounter, for the first time, a new and original phrase,— *the Holy Ghost,* which occurs repeatedly, in all nearly a hundred times, is found in almost every book, and is used by every writer of the New Testament with the single exception of St. James, who, however, as we have seen, implies, in very remarkable words, the operation of the Holy Spirit. The natural inference, therefore, is, that this new phraseology is expressive of a new fact; and we know that the Apostles laid claim to the bestowal of the Holy Spirit as a new gift, and appealed to it as the most convincing proof that their message was a true one.

It is surely, then, incidental evidence of the reality of

---

[1] In the later Apocryphal books we have only in Wisdom ix. 17—"And thy counsel who hath known, except thou give wisdom, and send thy Holy Spirit from above?" And in 2 Esdras xiv. 22: "But if I have found grace before thee, send the Holy Ghost into me." Cf. the statement of St. John vii. 39: "The Holy Ghost was *not yet,* because that Jesus was ot yet glorified."

the new gift they claimed to bestow, that their writings are so full of allusions to it which are couched in language that is also new. There is nothing even in the Old Testament answering to the continual reference to the Holy Spirit in the New. The idea exists there in germ, as does also the idea of the Christ; but the full development of both ideas is the great literary fact of the New Testament, which is patent and demonstrable.

If, therefore, this new and original gift, which was confessed alike by Jew and Gentile, by Roman and Greek, by Barbarian, Scythian, bond and free, and has left for all ages its indelible mark and its indestructible monument in the literature of the New Testament, was, as a matter of fact, the product of the acknowledgment of Jesus as the Christ, and its accompaniment;—if, as an historic result, which there is no denying, the confession of Jesus as the Christ, and that alone, was the origin of this literature, and the effects to which it witnesses—may we not affirm that the credit of the Spirit of truth, which is also the Spirit of promise, is, in a manner, staked upon the validity and truth of that to which He so clearly testified —namely, that Jesus was the Christ, the chosen of God, who was *declared to be the Son of God with power, according to the Spirit of holiness, by the resurrection from the dead.*[2]

It must be borne in mind that the broad issue thus presented is virtually independent of a variety of questions which may be proposed as to the authorship and date of various books. The acknowledged Epistles of St. Paul are themselves a mine of testimony to the nature of early Christian belief, and the facts on which it rested. They carry us back far within the limits of the generation in which Jesus lived and died, and they show the kind of effect which belief in Him had produced. Whether this

[2] Rom. i. 4.

or that other Epistle is by him, or when it was written, does not really affect the main issue, which is clear enough without. Putting the extreme case that the name of Peter has been wrongly affixed to the first Epistle bearing it, the whole value of the document as a witness to Christ does not turn upon that. We may still believe that it truly represents the condition and faith of many *scattered throughout Pontus, Galatia, Cappadocia, Asia, and Bithynia,*[3] who, being the *elect* of God *as lively stones* had been *built up a spiritual house, a holy priesthood, to offer up spiritual sacrifices acceptable to God by Jesus Christ.*[4] The patent phenomena of it as a literary monument have still to be accounted for. And taken only as such it is one witness more to the marvellous effects brought about by belief in Jesus as the Christ, which from other sources were sufficiently plain already.

Nor is it possible that this position can be seriously affected by the most that can be made out of the obvious divergencies of Christian teaching, as, for example, those of St. James and St. Paul. It is not the divergencies that are the most remarkable feature. These exist in the acknowledged writings of St. Paul himself, and they must exist in the writings of any man. The common foundation of underlying fact that is apparent, and the implicit unity of originating motive at work, in both, are the points of real moment to be observed. And these are no less patent in one than in the other; and the conclusion to which they lead us is the same, that the Jesus who was glorified and would return to judgment was acknowledged as the Christ, and that belief in Him was an obligation to consistent holiness of life.

Thus the books of the New Testament present us with the full development and expansion of an idea which existed in germ in the Old Testament, the idea, that is, of

<hr>

[3] 1 St. Peter i. 1.   [4] ii. 5.

the Christ or the Messiah. The historic growth of this idea is distinctly traceable in the ancient Scriptures. The earliest indications of it are to be found in Genesis, the latest in Daniel, and the post-captivity prophets. Each successive stage of the history and each successive period of the literature added its own contribution to the thought, till the actual result of the whole was the undefined and yet definite expectation of the Messiah which was rife in the Jewish nation long before the commencement of the Christian era. As, however, it was impossible that any one element in the Old Testament conception should have been the natural parent of any other,—that the fifty-third of Isaiah, for instance, should have been suggested by or grown out of the twenty-second Psalm, or Daniel's prophecy of the Messiah have been originated by Jeremiah's prediction of the captivity, or the like—so also is it impossible that all these elements combined should have created that full development of the conception which is presented in the collective books of the New Testament.

At the close of the reign of Tiberius Cæsar all that the world knew of this Messianic conception was contained in the sacred writings of the Jews and the popular faith derived from them. Within the space of two generations afterwards, that doctrine of the Christ, as it is contained in the bulk of the New Testament literature, existed in its integrity. That the seed had expanded into the tree of mighty growth, is an undoubted fact both of history and of literature. For it is with literary monuments that we are now dealing. The four great Epistles of St. Paul are impossible phenomena if they had nothing but the Old Testament to rest on. As a matter of fact, the one could not have originated the other. And yet the Pauline letters could not have existed without the Old Testament Scriptures. Between these two great literary facts, as an inevitable and connecting link, there occurred the historic fact of the human life and death of Jesus. As that human life and death can alone account for the relation subsisting between the two, so is it also the one historic and originating cause without which these Epistles could not have existed. But the mere life and death of a Man who Himself left no abiding memorial behind Him, could not, together with the Scriptures of the Old Testament, have given birth to a new and unique literature, unless there were elements in His character and history as unique as the results which they produced. That Jesus was the Christ is the uniform and consistent testimony of the New Testament writers, and the belief that He was is the only occasion for their existence as writers. That He, being the Christ of prophecy, contained in Himself the fulfilment of all the past and the promise of all the future—that He was at once the *root and the offspring of David,* and *the bright and morning star,*[4] the realisation of the old and the inaugurator of the new dispensation, the fountain of eternal life and the giver of the Holy Ghost, and thus should have been the adequate and sufficient origin of effects so mighty and so marvellous, is conceivable; but that the effects, being no less mighty and marvellous than they are, should have been produced when His alleged character was a fiction, and His personal influence an unreality, is not conceivable, and reduces us to the necessity of rejecting a cause commensurate with the effect in order that we may choose one which would be altogether and wholly inadequate.

As, moreover, the Epistles of St. Paul are unfaltering and decisive in their testimony to the reality of the human life of Jesus, so also do they contain within themselves the germ of the perfect conception of His character as the Christ. That character is of necessity an ideal because it is a spiritual one. Christ as He was known after the flesh

<hr>

[4] **Rev. xxii. 16.**

was the son of Mary who was crucified through weakness. The conditions of His natural life were confounding to flesh and blood, and they culminated in the offence of the cross. The very assertion that He was the Christ involved a certain idealisation of those spiritual functions the title implied, which could not be discernible by flesh and blood. The priesthood of Christ, His eternal Sonship, His future return to judgment, even His resurrection and ascension, to some extent appealed to the imagination and to the spiritual faculties to apprehend them. They could not be the objects of experience to the natural senses. Their contemplation involved the exercise of other powers. The fact that it was these topics that the Epistles dealt with, would itself explain the marked difference existing between them and the Gospels or the Acts. The Christ was of necessity an internal conception endued with all the glory and majesty which was hidden from the natural eye in the human Jesus. It was the discovery of the one in the other, and the fulfilment in Jesus of the ideal character of the Christ that produced the phenomena of conversion, and gave the impulse to those mighty results of which the Epistles themselves are the lasting monument and the abiding proof.

But then these results were the very last that the Scriptures of the Old Testament would have produced. It was the person of Jesus acting through those Scriptures that produced the results. It was His life, His death, His resurrection, His ascension, but pre-eminently the Holy Spirit which He promised to send, that awoke in those ancient writings their latent fire, and produced, through their agency and through the answer given to their prophetic promises and hopes, those phenomena of new and spiritual life of which the New Testament itself is the greatest witness.

And this is what we mean by the historic development

of the Christ-conception or of the religion of the Christ. Within thirty years after the death of Jesus, all the essential features of that doctrine or conception were fully developed. Whatever was added afterwards by the Revelation of St. John, for example, or by other books, was not a substantive addition; it had existed long before in the faith of believers and in the record of their belief. This is a matter of history, resting upon documentary evidence which is unexceptionable.

It is plain, moreover, that the effects which followed the acknowledgment of Jesus as the highest and complete fulfilment of prophecy, were not only unique as a matter of history, but also that there is no other life or character which could have produced the same results through the operation of the same means. There is no other person in the annals of history, who being contemplated in connection with the same writings of the Old Testament, is capable of producing such a combination as would effect a similar result. Nor have we any reason to believe there ever will be. But, as an unquestionable historic fact, these great results were the direct and immediate fruit of belief in Jesus as the Christ. It is hard indeed, therefore, to resist the cogency of the apostolic assertion that *the testimony of Jesus is the spirit of prophecy.*[5] We are constrained to acknowledge that the unity and completeness of the full conception of the Christ, the marvellous way in which it fits into the anticipations of the Old Testament, and more than fills up the measure of its significance, and yet from this very fact could not have been suggested by those writings, as it historically was not, is its own witness. This could not have been, as it assuredly was not, the work of man. Here, if anywhere, is to be seen the finger of God. By these indestructible facts of history and of literature, even more plainly than by a voice from

<hr>

[5] Rev. xix. 10.

heaven, He has declared of Jesus, *This is my beloved Son, in whom I am well pleased,*[6] and has set the seal of His Divine approval to the testimony of Apostles and Evangelists that He was the Christ.

We are precluded, then, from regarding the Christ-doctrine, even as it is expressed in St. Paul's Epistles, as a merely Pauline conception, because some of the most essential features of that doctrine—such as the Messiahship, the glorification, and the future return of Jesus—are as characteristic of St. James as they are of St. Paul; and because other features no less prominent in him are common with him to the other writers of the New Testament. These are, the belief in Jesus as the Christ, the fulfilment in Him which that implied of the Scriptures of the Prophets; the life, death, resurrection, ascension, and final manifestation of Jesus; His perpetual priesthood, or the mystic power to cleanse from sin involved and inherent in His death; the sanctification of the Holy Spirit, which was the natural and yet the supernatural consequence of belief in Him; and the requisite consistency in holiness of life enjoined upon and commonly produced in those who became followers of Him, as well as the union of believers with God and with one another through their union with Him.

And to this historic and literary development of the Religion of the Christ, arising as it did out of the facts of the life of Jesus, and the light which was shed by them on the Scriptures of the Prophets, we point as a sufficient and conclusive evidence of its origin.

The variety, the independence, and the gradual development of the materials existing in the Old Testament, which supplied the foundation of it, are facts that cannot be gainsaid. Neither can their existence, regarded merely as literary phenomena, be accounted for on purely

----

[6] St. Matt. iii 17; xvii. 5.

natural principles. The ordinary impulses of human authorship or flights of human genius will not account for or explain the mysterious utterances of an Isaiah or a Zechariah. There is that in them which no theory of merely human causation will resolve. Each separate stage in the marvellous growth is a witness to the existence of the earlier one, but not the natural or the necessary result of it. Each individual writer stands out in his own clearly-marked and characteristic personality, spontaneously but unconsciously adding his own fragment to the mass; and not till the last echoes of the latest Prophet have died away is the result seen to be a uniform and consistent whole. Not till the Son of man has come, and died and risen and been glorified, is it perceived, because before it could not be, that His portraiture was sketched of old by the Prophets.

And when we come to that life itself, it is not till we find the impress of the seal on the plastic clay of human life which has been regenerated, renewed, and elevated, recreated, cleansed, and glorified, that we discover what the seal itself had been. The death which could communicate itself to a corrupt and sinful nature, and prove the destruction of the old man, could have been no ordinary death. It must have been the death of Him on whom the Lord had laid the iniquity of us all, and who had made His soul an offering for sin. The resurrection of Him who had bestowed spiritual life on others, which had brought forth such fruit in them as the Epistles to Rome and Ephesus are samples of, must have been itself a reality, the demonstration of an inherent principle of eternal life which was undying and had cast out death. To Him who had shed forth on the new society gifts of the Spirit so unmistakable and so abundant, the Spirit itself must have been given without measure. He had indeed received gifts for men, yea even for His enemies, because He had ascended up on high, and· had led captivity captive, that the Lord God might dwell among them.

· And lastly, in the historic development of the religion and doctrine of the Christ, appearing as it does first in the Prophets in a form inchoate and germinal, next in the Epistles in a form fully matured and complete, and lastly in the historic books of the New Testament, which endeavour to recall the image of the living Jesus in the form of reminiscences of an actual human life, we have the clearest possible proof of the real origin of that doctrine. The Epistles of necessity presuppose the fact of a previously-existing human life in all material points identical with that portrayed in the Gospels. It cannot be alleged that these Epistles owe their existence to the prior existence of the Gospels. On the contrary, they exhibit the central fact of the Gospels in active operation, probably, or at least possibly, long before they were any one of them written. At all events, their testimony is entirely independent, as from the nature of the case it is undesigned. We have then to account for the phenomena they present without drawing upon any existing sources, or sources known to have existed, except those which already existed in the Scriptures of the Old Testament.

But these of themselves are manifestly inadequate to account for them. We must throw in the human life of Jesus, including the central and essential facts of that life, without which it alone would have been inadequate to account for them. If the Epistles could possibly be regarded merely as the expression of individual sentiment and opinion, the case would of course be very different. But they cannot be so regarded. They are themselves the evidence of certain facts, as also is the personal history of their author. His early, no less than his later career, is only to be accounted for on the supposition of the reality of the life of Jesus. His writings show us that life, operating not as a past but as a present influence, not only in himself but in others. They spring from no morbid attachment to a dead man, but are instinct with the Almighty power and with the Divine Spirit of a risen and triumphant Saviour. Judged, therefore, merely as literary results, they can only be assigned to delusion or to madness, if their real origin is not that which it claims to be. The hypothesis of delusion is untenable, because it demands too wide an area. The hypothesis of madness was long ago anticipated and precluded in a defence attributed to the writer himself—*I am not mad, most noble Festus, but speak forth the words of truth and soberness.*[7]

The historic development, therefore, of the Christ-doctrine is a manifest proof of the historic origin of Christianity, of that religion of which it is the essential basis. In Christianity we are brought face to face with a religion which as a matter of fact sprang from facts, and was based upon the foundation of a human life. All evidence is fatal to the notion that it was a congeries of coagulated sentiment. It was no cobweb of fictions spun from the brain of overwrought and deluded preachers. We cannot trace it home to any such origin or birthplace. Its simplest and most elementary expression was *Jesus is the Christ.* And this was not only simple and elementary, but it was essential and uniform. There was and could be no Christianity where this expression did not obtain. If the Christ was an ideal conception, it was one which owed more than half its existence and all its glory to the realities of the life of Jesus. That life was the vital spark, which, falling on the prepared substance of ancient prophecy, produced a conflagration which set the whole world in a blaze. *I am come to send fire on the earth, and what will I if it be already kindled ?*[8]

But that the material was prepared beforehand, was the

---

[7] Acts xxvi. 25.   [8] St. Luke xii. 49.

work of God, and not of man, and that the vital spark was deposited in a human life which through death could destroy him that had the power of death, is evidence that that human life was the gift of God, and derived from God as no other life could be. *This is my beloved Son, in whom I am well pleased.*[9] No other fact of history, no other human life, falling on the same substance, could have produced the same result, nor would this human life, falling upon any similar substance not similarly prepared. It was the union of these two, but of these two only, which resulted, or could have resulted, in the way it did.

What is the inference, therefore?—Verily, that the expression *Jesus is the Christ* was, as the Apostles declared it to be, and as the Holy Spirit testified, the utterance of the truth of God. This was the record that God gave of His Son.

But we find in this Christ-doctrine and Religion of the Christ not only an evidence of its historic origin in the world of fact, but an indication also of its destined permanence. It is independent alike of the changes of fortune and the chances of time. Empires may dissolve and monarchies may fall, but this religion will stand. No revelations of science in the future can reverse or unwrite the record of the past, which is deep graven in the facts of human literature and history. If as a matter of undeniable fact the consequence of the proclamation of Jesus as the Christ was what we have seen it to be, it becomes impossible to imagine that the Christ-doctrine was nothing more than a temporary and a transient feature of the movement. We cannot see in these results a marked indication of the finger of God, a setting of the seal of the Divine Spirit to the truth of a message proclaimed in obedience to the Divine will, and refuse to acknowledge that the message was something more than of temporary signifi-

<hr>

[9] St. Matt. xvii. 5.

cance and of transient import. If this was the Divine message in a way that no other message ever was Divine, then we can hardly venture to affirm that the essential terms of it were in their essence transitory. We can scarcely suppose that it will be a matter of indifference whether or not we cease to regard Jesus as the Christ. To take Him only as He is known to the wildest unbelief— as a human teacher of great originality, as a successful reformer, as an enthusiast who was Himself the victim of extraordinary delusions—will in no degree be compatible with the literary phenomena of the New Testament which we possess as the actual outcome and result of His personal influence, whatever His personal character may have been. If a similar estimate of the character of St. Paul will fail to account for the remarkable features of the Pauline writings, still less will this theory of the character of Jesus be consistent with those features, because it implies on His part not only delusion, but deliberate and energetic deception. The centre of Pauline teaching was Jesus, but the centre of the teaching of Jesus was Himself, and every estimate of His character is inadequate which does not recognise this fact. If, therefore, we cannot have the complete conception of the Christ-character without the human life of Jesus, so neither can we have any adequate or just notion of the personal life of Jesus without the essential elements of the Christ-character combined with it. Who was Jesus, if He was not the Christ? We are at a loss to determine. He was an anomaly in human history, standing out in remarkable relation to the ancient literature and history of His people, but having nothing to do with it, and assuredly not produced by it—shedding marvellous light on all other times and histories, but Himself dwelling in darkness—undeniably the centre and source of a unique collection of writings, to which there is no approximate parallel in literature, but presenting, in

His own character, the strongest possible contrast to the acknowledged tendency of those writings, because Himself indifferent to truth as a first requisite of virtue. If Jesus was not what the Gospels, Acts, and Epistles, agree in confessing Him to have been, we not only are unable to say what He was, but are at a loss to account for their existence as the actual product of the belief that He was the Christ. On the assumption that their combined testimony is true, His character at once becomes consistent and intelligible, and their existence is explained. They were the substantial and permanent bequest of Him who was the Mediator of the New Testament. They are the abiding proof of the reality and the fulfilment of that promise of the Holy Ghost which He made to His disciples. If it is asked, How do we know that He made it, except on the authority of these writings themselves? we can only reply, It is more in accordance with reason to suppose He did than it is, judging from the nature of the result itself, to imagine that the promise was invented to give the appearance of greater mystery to that which already was but too mysterious; to seem to account for that which, with or without it, was equally unaccountable.

The historic development, then, of the doctrine and religion of the Christ is a strong moral evidence of its origin. It was not invented by man. In the highest and truest sense it was God-given. It has all the characteristics of an actual and a genuine revelation. Not only was the character of Jesus the character of the Son of God, but the way in which His life gave vitality to the germinal elements of the Christ-idea latent in the ancient Scriptures, and the way in which that conception gathered strength and grew, as it were, naturally, and yet not without an energy at work which was other than natural, in the threefold and mutually independent forms of correspondence, history, biography, till, within the period of an ordinary human lifetime from the death of Jesus, it had attained its fullest development, and was substantially complete long before; and the way in which it wrought, like leaven, in the mass of a decaying and corrupt humanity, till the whole was leavened and renewed,—is the highest moral evidence we can have of the character of the energy at work, and of the nature of the Will whose operation it revealed.

No mere worship of humanity unredeemed and unregenerate can aspire to supersede the religion of Jesus as the Christ; no vague residuum of the various religions of the world, reduced to their common elements of morality and truth, can hope to supplant this, for it is possessed of special characteristics which mark it out as separate from all. No other religion has an origin so distinct and manifest as this. No other faith has the evidence of an inherent vitality like this. No other has the promise or the prospect of permanence like this. No other is capable of producing fruits that redound so much to the glory of God and to the good of man as this. No other religion may so fitly be called Divine, or so justly be attributed to God, as this; for none can so clearly establish her credentials or make good her claim.

It is no question, however, of mere superiority between this religion and any other. If Christianity is true, that is to say if the religion of Jesus as the Christ is true, it is true as no other is true. If God has indeed set His seal to this religion, He has set it in a way that He has not set it to any other. No other religion but this, saving only that from which it sprang, which must stand or fall with it, can point to anything like the same pedigree of fact. No other religion but these which are virtually both one as regards their origin, can point to monuments so enduring, so remarkable, so sublime, so holy. *Heaven and earth shall pass away; but my words shall not pass away,*[1] was a bold

---

[1] St. Matt. xxiv. 35; St. Luke xxi. 33.

and magnificent challenge; but it was something more, for it was a challenge, daring as it was, which may be safely left to vindicate and prove itself.

Lord, to whom shall we go? thou hast the words of eternal life,[2] is language that was addressed to Jesus, and which can be addressed to no human teacher. We may be uncertain as to its propriety when addressed to Him; but we can scarcely venture to address such words to any other. He is either worthy of them, or He is not; if He is not, then there is no one else that we can name in comparison of Him; but if He is worthy of them, then let us go to Him ourselves with them. Let us make them our own. Let us give ourselves in heart and soul and mind and strength to Him. Let us go to Him for the life which He alone can give, for the pardon of all the sinful past, for the light of the darkened present, for the hope of the endless future. Let us resolve that, while many are falling away, and some are making shipwreck of faith, and some are tossed to and fro with every wind of doctrine, and some have no steadfastness and no hope, and some are without God in the world, and while times are changing and things temporal are passing away, and things eternal are hastening on and drawing near, it shall be ours to cling fast to Jesus as the Christ, the chosen of God—to serve Him in health and strength, when all is bright and joyous, and the powers are vigorous and unimpaired, and to trust Him in the time of trouble when days are dark and dreary, and to believe in Him to the saving of the soul *now* and when the solemn hour of departure is at hand. There is no other friend but He who will not fail us now. There is no other friend but He whom we can dare to trust then; for He alone hath the promise of the life that now is, and of that which is to come.

Let us then not be too proud or too cold or too frivolous

[2] St. John vi. 68.

to adopt the conclusion of the men of Samaria—*We know that this is indeed the Christ, the Saviour of the World ;*[3] but with the fixed assurance that what is thus true once must inevitably be true for ever, let us go to Jesus ourselves, with the noble, the generous, the sublime confession of Simon Peter, and say to Him, as the heart-felt utterance of our own personal conviction and unchanging faith, *We believe, and are sure, that thou art that Christ, the Son of the living God.*[4]

[3] St. John iv. 42.   [4] vi. 69.

Itaque Tu Pater, qui lucem visibilem primitias creaturæ dedisti, et lucem Intellectualem ad fastigium operum tuorum in faciem hominis inspirasti; Opus hoc, quod à tua bonitate profectum, tuam gloriam repetit, tuere et rege. Tu postquam conversus es ad spectandum opera quæ fecerunt manus tuæ, vidisti quod omnia essent bona valdè; et requievisti. At homo conversus ad opera quæ fecerunt manus suæ, vidit quod omnia essent vanitas et vexatio spiritûs; nec ullo modo requievit. Quare si in operibus tuis sudabimus, facies nos visionis tuæ et Sabbati tui participes. Supplices petimus, ut hæc mens nobis constet: utque novis eleemosynis per manus nostras et aliorum, quibus eandem mentem largieris, familiam humanam dotatam velis.

THE END.